Pearson Revise

Pearson Edexcel GCSE

French

Revision Guide

Author: Stuart Glover

This book includes Pearson Revise Online access with a revision planner, retrospective tracker, plus make your own flashcards!

Quizzes, videos and flashcards to boost your progress – on every page!

Scan the **Digital resources QR codes** for more ways to revise.

Digital resources

- **Quick quizzes**: Quick-fire practice to check your knowledge.
- **Vocabulary quizzes**: Improve your understanding and retention of all the required vocabulary with just a few minutes' practice each day.
- **Videos**: Help with tricky grammar and tips for the exams.
- **Vocab flashcards**: Test your understanding of all the required vocabulary with ready-made flashcards

Audio for Speaking and Listening at your fingertips

Scan the **green audio QR codes** to immediately launch high-quality recordings of native speakers.

Listen to the recording

- **Exam-style tracks** for realistic assessment practice
- **Targeted pronunciation practice** of French sounds helps build your confidence.
- **Answer-section audio** brings Speaking activities to life.

Transcripts for all audio files can be accessed on the Pearson Revise Online platform.

Higher and Foundation tiers

You can use this book no matter which tier you are doing.

Higher tier vocabulary and grammar are highlighted with the purple background or H symbol.

Everything else is relevant for both Foundation and Higher tier.

état (m)	state
pression (f)	pressure
régime (m)	diet
souffrir	to suffer
stressé(e)	stressed

H ONLY **Before and after** — Grammar page 115

avant de **+ infinitive** before doing something
Avant d'aller au collège, je prends le petit-déjeuner.
Before going to school, I have breakfast.

Difficulty scale

The icon next to each exam-style question tells you how difficult it is. Some questions cover a range of difficulties.

Target grade **4**

Target grade **7-8**

Also available:

The Revision Workbook provides additional practice with hundreds more exam-style questions along with hints on writing the most effective responses PLUS a the full set of practice papers – one for each of Foundation and Higher tier – at the back of the book.

How can this book help me revise?

On the page…

1 **Topics** make vocabulary easier to revise.

✓ Revise the words, then see and use them again in many topics!

2 Key **vocabulary**, taken from the approved vocabulary list.

✓ Check which words you already know and learn some new words.

✓ Refer to vocabulary pages at the back of the book for a complete list.

Words/grammar which will only appear on the Higher tier papers look like this: souffrir . The rest may appear on either paper.

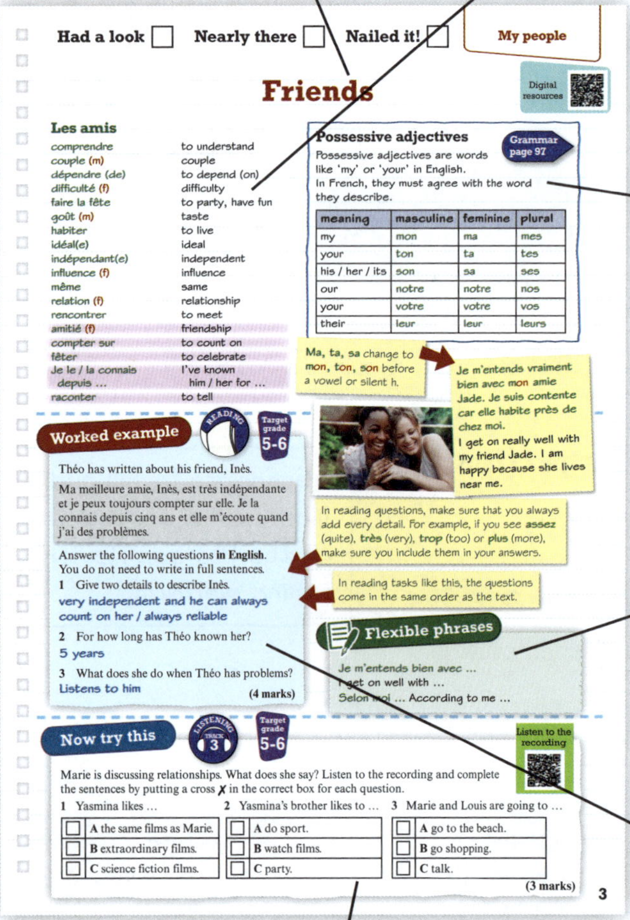

3 Short reminders on **grammar** points help you revise how to form the language correctly and add 'complexity' to aim for higher grades. Grammar points which are only needed on the Higher papers are marked **H** . **Videos** cover key or tricky areas.

✓ If you need more detail, you can look in the longer grammar section on pages 94–117, watch one of the accompanying videos, or ask your teacher.

4 **Flexible phrases** can be used in many contexts.

✓ Learn these to use in your writing and speaking exams to help boost your confidence.

5 Now, look at the **Worked examples** to see how a student might use this language in an exam-style question. Hints tell you how to approach similar questions, things to look out for and how to improve your answer.

✓ Use some of the language you've learned to answer this question.

6 Then put it all into practice. The **Now try this** is an exam-style question to help you bring everything together and have a go yourself.

✓ Check your answer with the model answer in the answer section – this may include an audio file to help with pronunciation.

You'll see a range of question types – **Speaking**, **Listening**, **Reading** and **Writing** – including the new read aloud and dictation tasks, plus audio files for Listening and Speaking questions.

Sample page content

Had a look ☐   Nearly there ☐   Nailed it! ☐   My people

Digital resources

Friends

Les amis

comprendre	to understand
couple (m)	couple
dépendre (de)	to depend (on)
difficulté (f)	difficulty
faire la fête	to party, have fun
goût (m)	taste
habiter	to live
idéal(e)	ideal
indépendant(e)	independent
influence (f)	influence
même	same
relation (f)	relationship
rencontrer	to meet
amitié (f)	friendship
compter sur	to count on
fêter	to celebrate
Je le / la connais depuis …	I've known him / her for …
raconter	to tell

Possessive adjectives   Grammar page 97

Possessive adjectives are words like 'my' or 'your' in English. In French, they must agree with the word they describe.

meaning	masculine	feminine	plural
my	mon	ma	mes
your	ton	ta	tes
his / her / its	son	sa	ses
our	notre	notre	nos
your	votre	votre	vos
their	leur	leur	leurs

Ma, ta, sa change to mon, ton, son before a vowel or silent h.

Je m'entends vraiment bien avec mon amie Jade. Je suis contente car elle habite près de chez moi.
I get on really well with my friend Jade. I am happy because she lives near me.

Worked example   READING   Target grade 5–6

Théo has written about his friend, Inès.

Ma meilleure amie, Inès, est très indépendante et je peux toujours compter sur elle. Je la connais depuis cinq ans et elle m'écoute quand j'ai des problèmes.

In reading questions, make sure that you always add every detail. For example, if you see assez (quite), très (very), trop (too) or plus (more), make sure you include them in your answers.

Answer the following questions **in English**. You do not need to write in full sentences.

1 Give two details to describe Inès.
very independent and he can always count on her / always reliable

In reading tasks like this, the questions come in the same order as the text.

2 For how long has Théo known her?
5 years

3 What does she do when Théo has problems?
Listens to him   (4 marks)

Flexible phrases

Je m'entends bien avec …   I get on well with …
Selon moi … According to me …

Now try this   LISTENING TRACK 3   Target grade 5–6   Listen to the recording

Marie is discussing relationships. What does she say? Listen to the recording and complete the sentences by putting a cross ✗ in the correct box for each question.

1 Yasmina likes …
☐ A the same films as Marie.
☐ B extraordinary films.
☐ C science fiction films.

2 Yasmina's brother likes to …
☐ A do sport.
☐ B watch films.
☐ C party.

3 Marie and Louis are going to …
☐ A go to the beach.
☐ B go shopping.
☐ C talk.

(3 marks)

3

On Pearson Revise Online…

7 Give your knowledge a quick check with the **quick quiz!**

✓ Scan the QR code to access a set of multi-choice questions relating to what you've just revised.

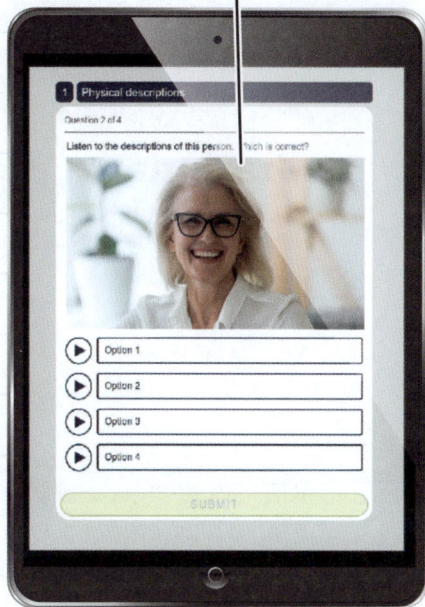

8 Power up your vocabulary with the **vocab test!** Scan the QR code for quick-fire questions to boost your knowledge.

✓ Do this every day to really build your vocabulary – and see your progress grow!

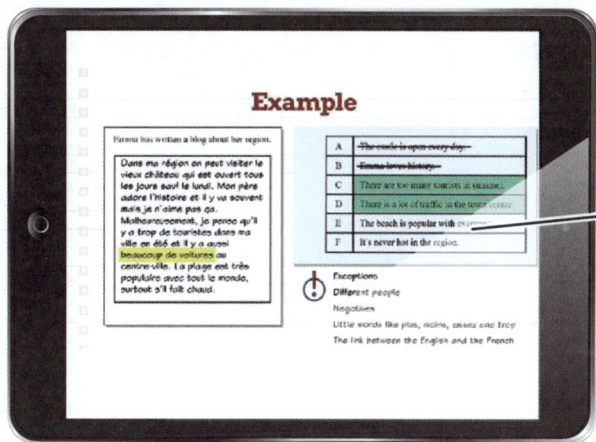

9 **Videos** help you focus in on mastering your grammar, plus provide overall tips from experienced teachers and examiners.

10 Ready made flashcards covering all the required vocabulary help you test your understanding at the touch of a button.

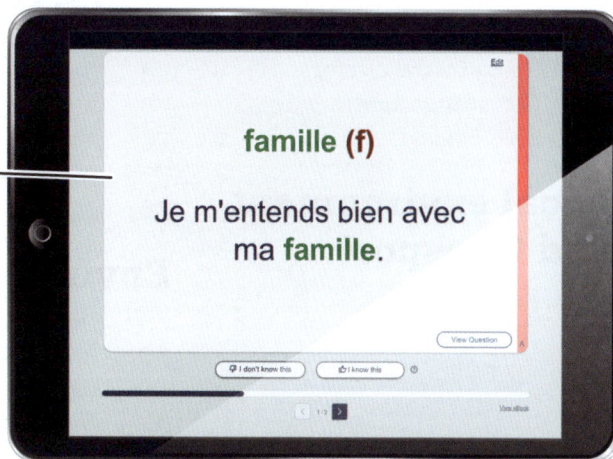

Pearson Revise

Your Pearson Revise Online access also includes a revision planner, progress tracker, plus make your own flashcards!

Contents

. . . .

A small bit of small print:
Pearson Edexcel publishes Sample Assessment Material and the Specification on its website. This is the official content and this book should be used in conjunction with it. The questions in Now try this have been written to help you practise every topic in the book. Remember: the real exam questions may not look like this.

Physical descriptions

Digital resources

Décris-toi

beau / belle	handsome / beautiful
cheveux (mpl)	hair
Elle a les yeux bleus.	She has blue eyes.
Il a les cheveux courts / longs.	He has short / long hair.
Il a les cheveux roux / blonds / marron / noirs.	He has red / blond / brown / black hair.
Il est plus grand que moi.	He is bigger than me.
Je suis grand(e) / petit(e)	I am tall / small
jeune	young
lunettes (fpl)	glasses
plus ... que	more ... than
porter	to wear
vieux / vieille	old
yeux (mpl)	eyes
ressembler à	to look like

Adjectives

Grammar page 96

Remember that adjectives usually come after the word they describe in French and must **agree** (change spelling) with that word.
Regular adjectives add an -e for the feminine, -s for the plural and -es for the feminine plural.

adjective	singular		plural	
	masculine	feminine	masculine	feminine
tall	grand	grande	grands	grandes

However, if the adjective already ends in an -e, like jeune, no extra -e is added for the feminine.
If the adjective already contains an -s, like gris, no extra -s is added for the masculine plural.
See page 96 for more on adjective endings.

Elle est jeune. She is young.

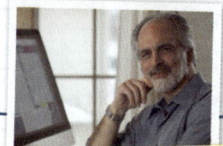

Il a les cheveux gris. He has grey hair.

This question could be part of the conversation part of the Speaking exam where you can give a detailed answer.

The example uses modifiers like **assez** (quite) and **très** (very) to make the answer more interesting and complex. It also uses a nice phrase, **On dit que**, so that you are not always using **je**. In addition, by saying what the person used to look like, a different tense (the imperfect) is used and this makes the answer more complex.

Worked example

SPEAKING TRACK 1

Target grade 3-6

Décris-toi.
Je suis très grand, j'ai les cheveux noirs et les yeux marron. On dit que je suis assez beau.

Quand j'étais plus jeune, je portais des lunettes et j'étais plus petit. Je pense que je ressemble à mon frère aîné.

With colours, **marron** (brown) never changes its spelling.

Listen to the recording

This sentence uses some higher-level vocabulary.

Now try this

WRITING

Target grade 1-5

Describe the photo. Write four short sentences **in French**.

(8 marks)

Make sure that all your adjectives agree.

Flexible phrases

Je pense que ...	I think that ...
Je le / la trouve ...	I find him / her ...
On dit que ...	People say that ...

Digital resources

Character descriptions

La personnalité

actif / active	active
agréable	pleasant
amusant(e)	funny, fun
calme	quiet
faible	weak, poor at
fort(e)	strong, loud, good at
fou / folle	crazy, wild
heureux / heureuse	happy
patient(e)	patient
sérieux / sérieuse	serious
sportif / sportive	sporty
strict(e)	strict
sympa	nice, kind
travailleur / travailleuse	hard-working
triste	sad
fidèle	faithful, loyal
fier / fière	proud
se comporter	to behave
se soucier de	to show concern for
sévère	severe, strict, harsh
stressé	stressed

Direct object pronouns

Grammar page 101

Using pronouns can help you avoid repeating nouns.

me	me	us	nous
you	te	you (formal or polite)	vous
him / it	le	them	les
her / it	la		

Mon ami s'appelle Lucas. Je **le** trouve amusant.
My friend is called Lucas. I find him funny.

me, te, le, la + vowel / silent h = m', t', l'

Le sport ne **m'**intéresse pas.
Sport doesn't interest me.

Flexible phrases

À mon avis … In my opinion …
… m'intéresse beaucoup. … interests me a lot.
… ne m'intéresse pas. … doesn't interest me.

Aiming higher

Try to use adverbs like toujours (always), souvent (often) or de temps en temps (from time to time) to make your work more interesting and complex.

Look out for negatives like **ne … pas** and **ne … jamais**.
All adjectives need to agree with the noun they are describing. Here the adjective **travailleur** has become **travailleuse** and **sportif** has become **sportive** because Emma is female.

Worked example

READING   Target grade 2-3

Read the description of Emma.

Emma est très travailleuse mais à mon avis, elle n'est jamais stricte. Je pense qu'elle est toujours sympa, mais elle n'est pas sportive. On dit qu'elle est amusante aussi.

Which adjectives describe her?
Put a cross ✗ in each one of the **three** correct boxes.

✗	**A** funny		☐	**D** strict
✗	**B** hard-working		☐	**E** sporty
✗	**C** kind		☐	**F** quiet

(3 marks)

Now try this

LISTENING TRACK 2   Target grade 5-6

Listen to someone describing Emma's friend, Louis.

Which adjectives describe him? Listen to the recording and put a cross ✗ in each one of the **three** correct boxes.

Listen to the recording

☐	**A** loyal		☐	**D** fun
☐	**B** hard-working		☐	**E** proud
☐	**C** stressed		☐	**F** loud

(3 marks)

Friends

Digital resources

Les amis

comprendre	to understand
couple (m)	couple
dépendre (de)	to depend (on)
difficulté (f)	difficulty
faire la fête	to party, have fun
goût (m)	taste
habiter	to live
idéal(e)	ideal
indépendant(e)	independent
influence (f)	influence
même	same
relation (f)	relationship
rencontrer	to meet
amitié (f)	friendship
compter sur	to count on
fêter	to celebrate
Je le / la connais depuis …	I've known him / her for …
raconter	to tell

Possessive adjectives

Possessive adjectives are words like 'my' or 'your' in English.
In French, they must agree with the word they describe.

Grammar page 97

meaning	masculine	feminine	plural
my	mon	ma	mes
your	ton	ta	tes
his / her / its	son	sa	ses
our	notre	notre	nos
your	votre	votre	vos
their	leur	leur	leurs

Ma, ta, sa change to **mon, ton, son** before a vowel or silent h.

Je m'entends vraiment bien avec mon amie Jade. Je suis contente car elle habite près de chez moi.

I get on really well with my friend Jade. I am happy because she lives near me.

Worked example

READING   **Target grade 5-6**

Théo has written about his friend, Inès.

Ma meilleure amie, Inès, est très indépendante et je peux toujours compter sur elle. Je la connais depuis cinq ans et elle m'écoute quand j'ai des problèmes.

Answer the following questions **in English**. You do not need to write in full sentences.

1   Give two details to describe Inès.

very independent and he can always count on her / always reliable

2   For how long has Théo known her?

5 years

3   What does she do when Théo has problems?

Listens to him

(4 marks)

In reading questions, make sure that you always add every detail. For example, if you see **assez** (quite), **très** (very), **trop** (too) or **plus** (more), make sure you include them in your answers.

In reading tasks like this, the questions come in the same order as the text.

Flexible phrases

Je m'entends bien avec …
I get on well with …
Selon moi … According to me …

Now try this

LISTENING TRACK 3   **Target grade 5-6**

Listen to the recording

Marie is discussing relationships. What does she say? Listen to the recording and complete the sentences by putting a cross ✗ in the correct box for each question.

1   Yasmina likes …

☐ **A** the same films as Marie.
☐ **B** extraordinary films.
☐ **C** science fiction films.

2   Yasmina's brother likes to …

☐ **A** do sport.
☐ **B** watch films.
☐ **C** party.

3   Marie and Louis are going to …

☐ **A** go to the beach.
☐ **B** go shopping.
☐ **C** talk.

(3 marks)

Digital resources

Family

La famille

beau-père (m)	stepfather
belle-mère (f)	stepmother
demi-frère (m)	stepbrother / half brother
demi-sœur (f)	stepsister / half sister
enfant unique (m/f)	only child
femme (f)	wife
fille (f)	daughter
fils (m)	son
frère (m)	brother
grand-mère (f)	grandmother
grand-père (m)	grandfather
mari (m)	husband
mère (f)	mother
oncle (m)	uncle
parents (mpl)	parents
partenaire (m/f)	partner
père (m)	father
respecter	to respect
s'amuser	to enjoy oneself
sœur (f)	sister
tante (f)	aunt
aîné(e)	older
Je m'occupe de mon petit frère.	I look after my little brother.
jumeau (m) / jumelle (f)	twin
s'occuper de	to look after

Question words

Grammar page 117

Qui?	Who?
Que / Qu'est-ce que?	What?
Comment?	How? What?
Où?	Where?
Combien?	How much / How many?
Quand?	When?
Avec qui?	With whom?
Pourquoi?	Why?
À quelle heure?	At what time?
Quel(le)?	What / which?
Comment s'appelle ton père?	What's your father's name?
Quand est-ce que vous sortez?	When do you go out?
Qu'est-ce que c'est qu'un bon frère?	What is a good brother like?

Qui prépare les repas?
Who makes the meals?

Worked example

WRITING

Target grade 1-5

Translate the following five sentences **into French**.

1 My family is quite big.
2 I have two brothers and one sister.
3 I respect my parents because they are kind.
4 I like playing football with my uncle.
5 Yesterday I went to town with my aunt.

(10 marks)

1 Ma famille est assez grande.

2 J'ai deux frères et une sœur.

3 Je respecte mes parents car ils sont sympa.

4 J'aime jouer au football avec mon oncle.

5 Hier je suis allé(e) en ville avec ma tante.

Remember that the word for 'my' depends on the gender of what it is describing. **Mon** père, **ma** mère, **mes** frères.

Famille is feminine, so don't forget the **-e** on 'grande'.

Don't forget the **-s** on **frères** as it's plural.

Now try this

SPEAKING

Target grade 3-6

1 Comment est ta famille?
2 Qu'est-ce que vous faites ensemble?

Relationships

Digital resources

Les relations

aider	to help
améliorer	to improve
chez	at the house of
émotion (f)	emotion
en commun	in common
gay	gay
hétéro(sexuel)	straight
inspirer	to inspire
lutter	to struggle, fight
partenaire (m/f)	partner
respecter	to respect
se marier	to get married
traiter	to treat
voisin (m)	neighbour
accueillir	to welcome
adopter	to adopt
confiance (f)	trust
il / elle m'inspire	he / she inspires me
J'ai de bonnes relations avec …	I have a good relationship with …
menacer	to threaten
pression (f)	pressure
soin (m)	care
soutien (m)	support

Relative pronouns

Grammar page 103

You may need to link parts of your sentence with the words who, which or that. To do this you use the French words qui or que.

- Qui replaces the **subject** of the sentence.

  J'ai un voisin qui m'inspire. Il lutte contre la destruction des forêts pour améliorer notre planète.

  I have a neighbour who inspires me. He fights against the destruction of forests in order to improve our planet.

- Que replaces the **object** of the sentence.
- Que changes to qu' before a vowel.

J'ai un nouveau chien que j'adore. J'ai organisé une fête pour l'accueillir dans ma famille!

I have a new dog that I adore. I organised a party to welcome it into our family!

C'est l'enfant qu'ils ont adoptée. Ils prennent bien soin d'elle.

That's the child that they adopted. They take good care of her.

Worked example

WRITING · Target grade 4-6

Write to your friend about relationships. You must include the following points:
- a description of a good friend
- why you get on well with this friend
- what you did together recently
- what you will do together this weekend.

Write your answer **in French**. You should aim to write between 80 and 90 words. **(18 marks)**

Mon meilleur ami s'appelle Louis. Il est grand et vraiment sportif. Nous avons beaucoup de choses en commun.

Il m'inspire parce qu'il est sympa et amusant. Nous jouons au football après l'école et nous aimons écouter de la musique et danser.

Récemment, je suis allé à un concert avec lui et nous nous sommes très bien amusés.

Le week-end prochain, je vais faire du camping avec lui et toute sa famille à la campagne et j'espère qu'il ne pleuvra pas!

Try to give reasons and make your sentences more complex by using connectives like **car** or **parce que**.

Using pronouns is another way of showing complexity. Here the student has used **lui** (to him/him) and **m'** (me). Note that **lui** can also mean 'to her/her'.

Now try this

SPEAKING · Target grade 3-6

1 Qu'est-ce que tu aimes faire avec ta famille ou tes amis?
2 Qu'est-ce que c'est qu'un bon ami?

5

Digital resources

Helping friends with problems

Aider les amis

crise (f)	crisis
danger (m)	danger
dangereux / dangereuse	dangerous
effet (m)	effect
effort (m)	effort
en forme	fit / healthy
énergie (f)	energy
forme (f)	shape / fitness
malsain(e)	unhealthy
médical(e)	medical
médicament (m)	medicine
mental(e)	mental
pleurer	to cry
responsable	responsible
sain(e)	healthy
se lever	to get up
victime (f)	victim
violence (f)	violence
état (m)	state
pression (f)	pressure
régime (m)	diet
souffrir	to suffer
stressé(e)	stressed

To have to

Grammar page 108

To say that something must or has to happen, you can use:

- **il faut** + **infinitive** (it is necessary to)
  Il faut toujours aider les amis.
  You must always help your friends.

- the irregular verb **devoir** + infinitive.

je dois	I must / have to
tu dois	you must / have to
il doit	he / it must / has to
elle doit	she / it must / has to
on doit	one must / has to
nous devons	we must / have to
vous devez	you must / have to
ils / elles doivent	they must / have to

Je dois aider mes amis.
I must help my friends.

Il doit aider.
He has to help.

You might need to use devoir in other tenses.
e.g. J'ai dû aider mes amis.
I had to help my friends.

Worked example

LISTENING TRACK 4   **Target grade 1-3**   **Listen to the recording**

Listen to Ana talking about what she does to help her friends.

> J'aide mon ami Mathis avec ses devoirs.
>
> Mon amie, Léa, est très stressée. J'aime l'aider quand elle a des problèmes.
>
> Ma meilleure amie Lucie pleure tout le temps et je suis triste quand je la vois.

Complete the sentences by putting a cross ✗ in the correct box for each question.

1 Ana helps Mathis ...

✗	**A** with his homework.
☐	**B** with his health.
☐	**C** with his friendships.

2 Léa is ...

☐	**A** helpful.
✗	**B** stressed.
☐	**C** happy.

3 Lucie always ...

☐	**A** smiles.
☐	**B** laughs.
✗	**C** cries.

(3 marks)

Il faut être en forme.
You have to be fit.

Remember that although the question is asked in the present tense, you could talk about the past and the future as well as using the present tense.

Now try this

SPEAKING

Qu'est-ce que tu fais pour aider tes amis?

Target grade 6-7

When I was younger

Digital resources

You may need to be able to use the imperfect tense to talk about when you were younger.

Dans le passé

À l'âge de …	At the age of …
… c'était …	… it was …
… il y avait …	… there was / were …
… j'allais …	… I used to go …
… je faisais …	… I used to do …
… je jouais …	… I used to play …
… je participais à …	… I used to participate / participated in …
Il y a cinq / dix ans …	5 / 10 years ago …
Quand j'avais dix ans …	When I was 10 years old …
Quand j'étais petit(e) / plus jeune …	When I was little / younger …

The imperfect tense

Grammar page 111

You use the imperfect tense to express what used to happen in the past.

Forming the imperfect tense

1 Take the **nous** form of the present tense, remove the -ons ending.

nous habit~~ons~~

2 Add the following endings:

je	-ais	nous	-ions
tu	-ais	vous	-iez
il / elle / on	-ait	ils / elles	-aient

habiter to live	
j'habitais	nous habitions
tu habitais	vous habitiez
il / elle / on habitait	ils / elles habitaient

All verbs except **être** are **regular** in the imperfect tense. For **être**, use the stem **ét-** and add the endings above.

être to be	
j'étais	nous étions
tu étais	vous étiez
il / elle / on était	ils / elles étaient

So j'étais means 'I was' or 'I used to be'.

Translating the imperfect tense

When you translate 'used to', remember that there won't be any French words for these two English words, as you just use the imperfect tense. 'He used to play' is just il jouait. Note that this can also be translated as 'He was playing' and 'He played' (a continuous action, e.g. Il jouait toute la journée. He played all day).

Worked example

READING

Target grade 4-5

Maxime is writing about the past.

> Quand j'étais plus jeune, j'habitais dans une grande maison au bord de la mer avec mes parents et mon chien, mais maintenant nous habitons dans une petite ville à la campagne. J'étais plus calme, travailleuse et je lisais beaucoup, mais j'étais aussi très contente parce que ma vie était plus simple.

Complete the sentences below.
Put a cross ✗ in the correct box for each question.

1 Maxime used to live …

☒	**A** at the seaside.
☐	**B** in a small house.
☐	**C** in the countryside.

2 She used to be …

☐	**A** more active.
☐	**B** less hard working.
☒	**C** quieter.

3 She used to …

☒	**A** read a lot.
☐	**B** be unhappy.
☐	**C** live a complicated life.

(3 marks)

Now try this

SPEAKING

Target grade 5-6

Ta vie était comment quand tu étais plus jeune?

You might be asked to talk about what you were like when you were younger.

Digital resources

Identity

L'identité

ambition (f)	ambition
gay	gay
handicapé(e)	disabled
hétéro, hétérosexuel(le)	straight
lesbien(ne)	lesbian
mériter	to deserve
non-binaire	non-binary
personnalité (f)	personality
religieux / religieuse	religious
respecter	to respect
sexisme (m)	sexism
accueillir	to welcome
combattre	to fight
compétence (f)	ability, skill
également	also / too / as well / equally
liberté (f)	freedom
lutte (f)	fight
s'identifier à	to identify with
s'intégrer	to integrate, fit in
unité (f)	unity

Flexible phrases

Je crois que … I believe that …
Je dirais que … I would say that …

Formality

There are two words for 'you': tu and vous
Use tu when you are:
- being friendly or informal
- talking to your own family and friends
- talking to people roughly your age or younger.

Use vous when you are:
- being polite or formal
- speaking to someone you don't know
- addressing someone older than you
- referring to more than one person.

Exam alert

Your teacher will address you as vous in the **role play**. However, you can use either tu or vous in your responses to them.

Que signifie l'identité, pour toi?
Pour moi, c'est ma personnalité, mes choix, mes amis, mes ambitions et ma religion.
What does identity mean, for you? For me, it's my personality, my choices, my friends, my ambitions and my religion.

Worked example

READING — Target grade 5-7

Read what Mehdi says about his life.

Je dirais que ma vie est assez difficile. Je suis gay et il y a beaucoup de personnes qui ne respectent pas ça. Je suis né en Algérie et quand j'y habitais, j'ai dû combattre le racisme et le sexisme. Selon moi, la lutte pour l'unité est vraiment importante.

Answer the questions **in English**. You do not need to write in full sentences.

1 Why does Mehdi think that being gay is an issue in his life?
Lots of people don't respect this.

2 Give one problem he faced in the past.
racism OR sexism

3 What does he want to fight for?
unity   (3 marks)

Now try this

READING — Target grade 7-9

Sofiane has written this passage:

Je viens d'écrire un roman où je raconte l'histoire de la vie d'un homme, Nathan, qui avait plein de problèmes dans sa vie. Il est arrivé en France à l'âge de vingt-deux ans de son pays, en Afrique. Il était très religieux et personne ne l'a accueilli.

What does Sofiane tell us?

Put a cross ✗ next to each one of the **three** correct statements.

☐	**A** He is going to write a novel.
☐	**B** Nathan is French.
☐	**C** Nathan had many problems.
☐	**D** Nathan was born in Africa.
☐	**E** Nathan was religious.
☐	**F** Nathan received a warm welcome.

(3 marks)

Everyday life

La vie quotidienne

alors	so, well, then
après-midi (m)	afternoon
déjeuner (m)	lunch
devoirs (mpl)	homework
fois (f)	time
matin (m)	morning
petit-déjeuner (m)	breakfast
quitter / partir	to leave
rentrer	to return / go home
se lever	to get up
soir (m)	evening
sortir	to go out
vie (f)	life
ailleurs	somewhere else
quotidien / quotidienne	daily

Before and after

H ONLY

Grammar page 115

avant de + infinitive before doing something
Avant d'aller au collège, je prends le petit-déjeuner.
Before going to school, I have breakfast.
après avoir + past participle after doing something
Après avoir pris mon petit-déjeuner, je suis allé au collège.
After having breakfast, I went to school.

Describing when

généralement	generally	avant	before
normalement	normally	ensuite	then (next)
souvent	often	finalement	finally
chaque jour	every day	auparavant	previously
de temps	from time	parfois	sometimes
en temps	to time	puis	then / next
quelquefois	sometimes	enfin	finally
après	after		

Worked example

SPEAKING TRACK 5   Target grade 3-5

Décris une journée ordinaire le week-end.

Listen to the recording

Le matin, je me lève à huit heures et je prends le petit-déjeuner. Avant de quitter la maison, je regarde la télé ou j'écoute de la musique. L'après-midi, je vais en ville avec mes amis où on fait des achats.

Le soir, je reste chez moi ou je sors avec ma famille. On va souvent au cinéma parce que ma mère adore regarder des films amusants.

You might have to answer questions about your daily routine.

Je me lève tôt le matin et ensuite, je prends mon petit-déjeuner. I get up early every morning and then, I have my breakfast.

Aiming higher

You might want to use verbs which use être as the **auxiliary** verb like aller or arriver. When you say 'after doing something', you use être instead of avoir and the past participle must agree with the subject.
Après être arrivé, il a mangé son déjeuner.
After arriving, he ate lunch.
BUT
Après être arrivée, elle a mangé son déjeuner.
After arriving, she ate lunch.

You won't meet the **après être** form in your Reading or Listening exams, but you can use it yourself if you wish.

Listen to the recording

Now try this

LISTENING TRACK 6   Target grade 5-6

Listen to Yasmina describing her day. Complete the gap in each sentence using a word or phrase from the box below.

car	coach	bike	foot
lunch	break	breakfast	dinner
see a pet	do her homework	eat sweets

There are more words / phrases than gaps.

1 Yasmina goes to school by _____ .
2 There are two lessons before _____ .
3 She chats with her friends at _____ .
4 Yesterday she went to her aunt's house by _____ .
5 She went there to _____ .

(5 marks)

Digital resources

Meals at home

Les repas à la maison

allergique	allergic
avoir faim	to be hungry
baguette (f)	French stick
boîte (f)	box, tin
café (m)	coffee
couteau (m)	knife
cuillère (f)	spoon
cuisine (f)	cooking, kitchen
eau (f)	water
faim (f)	hunger
fourchette (f)	fork
fruit (m)	fruit
lait (m)	milk
légume (m)	vegetable
pain (m)	bread
thé (m)	tea
viande (f)	meat
boisson (f)	drink
goûter	to taste, try (food)
verre (m)	glass

Connectives / conjunctions

You can use these to make your sentences longer and more complex to help improve your answer.

et	and	parce que	because
ou	or	quand	when
mais	but	alors	so, then, well
donc	so, therefore	aussi	also, as well
car	because	où	where

J'aime manger des fruits mais je déteste les légumes parce qu'ils sont dégoûtants.
I like eating fruit, but I hate vegetables because they are disgusting.

In this task, where you write four sentences about a photo, keep your sentences short and simple. Use constructions you know, like **il y a** (there is / are) or **je vois** (I see).

Worked example

WRITING   Target grade 1-2

Describe the photo. Write four short sentences **in French**. **(8 marks)**

1 Il y a quatre personnes.
2 Je vois une table.
3 La fille est contente.
4 Je vois du pain sur la table.

Flexible phrases

Ce que j'aime c'est …
What I like is …

Ce que je n'aime pas, c'est …
What I dislike is …

On s'amusera bien.
We will have fun.

Now try this

READING   Target grade 4-6

Morgane is talking about eating at home.

Chez moi, on mange le repas du soir, assis à table. Mon père est allergique au poisson, alors on n'en mange pas à la maison. Je suis assez triste car j'adore le poisson. Mon frère est végétarien mais mes parents aiment bien la viande. On mange toujours à huit heures. Moi, je pense que c'est trop tard! Ma mère cuisine bien.

Put a cross ✗ in each one of the **three** correct boxes.

☐	**A** Morgane is allergic to fish.
☐	**B** Morgane is sad that the family doesn't eat fish.
☐	**C** Her dad is a vegetarian.
☐	**D** They always eat their evening meal at the same time.
☐	**E** Morgane would like to eat earlier.
☐	**F** Her mother is not a good cook.

(3 marks)

Celebrations

Digital resources

Les fêtes

anniversaire (m)	birthday
Bon anniversaire!	Happy birthday!
cadeau (m)	present
carte (f)	card
donner	to give
faire la fête	to party, have fun
fête (f)	party, celebration, festival
habiller	to dress
mariage (m)	marriage
Nouvel An (m)	New Year
recevoir	to receive
s'amuser	to enjoy oneself
s'habiller	to get dressed
Saint-Sylvestre (f)	New Year's Eve
se marier	to get married
fêter	to celebrate

Vouloir (to wish, want)

Grammar page 108

This verb is irregular but you might need to use it a lot, so it will be a good idea to learn it.

je veux	I want
tu veux	you want
il / elle / on veut	he / she / it / one wants
nous voulons	we want
vous voulez	you want
ils / elles veulent	they want

It is often followed by an infinitive.

Je veux fêter le Nouvel An avec mes amis.
I want to celebrate New Year with my friends.

Remember that in the perfect tense, the past participle is voulu.

J'ai voulu y aller. I wanted to go there.

Je voudrais (I would like) is also a part of this verb.

📝 Flexible phrases

À vrai dire, c'était le plus beau jour de ma vie.
To tell you the truth, it was the happiest day of my life.

C'était une expérience unique.
It was a once-in-a-lifetime experience.

Nous voulons organiser une grande fête pour fêter le mariage de mon frère.
We want to organise a big party to celebrate my brother's wedding.

You could use these phrases to talk or write about celebrations, holidays, friends and more!

It's quite easy to use a future time frame using Je voudrais!

Worked example

SPEAKING TRACK 7 · Target grade 5

Aiming Higher Que fais-tu pour fêter ton anniversaire?

Normalement je fête mon anniversaire, qui est le 30 avril, en famille. Pour mon prochain anniversaire, mes parents veulent organiser une fête spéciale pour moi et je trouve ça vraiment sympa. Je voudrais inviter tous mes amis.

Listen to the recording

Aiming higher

This is an example of a question your teacher might ask you in the conversation part of your exam. In this part of the exam, try to develop your answers to use different time frames and opinions with reasons.

Remember to develop your answers and use different time frames.

Note that here the student has developed sentences using qui and et. There are also adjectives, an adverb and an intensifier (vraiment).

Now try this

SPEAKING · Target grade 5-9

1 Comment est-ce que tu fêtes l'anniversaire de ton meilleur ami?

2 Parle-moi d'une fête récente.

Digital resources

Food and drink

À manger et à boire

acheter	to buy
boire	to drink
caisse (f)	checkout, till
chocolat (m)	chocolate
fromage (m)	cheese
gâteau (m)	cake
glace (f)	ice cream
J'ai soif	I'm thirsty
malade	sick, ill
manger	to eat
payer	to pay (for)
recette (f)	recipe
végan(e) (m/f)	vegan
végétarien (m) / végétarienne (f)	vegetarian
aigre	sour
goûter	to taste
sec / sèche	dry
sucré(e)	sugary, sweet

Using on

The French often use the word on to translate 'you', 'we', 'they' or even 'people'. The literal translation is 'one': that can sound a bit posh in English, but it's not in French. It is the same part of the verb as il and elle. You should try to use it in speaking and writing as it sounds and looks very French.

On mange … We / They / You / People eat …

On aime boire … We / They / You / People like to drink …

En France, on peut manger beaucoup de fromages délicieux.
In France you can eat lots of delicious cheeses.

Worked example

READING

Target grade 5-6

Hugo is talking about his holiday food.

Answer the questions in English. You do not need to write in full sentences.

> Je viens de rentrer de vacances en Martinique. J'étais chez mon oncle. Ce qui m'a plu le plus, c'était la cuisine traditionnelle de la région. On mange beaucoup de plats sucrés et j'ai adoré le blanc manger coco*.

*A dessert using coconut milk, vanilla and sugar.

1   What did Hugo like best about his holiday?

the traditional cooking of the area

2   What does he say they eat lots of?

sugary dishes

(2 marks)

Don't give too much information in your answers; you only need to answer the question being asked and you don't need to write in full sentences.

In reading texts, read the whole passage first to make sure that you have a general idea of the meaning before looking at individual questions.

Now try this

READING

Target grade 5-6

Hugo continues:

> Le dernier jour des vacances, j'ai goûté un gâteau qui n'était pas sec et qui était vraiment délicieux mais mon ami a préféré les glaces. On est allés manger chez un ami de mon oncle et il était végan. Moi, j'ai trouvé les plats sans viande assez ennuyeux.

Answer the questions in English. You do not need to write in full sentences.

1 When did Hugo try the cake?

2 How does he describe the cake? (1 detail)

3 What did his friend prefer?

4 What did Hugo think of vegan cuisine?

(4 marks)

Healthy diets

Digital resources

Bien manger

commander	to order (food)
consommation (f)	consumption
frais / fraîche	fresh, cool
malsain(e)	unhealthy
sain(e)	healthy
santé (f)	health
grave	serious
inquiétant(e)	worrying
limiter	to limit
malgré	despite
nourriture (f)	food
nuire	to harm
régime (m)	diet
savoureux / savoureuse	tasty

-er verbs in the present tense

Grammar page 104

Regular -er verbs such as commander (to order) follow these rules:

1 Take off the -er from the infinitive.

2 Add the endings of the present tense:

je commande	I order
tu commandes	you order
il / elle / on commande	he / she / one orders
nous commandons	we order
vous commandez	you order
ils / elles commandent	they order

Manger (to eat) is slightly different as it has an extra e in the nous part to soften the g sound: nous mangeons.

Worked example

READING — Target grade 2-3

Tom is talking about what he eats.

Pour moi, il est important de bien manger. Je mange beaucoup de fruits et de légumes et je suis végétarien. Mes amis ne mangent pas bien. Ils adorent les frites!

Complete the sentences below. Put a cross ✗ in the correct box for each question.

1 Tom thinks it's important to …

✗	A eat well.
☐	B drink water.
☐	C eat regularly.

2 He eats …

☐	A meat.
☐	B fruit and chips.
✗	C fruit and vegetables.

3 His friends …

☐	A are vegetarians.
✗	B love chips.
☐	C never eat chips.

(3 marks)

Worked example

READING — Target grade 7-8

Read this extract from an article in a school magazine about healthy eating.

Aujourd'hui, beaucoup de maladies sont le résultat de la consommation de nourriture malsaine. Nous devons essayer de limiter notre consommation de boissons sucrées et manger plus de légumes: si vous les préparez bien, ils peuvent être vraiment savoureux. On peut ainsi rester en forme sans avoir besoin de suivre un régime.

Answer the following questions in English. You do not need to write in full sentences.

1 What is the cause of many illnesses today?
Eating food which is bad for you.

2 What should we try to limit?
Our consumption of sugary drinks.

3 How can you make vegetables tasty?
By preparing them well.   (3 marks)

Even when you don't have a lot to say, it's easy to give an opinion and say why you feel that way.

Now try this

SPEAKING — Target grade 1-5

1 Qu'est-ce que tu aimes manger et boire?
2 Qu'est-ce qu'on doit manger pour être en bonne santé?

13

Sport and exercise

Le sport et l'exercice

basket (m)	basketball
cheval (m)	horse
club (m)	club
danse (f)	dance
en forme	fit, in shape
équipe (f)	team
exercice (m)	exercise
foot(ball) (m)	football
handball (m)	handball
jeu (m)	game
match (m)	match
natation (f)	swimming
sport (m)	sport
stade (m)	stadium
tennis (m)	tennis
terrain (m)	ground
tomber	to fall
vélo (m)	bicycle
athlétisme (m)	athletics
foule (f)	crowd
gymnase (m)	gym

Jouer à or faire de?

Grammar page 108

When you are talking or writing about participating in sport, you need to use either jouer à or faire de in French.

If we use **to play** in English, use jouer à.

Ils jouent au handball. They play handball.

If you don't say **play** in English, use faire de.

Elle fait de la natation. She goes / does swimming.

Il fait du vélo. He goes cycling.

J'aime jouer …   I like to play / playing …
J'aime faire …   I like doing / going …

Je n'aime pas faire de la danse mais j'aime bien jouer au tennis.
I don't like dancing but I really like playing tennis.

Worked example

READING   Target grade 1-3

Read these comments from an internet forum.

Jules: Mon sport préféré, c'est le football mais je déteste faire du vélo car c'est nul.
Léa: Ma passion, c'est le tennis. Demain, je vais regarder un match avec mes amis.
Zoé: Je fais de la danse mais j'aime mieux jouer au basket parce que c'est passionnant.

Who says what? Choose the correct answers. Put a cross ✗ in the correct column for each question.

	Who …	Jules	Léa	Zoé
(a)	… loves tennis?		✗	
(b)	… loves basketball?			✗
(c)	… hates cycling?	✗		
(d)	… will watch a match?		✗	
(e)	… dances?			✗
(f)	… likes football?	✗		

(6 marks)

Using time phrases

Improve your speaking and writing answers by using different tenses. You can also use time phrases:

Past	hier (yesterday)
	la semaine dernière (last week)
	il y a deux semaines (two weeks ago)
Present	normalement (normally, usually)
	en ce moment (at the moment)
	maintenant (now)
	toujours (always)
	toutes les semaines (every week)
	chaque année (each year)
Future	la semaine prochaine (next week)
	demain (tomorrow)
	bientôt (soon)

Now try this

SPEAKING   Target grade 5-9

1 Qu'est-ce que tu as fait récemment comme exercice?
2 Quels sports vas-tu faire la semaine prochaine?

Physical wellbeing

Digital resources

La santé physique

actif / active	active
activité (f)	activity
aider	to help
améliorer	to improve
causer	to cause
cœur (m)	heart
corps (m)	body
effet (m)	effect
malade	ill
maladie (f)	illness
marcher	to walk
réduire	to reduce
santé (f)	health
besoin (m)	need
résoudre	to solve, resolve
s'entraîner	to train

Flexible phrases

J'ai l'intention de …	I intend to …
J'ai envie de …	I want to …
Je rêve de …	I dream of …

H ONLY

Expressing the future

Grammar page 112

You can use:
- the future tense
  J'irai à l'école à pied.
  I will go to school on foot.
- aller + infinitive to be going to
  Je vais améliorer ma condition physique.
  I am going to improve my fitness.
- avoir l'intention de to intend to
  J'ai l'intention de faire de la natation.
  I intend to go swimming.
- avoir envie de to want to
  J'ai envie de faire du vélo demain.
  I want to go cycling tomorrow.
- rêver de to dream of
  Je rêve d'être en forme.
  I dream of being fit.
- je voudrais / j'aimerais I'd like to
  Je voudrais être plus sain(e).
  I'd like to be more healthy.

Je vais réduire le temps que je passe en voiture. Marcher, c'est meilleur pour la santé, surtout pour le cœur.
I'm going to reduce the time I spend in the car. Walking is better for your health, especially for the heart.

Worked example

LISTENING TRACK 8 **Target grade 5-6**

Listen to Lola talking about physical wellbeing.

Chaque soir, pour rester en forme, je marche pendant une heure avec mon chien dans le parc qui est près de chez moi. J'ai l'intention de ne plus boire de café car c'est mauvais pour la santé et je vais aller au gymnase où je ferai des activités physiques.

Answer the following questions **in English**. You do not need to write in full sentences.

1 When does Lola go for a walk?
every evening

2 What does she no longer intend to do?
drink coffee

3 Why?
It's bad for your health.

Listen to the recording

(3 marks)

Make sure you read the question carefully. For example in Question 1, it's **when** not **where**.

Look and listen for key words to help you locate the correct answer to a question in listening and reading tasks. For example, listen for **ne … plus** (no longer) to find the answer to Question 2.

Now try this

WRITING **Target grade 1-5**

Translate the following five sentences **into French**.

1 I like to be fit.
2 My favourite sport is swimming.
3 It's good for my health.
4 Yesterday I went to the swimming pool.
5 I like to walk every day and at the weekend I walk for two hours with my dogs.

(10 marks)

Digital resources

Mental wellbeing

La santé mentale

bruit (m)	noise
crise (f)	crisis
danger (m)	danger
dormir	to sleep
émotion (f)	emotion
examen (m)	exam
mental(e)	mental
protéger	to protect
responsable	responsible
sauver	to save
cacher	to hide
écran (m)	screen
harcèlement (m)	bullying
pression (f)	pressure
s'intégrer	to fit in
stressé(e)	stressed

Negatives

Grammar page 114

In English, verbs are made negative by adding 'not'.

In French you need to put ne ... pas around the verb.

Je regarde la télé. ➡ Je **ne** regarde **pas** la télé.

I watch TV ➡ I do not / don't watch TV.

In the perfect tense the ne ... pas goes around the part of avoir or être.

Elle a bien dormi. She slept well.

Elle n'a **pas** bien dormi. She didn't sleep well.

Nous sommes arrivés. We arrived.

Nous **ne** sommes **pas** arrivés. We didn't arrive.

Other negatives include:

ne ... jamais never

ne ... rien nothing

ne ... personne nobody / no-one

Worked example

LISTENING TRACK 9

Target grade 1-3

Ahmed, Myriam and Clément are talking about their mental wellbeing. What do they say?

Listen to the recording and complete the sentences by putting a cross ✗ in the correct box for each question.

Listen to the recording

Ahmed: J'ai trop d'examens. C'est nul et la pression peut causer des problèmes de stress.
Myriam: Internet, c'est mauvais pour la santé mentale et malheureusement c'est facile de voir qu'il a une influence négative sur les jeunes.
Clément: Je dépends trop de mon portable. Mes parents et mes amis pensent que ce n'est pas bon pour moi.

Je me sentais seul et je pensais que **personne ne** pouvait m'aider.

I felt alone and I thought that no-one could help me.

H ONLY

Here **personne** is used as a subject: Personne ne pouvait m'aider.

1 Ahmed has …

☐	**A** no stress.
☒	**B** too many exams.
☐	**C** a minor illness.

2 Myriam says the internet …

☐	**A** has a positive influence.
☐	**B** is easy to use.
☒	**C** is bad for mental health.

3 Clément is dependent on his …

☒	**A** mobile.
☐	**B** parents.
☐	**C** friends.

(3 marks)

Now try this

READING

Target grade 5-6

Fatima has written a diary.

Je ne peux pas dormir parce que je suis trop stressée. J'ai caché mes émotions et je sais que j'ai passé trop de temps devant un écran. J'ai peur de parler à mes parents car je pense qu'ils ne me comprendront pas.

Put a cross ✗ next to each one of the **two** correct statements.

☐	**A** Fatima shows her emotions.
☐	**B** Fatima cannot sleep.
☐	**C** Fatima wants to spend more time on her computer.
☐	**D** Fatima thinks her parents won't understand her.

(2 marks)

Feeling unwell

Digital resources

Être malade

bouche (f)	mouth
bouger	to move
bras (m)	arm
cœur (m)	heart
se couper	to cut oneself
doigt (m)	finger
dos (m)	back
gorge (f)	throat
jambe (f)	leg
main (f)	hand
malade	sick, ill
maladie (f)	illness
nez (m)	nose
oreille (f)	ear
pharmacie (f)	chemist
pied (m)	foot
tête (f)	head
ventre (m)	stomach
yeux (mpl)	eyes
se blesser	to injure oneself
se brûler	to burn oneself
fièvre (f)	fever, temperature
peau (f)	skin
souffrir	to suffer

Je ne peux pas … I can't …

Je ne peux pas courir.
I can't run.

Aiming higher

In tasks where you have to fill gaps, make sure what you select makes sense when you read the sentence back to yourself.

Avoir mal à to ache, hurt

Grammar page 95 & 106

In French, to say that something hurts or aches, you need to used J'ai mal à + the part of the body affected.
If the word is masculine, use au.
If the word is feminine, use à la.
If the word is plural, use aux.
J'ai mal au dos. I have a sore back. / My back hurts / aches.
Elle a mal à la jambe. She has a sore leg. / Her leg hurts / aches.
Il a mal aux yeux. His eyes hurt / are sore.

Worked example

READING

Target grade 3-5

Maxime has written a diary entry.

> Ma mère est malade et elle est allée chez le médecin. J'ai cherché des médicaments en ville. Ce soir elle a toujours mal à la gorge et elle n'est pas contente.

Complete the gap in each sentence using a word from the box below. There are more words than gaps.

chemist	doctor	church
medicine	help	sweets
ear	back	throat

1 Maxime's mum went to see the ...... doctor ......
2 Maxime fetched some ...... medicine ......
3 Her mother has a sore ...... throat ......

(3 marks)

Now try this

LISTENING TRACK 10

Target grade 5-9

Listen to the recording

Dictation

You are going to hear someone talking about feeling unwell.
Sentences 1–2: write down the missing words in the gaps provided. In each gap, you will write one word **in French**.

1 Mon _____ a _____ mal aux _____ .
2 Il _____ , donc il est _____ acheter des médicaments _____ en ville.

Sentences 3–6: write down the full sentences that you hear in the spaces provided, **in French**.

3 _____ .
4 _____ .
5 _____ .
6 _____ .

(10 marks)

Digital resources

Equality and sporting role models

L'égalité et le sport

carrière (f)	career
divers(e)	diverse
égal(e)	equal
égalité (f)	equality
femme (f)	woman
handicapé(e)	disabled
homme (m)	man
identité (f)	identity
juste	fair, just, only
lutter	to fight
modèle (m)	role model
racisme (m)	racism
sexe (m)	gender
sexisme (m)	sexism
valeur (f)	value
agir	to act
citoyen (m)	citizen
discrimination (f)	discrimination
inquiétude (f)	worry, anxiety
justice (f)	justice
unité (f)	unity

Adjectives ending in -e and -é

Grammar page 96

Even though adjectives usually add an -e to make them feminine, if the adjective already ends in -e, a second -e is not added.

La discrimination n'est pas juste. Discrimination is not fair. The adjective juste already ends in -e so remains the same as for masculine nouns.

However, if an adjective ends in -é, an extra -e is added in the feminine.

une femme handicapée a disabled person (female)

Flexible phrases

Je veux / voudrais être comme …
I want / would like to be like …

Mon modèle est … My role model is …

Je veux rendre le monde plus juste / sûr / propre.
I want to make the world a fairer / safer / cleaner place.

Je veux être comme Hannah Cockroft qui est une sportive extraordinaire et qui lutte contre les discriminations.
I want to be like Hannah Cockroft who is an extraordinary sportswoman and who fights against discrimination.

Worked example

READING   Target grade 5-6

Sacha has posted this on an internet website about sporting role models.

> Je voudrais être comme Serena Williams qui a dû combattre la discrimination et qui a un don spécial pour le tennis, mon sport préféré.
>
> Elle a trouvé sa propre identité et elle respecte la justice et l'unité. Pour elle, l'argent n'est pas très important.

Complete the sentences below.
Put a cross ✗ in the correct box for each question.

1   According to Sacha, Serena Williams had to …

☒	A fight against discrimination.
☐	B change her identity.
☐	C be more determined.

2   Sacha says that Serena Williams …

☒	A has a special talent for tennis.
☐	B did not stand up for justice.
☐	C caused disunity.

3   Sacha says that Serena Williams …

☐	A is motivated by money.
☐	B is scared of her identity.
☒	C doesn't think money is very important.

(3 marks)

Exam alert

In your Speaking exam, your teacher will ask you questions.

- In the follow-up questions after the **role play**, **read aloud** and **picture task**, limit each of your answers to a short sentence (with a verb).
- In the **conversation**, develop your responses by adding two or three pieces of extra information.

Now try this

SPEAKING   Target grade 3-5

Qui est ton modèle? Pourquoi?

Sporting events

Digital resources

Les événements sportifs

billet (m)	ticket
but (m)	goal
durer	to last
événement (m)	event
fan (m/f)	fan, supporter
gagner	to win
passion (f)	passion
résultat (m)	result
Tour de France (m)	Tour de France
victoire (f)	victory
concours (m)	competition
professionel(le)	professional
public (m)	public

Translating -ing words

Grammar page 115

English uses lots of words which end in **-ing** and these are often translated into French by using an infinitive.

J'aime regarder le football.
I like **watching** / **to watch** football.

Je déteste aller au stade en train.
I hate **going** to the stadium by train.

Je préfère gagner le match!
I prefer to win the match!

Flexible phrases

C'est du moins mon opinion.
At least, that's my opinion.

En ce qui me concerne …
As far as I'm concerned …

Je suis d'accord. I agree.

En ce qui me concerne, le Tour de France est l'événement le plus passionnant.
As far as I'm concerned, the Tour de France is the most exciting event.

Worked example

SPEAKING TRACK 11   Target grade 4-7   Listen to the recording

Parle-moi d'un événement sportif récent.

La semaine dernière, je suis allé voir un match de football au stade de Liverpool puisque je suis fan de cette équipe.

On a gagné 4-0 contre Manchester United et c'était vraiment génial.

J'irai encore au stade le mois prochain et j'espère voir une autre victoire de mon équipe préférée.

This answer uses three time frames (past, present and future) and a variety of vocabulary including opinions with reasons. This answer shows both complexity and variety of language.

Using an infinitive after verbs expressing an opinion can help improve your answer.

Now try this

WRITING   Target grade 6-9

You could jot down some notes before you begin about some things you might try to include. For example, après avoir + a past participle.

If you haven't had personal experience of something in a question, make up your answer to show your knowledge of French.

Write about sporting events for an online magazine. You must include the following points:
- why sporting events are important
- what problems there might be with sporting events
- a sporting event you recently attended
- your future plans for sporting events.

Write your answer **in French**. You should aim to write between 130 and 150 words.

(22 marks)

Had a look ☐ Nearly there ☐ Nailed it! ☐

Digital resources

Me and my mobile

Moi et mon portable

acheter	to buy
appli(cation) (f)	app
charger	to charge
e-mail (m)	email
film (m)	film
joueur (m)	player
médias (mpl)	media
message (m)	message
portable (m)	mobile
social(e)	social
streaming (m)	streaming
données (fpl)	data
écran (m)	screen
limiter	to limit

> Regarde ce message! C'est vraiment amusant! Look at this message! It's really funny.

Adverbs

Grammar page 100

Adverbs describe verbs by telling you how, when or where something happens. Many adjectives end in **-ly** in English and **-ment** in French.

To form a regular adverb, take the feminine of the adjective and add **-ment**.

exacte ➡ exactement (exactly)

Il y a seulement … There is / are only …

However, some adverbs are irregular (like vraiment) or don't come from an adjective (like quelquefois). You just need to learn them.

C'est vraiment … It's really …

Flexible phrases

À mon avis, il faut absolument …
In my opinion, it's absolutely necessary …

À mon avis, il faut absolument avoir un portable.
In my opinion, it's absolutely necessary to have a mobile.

Worked example

SPEAKING TRACK 12

Target grade 4-7

Listen to the recording

1 Qu'est-ce que tu as fait sur ton portable, récemment?

Hier, j'ai regardé un film en ligne avec mes amis dans ma chambre et j'ai téléchargé beaucoup de chansons car j'adore la musique.

2 Est-ce que les portables sont dangereux?

Je dépends beaucoup de mon portable et je ne voudrais jamais le perdre. Cependant, on pourrait passer trop de temps sur un portable et c'est vraiment mauvais pour la santé.

> In speaking or writing tasks, make sure you answer the question asked.

> The student has used a direct object pronoun for 'it' (**je ne voudrais jamais le perdre**) which shows complexity and a good knowledge of grammar.

Aiming higher

Try to use adverbs as they make sentences more complex, so instead of saying j'écoute de la musique, you could say how often this happens, using de temps en temps, quelquefois or souvent for example.

Now try this

LISTENING TRACK 13

Target grade 1-3

Clément is talking about using technology. What does he say? Complete the gap in each sentence using a word or phrase from the box below.

There are more words / phrases than gaps.

Listen to the recording

> brother   half brother   half sister
> from time to time   often   rarely
> uses social media   downloads films
> watches films

1 On his phone, Clément speaks to his _____ .

2 He downloads videos _____ .

3 He never _____ .

(3 marks)

Social media

Digital resources

Les réseaux sociaux

choisir	to choose
commentaire (m)	comment, remark
danger (m)	danger
dangereux / dangereuse	dangerous
image (f)	picture, image
influence (f)	influence
médias (mpl)	media
message (m)	message
partager	to share
participer à	to take part in
populaire	popular
rapide	fast
risque (m)	risk
réseau (m)	network
réussir à	to succeed in
suivre	to follow
efficace	efficient
harcèlement (m)	bullying
nuire	to harm
virtuel(le)	virtual

-ir verbs

Regular -ir verbs like choisir (to choose) follow a fixed pattern.
To form the present tense of an -ir verb, take the -ir off the infinitive, and add these endings:

je choisis	I choose
tu choisis	you choose
il / elle / on choisit	he / she / one chooses
nous choisissons	we choose
vous choisissez	you choose
ils / elles choisissent	they choose

Grammar page 105

Elle choisit Instagram. She chooses Instagram.

Les influenceurs réuss**issent** à avoir un plus grand nombre d'amis en ligne. Influencers succeed in gaining a larger number of friends online.

Worked example

LISTENING TRACK **14**   Target grade **2-4**   Listen to the recording

Nadia, Tom and Manon are talking about social media.
What do they say?
Listen to the recording and complete the sentences by putting a cross ✗ in the correct box for each question.

Nadia: Je choisis Instagram où on peut regarder des photos de célébrités.

Tom: Je ne partage pas mes photos. C'est dangereux.

Manon: J'ai beaucoup d'amis virtuels.

Always take time to practise your reading aloud. In the exam you will be given one minute in the exam room with your teacher where you can practise reading this out loud to test out how the words sound.

1 Nadia says that you can …
 ☒ **A** look at photos.
 ☐ **B** follow celebrities.
 ☐ **C** message friends.

2 Tom says that sharing photos is …
 ☐ **A** a good choice.
 ☐ **B** possible.
 ☒ **C** dangerous.

3 Manon has …
 ☐ **A** no friends.
 ☒ **B** lots of virtual friends.
 ☐ **C** a few virtual friends.

(3 marks)

Now try this

SPEAKING   Target grade **5-9**

Read aloud
Thomas has contributed to a blog about social media.
Read out the text below.

> Je vais sur Internet chaque jour.
> Il est facile de trouver des copains et des copines sur les réseaux sociaux.
> À mon avis, il y a trop de harcèlement en ligne et je pense que c'est nul, surtout pour les jeunes.
> Je partage mes photos, je suis les célébrités et je m'amuse.

Remember that although spelt the same as in English, **Internet** is pronounced differently in French, with the **In-** sounding like the **-ain** in the French word **pain** (bread).

(8 marks)

21

The internet

Digital resources

Internet

acheter	to buy
communication (f)	communication
coûter	to cost
film (m)	film
genre (m)	type, kind, sort
gratuit(e)	free
influenceur (m)	influencer
loisir (m)	hobby, free time
ordinateur portable (m)	laptop
risque (m)	risk
scolaire	school
site (m)	site
utile	useful
virus (m)	virus
abonnement (m)	subscription
appareil (m)	device

Comparatives

Grammar page 98

In French you can use the words **plus** (more) and **moins** (less) before an adjective, and **que** (than) afterwards, to make a comparison.

petit	small
plus petit que ...	smaller than ...
moins petit que ...	less small than ...

Remember that the adjective still needs to agree with the noun:

Mon portable est **plus** utile **que** mon ordinateur portable.
My mobile is more useful than my laptop.

Les livres sont **moins** chers sur Internet.
Books are less expensive on the internet.

To say something is the same, use **aussi** ... **que** (as ... as).

Son portable est **aussi** grand **que** mon portable.
His mobile is as big as my mobile.

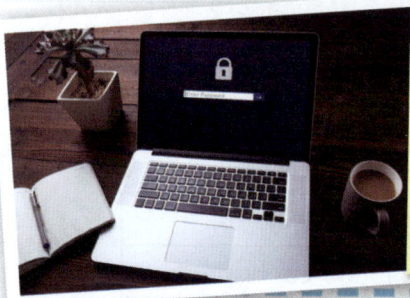

Il est **aussi** important d'utiliser un mot de passe fort pour protéger vos informations personnelles **que** de prendre soin de réduire le risque de télécharger un virus.
It is as important to use a strong password to protect your personal information as it is to take care to reduce the risk of downloading a virus.

Worked example

READING

Target grade 1-3

Read these comments on an internet forum.
Who says what? Choose the correct answers.
Put a cross ✗ in the correct column for each question.

Jade: Sur Internet on peut acheter des billets de train.
Yanis: En ligne les chemises et les pantalons sont moins chers.
Marie: Pour mes devoirs, Internet est pratique.

Who ...	Jade	Yanis	Marie
... talks about travel?	✗		
... talks about school?			✗
... talks about clothes?		✗	

(3 marks)

You will sometimes need to make a link between a specific item of vocabulary and a general word. So, in the worked example, **travel** links to **train**, **school** to **devoirs**, and **clothes** to **chemises** and **pantalons**.

When you are asked to answer a question in French in the conversation, make sure that you listen carefully to what is said and if you are not sure, don't be afraid to ask for the question to be repeated. **Peux-tu répéter la question, s'il te plaît?** Can you repeat the question, please?

Now try this

SPEAKING

1 Tu as souvent fait des achats en ligne?
2 Que fais-tu en ligne?

Target grade 5-6

Technology

Computer games

Digital resources

Les jeux vidéo

console (f)	games console
gagner	to win
jeu (m)	game
joueur (m)	player
loisir (m)	hobby
malsain(e)	unhealthy
ordinateur portable (m)	laptop
participer à	to take part in
perdre	to lose
personnage (m)	character
populaire	popular
risque (m)	risk
s'amuser	to enjoy oneself
santé (f)	health
sécurité (f)	security
tablette (f)	tablet
télécharger	to download
vidéo (f)	video
violence (f)	violence
virus (m)	virus
concours (m)	competition
écouteurs (mpl)	headphones
écran (m)	screen
harcèlement (m)	bullying
limiter	to limit
nuire	to harm
s'identifier à	to relate to
virtuel(le)	virtual

-re verbs

Grammar page 105

Regular verbs like perdre (to lose) follow a fixed pattern in the **present tense**.

1 Remove the -re from the infinitive.

2 Add the appropriate endings.

je perds	I lose / am losing
tu perds	you lose / are losing
il / elle / on perd	he / she / one loses / is losing
nous perdons	we lose / are losing
vous perdez	you lose / are losing
ils / elles perdent	they lose / are losing

e.g. Je perds souvent mes écouteurs.
I often lose my headphones.

In the **perfect tense** use perdu as the past participle.

J'ai perdu! I lost!

Worked example

READING — Target grade 7

Théo is writing about gaming.

L'année dernière, j'ai adoré jouer sur ma console de jeux. Je pouvais parler avec mes amis et je gagnais souvent des concours dans les mondes virtuels. Mais j'ai commencé à avoir mal à la tête à cause de l'écran, donc maintenant je limite le temps de jeu, sinon c'est malsain.

Il existe de très bons jeux qui sont très populaires, mais il y a également des risques: ils ne sont pas bons pour les jeunes enfants en raison de la violence et du harcèlement.

Answer the following questions **in English**. You do not need to write in full sentences.

1 Why did Théo like playing on his console? **(2 marks)**
He spoke to his friends and often won competitions.

2 Why did Théo limit his gaming? **(1 mark)**
He started to get headaches.

3 Why does he think some games are not suitable for young children? **(2 marks)**
Violence and bullying.

Worked example

LISTENING TRACK 15 — Target grade 3-4

Emma is talking about gaming. Which things does she mention? Listen to the recording and put a cross ✗ in each one of the **three** correct boxes.

Listen to the recording

J'ai une nouvelle console et elle est géniale. J'ai acheté des jeux en ligne et je voudrais participer à un concours.

☐	A videos	☐	D radio
✗	B console	✗	E competition
✗	C games	☐	F headphones

(3 marks)

Now try this

SPEAKING — Target grade 3-7

You might be asked a question like this in the conversation task.

Tu aimes participer à des jeux en ligne? Pourquoi or pourquoi pas?

Digital resources

Pros and cons of technology

La technologie – pour et contre

adolescent (m)	teenager
causer	to cause
célèbre	famous
danger (m)	danger
lien (m)	link
malsain(e)	unhealthy
mot de passe (m)	password
recherche (f)	research
risque (m)	risk
santé (f)	health
sécurité (f)	safety, security
victime (f)	victim
virus (m)	virus
yeux (mpl)	eyes
baisser	to lower
communiquer	to communicate
données (fpl)	data
harcèlement (m)	bullying
inconnu(e)	unknown
limiter	to limit
nuire	to harm
renseignement (m)	piece of information
vol (m)	theft

The perfect tense of regular verbs

Grammar page 109

To talk about what happened in the past, you will need to use the **perfect tense**. For all regular verbs, it has two parts:

1 the present tense of avoir

j'ai	I have
tu as	you have
il / elle / on a	he / she / one has
nous avons	we have
vous avez	you have
ils / elles ont	they have

2 a **past participle** from the verb you are using
Take the infinitive of the verb, then:
- for -er verbs, remove -er from the infinitive and add -é
  J'ai utilisé … I used …
- for -ir verbs, cross off the -ir and add -i
  Il a fini. He finished.
- for -re verbs, cross off the -re and add -u
  J'ai perdu. I lost.

Some verbs use the present tense of **être**, not **avoir**: see page 110.

For irregular verbs which use avoir, such as **écrire, vouloir, pouvoir, devoir** and **savoir**, see page 109. **H** ONLY

Worked example
SPEAKING TRACK 16 | Target grade 1-5

Tu aimes utiliser la technologie?
Oui, j'aime la technologie car ça m'aide à parler avec mes amis et aussi je peux acheter des choses en ligne. Je fais des recherches sur Internet pour mes devoirs.

Listen to the recording

Flexible phrases
Learn ways to give opinions in many scenarios.
J'aime Internet car c'est pratique.
I like the internet because it is practical.
À mon avis, il y a trop de dangers.
In my opinion there are too many dangers.

Worked example
SPEAKING TRACK 17 | Target grade 4-9

Quels sont les dangers de la technologie?
Il existe un lien entre la technologie et la santé des adolescents. Utiliser les écrans trop longtemps peut faire mal aux yeux. Il est possible pour les enfants de communiquer avec des inconnus ou de leur donner leurs mots de passe. C'est dangereux, à mon avis.

Listen to the recording

This is a high-grade conversation answer.

Now try this
WRITING | Target grade 5-9

Translate the following paragraph **into French**.

I like using the internet at home. My favourite social network is Instagram. I try to communicate with my friends every day. Last month I sent an email to my aunt who lives in Paris. Using new technology doesn't worry her and last year she bought a new laptop that she really likes.

(10 marks)

Hobbies

Digital resources

Les loisirs

aller au cinéma	to go to the cinema
chanter	to sing
cheval (m)	horse
club des jeunes (m)	youth club
danser	to dance
écouter de la musique	to listen to music
faire	to do, to go
faire du théâtre	to do drama
faire la cuisine	to do cooking
jouer au tennis / basket / foot	to play tennis / basketball / football
jouer de la musique	to play music
jouer sur ma console de jeux	to play on my games console
lire	to read
natation (f)	swimming
passer	to spend (time)
sortir	to go out
vélo (m)	bike, cycle
faire des achats (mpl)	to go shopping
foyer (m)	home

The verb faire

Grammar page 108

Faire means 'to do' or 'to make' but can also mean 'to go' with hobbies. (You can also use jouer à for playing sports: see page 14.)
Je fais mes devoirs. I do my homework.
Je fais un gâteau. I make a cake.
Je fais du vélo. I go cycling.

It is an irregular verb.

je fais	I do
tu fais	you do
il / elle / on fait	he / she / one does
nous faisons	we do
vous faites	you do
ils / elles font	they do

In the perfect tense faire is irregular but you still use avoir to help form this tense.
J'ai fait I did
The future is je ferai I will do

> This form of the future is for Higher tier only.

Worked example

SPEAKING TRACK 18
Target grade 1-9

Qu'est-ce que tu aimes faire le soir ou le week-end?

Listen to the recording

> This question could appear as part of the conversation in the Speaking exam, or as part of a writing task. Give as many opinions as you can. Don't forget to justify them.

Mon loisir préféré c'est la natation car c'est bon pour la santé. Je suis fort en natation! De temps en temps j'aime jouer au tennis avec mes amis en été car je trouve ça amusant.

Le week-end dernier je suis allé en ville faire les magasins et j'adore ça car la mode m'intéresse, mais demain je ferai du vélo avec ma sœur parce qu'elle adore passer du temps à la campagne.

> This is an answer of a student working at Grades 6–8.

Aiming higher

Skills page 87

Opinions and reasons allow you to show off a variety of vocabulary and structures.

> J'aime bien danser et chanter le week-end avec mes amis.
> I like dancing and singing at the weekend with my friends.

Now try this

LISTENING TRACK 19
Target grade 1-3

Listen to the recording

Ana is talking about her hobbies.
Listen to the recording and complete the following table **in English**.
You do not need to write in full sentences.

1 Her favourite hobby	
2 What she hates doing	
3 When she reads	

(3 marks)

Digital resources

Music and dance

La musique et la danse

chaîne (f)	channel
chanson (f)	song
chanter	to sing
chanteur (m) / chanteuse (f)	singer
classique	classical
concert (m)	concert
danse (f)	dance
danser	to dance
écouter	to listen to
festival (m)	festival
fort(e)	loud
groupe (m)	group, band
instrument (m)	instrument
jouer de	to play (a musical instrument)
musique (f)	music
populaire	popular
rythme (m)	rhythm
spectacle (m)	show
titre (m)	title
Je suis fan de …	I'm a fan of …
écouteurs (mpl)	headphones
paroles (fpl)	lyrics
son (m)	sound

'This' and 'that'

Grammar page 99

These words are adjectives and therefore, in French, they need to agree with the word they describe.

Ce means 'this' / 'that' and is used with **masculine singular words**.

ce groupe this / that group

Cette means 'this' / 'that' and is used with **feminine singular words**.

cette chanson this / that song

Cet means 'this' / 'that' and is used with **masculine singular words which start with a vowel or mute h**.

cet instrument this / that instrument

Ces means 'these' / 'those' and is used with **plural words whether masculine or feminine**.

ces chanteurs these / those singers
ces paroles these / those lyrics

La musique de **ce** festival est très **forte**.
The music at this festival is very loud.

In Reading texts, make sure that you look out for the correct tenses as they will often guide you to the correct answer.

Worked example

READING   Target grade 5-6

Toni has sent you an email.

> Hier soir je suis allée voir Ed Sheeran en concert avec mes amies et c'était génial. Je me suis très bien amusée et j'ai même dansé. Il a chanté ma chanson préférée, alors, je n'oublierai jamais cette soirée. Mon rêve est de voir Taylor Swift en concert car j'adore les paroles de ses chansons.

Complete the gap in each sentence using a word from the box below.

There are more words than gaps.

sang	danced	smiled
forget	improve	dream about
voice	stadium	lyrics

1 Toni enjoyed the concert and she even ....danced.... .
2 It was an evening that she will never ....forget.... .
3 She especially likes Taylor Swift's ....lyrics.... .

(3 marks)

Now try this

SPEAKING   Target grade 1-5

Tu préfères la musique ou la danse? Pourquoi?

In the conversation task it is important to develop your answer. Use past, present and future time frames, conjunctions like **mais** or **donc** and adjectives to add variety. Don't forget to give opinions with reasons to add complexity to your answer.

Digital resources

Arranging to go out

Sortir ensemble

centre commercial (m)	shopping centre
château (m)	castle
chez moi	at my house
cinéma (m)	cinema
inviter	to invite
musée (m)	museum
parc (m)	park
piscine (f)	swimming pool
plage (f)	beach
rencontrer	to meet (up)
sortie (f)	outing
sortir	to go out
stade (m)	stadium
ville (f)	town
disponible	available
foule (f)	crowd
pièce (f)	play

To learn vocabulary on any topic area, try this:
- Learn the words you want to remember.
- Cover the English words.
- Write the English words.
- Check how many you have got right.

Asking a question

Grammar page 117

You can:
- add **est-ce que** to the start of a statement
  Est-ce que tu veux aller en ville?
  Do you want to go into town?
- just use your voice to imply a question by going up in tone at the end of the sentence
  Tu veux aller en ville?
  Do you want to go into town?
- use **si on va … ?** to mean 'shall we go?'
  Si on va au stade?
  Shall we go to the stadium?
- reverse the verb and noun and hyphenate, and then go up in tone at the end of the sentence.
  Veux-tu sortir demain?
  Do you want to go out tomorrow?

Ways to respond

Oui je veux bien! Yes, I'd love to!

Oui bien sûr! Yes of course!

Je suis désolé(e), je ne peux pas venir parce que …
I'm sorry I can't come because …

Il me faut faire mes devoirs. I have to do my homework.

Il me faut aller voir ma tante. I have to visit my aunt.

Worked example

LISTENING TRACK 20   Target grade 1-2

Ahmed, Myriam and Clément are asking people to go out. What do they say?
Listen to the recording and complete the sentences by putting a cross ✗ in the correct box for each question.

1 **Ahmed:** Tu veux aller à la piscine ce soir?
2 **Myriam:** Si on va en ville cet après-midi?
3 **Clément:** Je veux aller au stade. Et toi?

Remember that in French you can often say **on** instead of **nous** (or other pronouns).

Listen to the recording

1 Ahmed is asking someone to go to the …

✗	A	swimming pool.
☐	B	supermarket.
☐	C	station.

2 Myriam suggests going out …

☐	A	this evening.
☐	B	this morning.
✗	C	this afternoon.

3 Clément wants to go to the …

☐	A	shopping centre.
☐	B	cinema.
✗	C	stadium.

(3 marks)

Now try this

LISTENING TRACK 21   Target grade 6

Listen to the recording

Myriam is talking about what she did last week. What does she say? Listen to the recording and put a cross ✗ in each one of the **three** correct boxes.

☐	A	She played football.
☐	B	She celebrated her friend's birthday.
☐	C	There was a big crowd.

☐	D	Her other friend came too.
☐	E	Her other friend played tennis.
☐	F	Her other friend acts in a play.

(3 marks)

Digital resources

Reading

La lecture

culture (f)	culture	livre (m)	book
culturel(le)	cultural	page (f)	page
genre (m)	type, genre	personnage (m)	character
		bibliothèque (f)	library
histoire (f)	story	emprunter	to borrow
journal (m)	newspaper	prêter	to lend
lecture (f)	reading	raconter	to tell
lire	to read	roman (m)	novel

C'est un livre …
… classique
… de voyage
… étonnant
… excellent
… intéressant
… populaire
… terrible
… utile

C'est une histoire …
… amusante
… complexe
… de comédie
… d'horreur
… de science-fiction
… étonnante
… extraordinaire
… grave
… historique
… inquiétante

> Elle a lu un article vraiment amusant.
> She read a really funny article.

🖋 Flexible phrases

Ce que j'aime le plus, c'est …
What I like best is …

The perfect tense: irregular verbs

Grammar page 109–110

Lire (to read) is one of the verbs with an irregular past participle in the perfect tense.
Hier, j'ai lu un roman historique.
Yesterday I read a historical novel.
Mes parents ont lu beaucoup de livres classiques.
My parents have read lots of classic books.
Some common irregular past participles:

avoir	eu	lire	lu
connaître	connu	mettre	mis
courir	couru	ouvrir	ouvert
écrire	écrit	prendre	pris
être	été	recevoir	reçu
faire	fait	rire	ri
découvrir	découvert	pouvoir	pu
devoir	dû	savoir	su
pleuvoir	plu	vouloir	voulu

H ONLY

Elle a eu peur parce que c'était une histoire d'horreur.
She was afraid because it was a horror story.
Je n'ai pas pu finir de lire le livre. **H ONLY**
  C'était terrible.
I wasn't able to finish reading the book. **H ONLY**
  It was terrible.
J'ai dû emprunter un livre à la bibliothèque.
I had to borrow a book from the library.

Worked example

SPEAKING TRACK 22   **Target grade 1-5**

Listen to the recording

Qu'est-ce que tu aimes lire?
J'aime lire des livres amusants.   **(2 marks)**

> Remember that the questions asked immediately after the read aloud and the picture task need to be short sentences. Don't try to extend the sentence, just answer it clearly. There are just 2 marks for full communication.

> You might be asked a question like this in your Speaking exam as a follow-up to the **read aloud** or the **picture task**.

Now try this

LISTENING TRACK 23   **Target grade 5-6**

Listen to the recording

Inès is talking about her hobby. What does she say?
Listen to the recording and complete the sentences by putting a cross ✗ in the correct box for each question.

1 She started reading …
☐ **A** five years ago.
☐ **B** when she was five.
☐ **C** five months ago.

2 She has just read …
☐ **A** a newspaper.
☐ **B** a boring novel.
☐ **C** an interesting novel.

3 One day she would like to write …
☐ **A** a play.
☐ **B** her own novel.
☐ **C** her mother's story.

(3 marks)

Television

Digital resources

La télévision

acteur (m)	actor
chaîne (f)	channel
comédie (f)	comedy
crime (m)	crime
émission (f)	programme
fan (m/f)	fan
film (m)	film
horreur (f)	horror
informations (fpl)	news
personnage (m)	character
police (f)	police
recommander	to recommend
science-fiction (f)	science fiction
série (f)	series, soap opera
télé(vision) (f)	television
tragédie (f)	tragedy, drama
critique (f)	review, criticism

Using the days of the week

lundi	Monday
mardi	Tuesday
mercredi	Wednesday
jeudi	Thursday
vendredi	Friday
samedi	Saturday
dimanche	Sunday

Note that unless they start a sentence, the days of the week don't have a capital letter in French.

There is no word for 'on' with days of the week in French so lundi can mean 'on Monday'.

To say you do something regularly on a certain day of the week, put le in front of the day:

le mardi … on Tuesdays …

'At the weekend' is just le week-end.

Le week-end, je regarde la télé.
At the weekend I watch TV.

Worked example

WRITING

Target grade **1-5**

Describe the photo. Write four short sentences **in French**.   **(8 marks)**

1 Il y a quatre personnes.

2 Ils regardent la télé.

3 Je vois des fruits.

4 Il y a une famille.

There is no need to try to use complex language in the Foundation Writing picture task as the marks are for communication only, but remember that you must not make a mistake which affects communication (a major error).
You could describe hair, eye colour and clothes in the picture task.

Now try this

SPEAKING

Target grade **5-9**

Read aloud

Jules has written a blog about TV. Read out the text below.

> J'aime bien regarder les émissions de science-fiction avec toute ma famille.
> Je les trouve vraiment sympa et ma sœur et moi n'avons jamais peur des personnages.
> J'essaie de ne pas regarder trop de télévision car c'est mauvais pour les yeux.
> Demain, mes copains vont venir chez moi et nous allons regarder un film d'horreur.

Don't forget to sound the previous -s before the start of the three words underlined (this is known as the s-liaison).

(8 marks)

Going to the cinema

Aller au cinéma

acteur (m)	actor
action (f)	action
billet (m)	ticket
célèbre	famous
cinéma (m)	cinema
comédie (f)	comedy
coûter	to cost
film (m)	film
genre (m)	type, sort, genre
histoire (f)	story
histoire (f) d'amour	love story
horreur (f)	horror
documentaire (m)	documentary
écran (m)	screen
séance (f)	screening, session

Using avoir to mean 'to be'

Grammar page 106

Avoir normally means 'to have', but, in certain French phrases, it means 'to be'.
J'ai 15 ans. I **am** 15 years old.
Learn the following expressions:

avoir faim / soif	to be hungry / thirsty
avoir tort	to be wrong
avoir besoin de	to need
avoir envie de	to feel like (doing something)
avoir lieu	to take place
avoir peur (de)	to be scared / frightened (of)

H ONLY

J'ai peur des films d'horreur.
I'm frightened of / by horror films.

Worked example

SPEAKING TRACK 24 | Target grade 1-5 | Listen to the recording

Describe the picture. Your description must cover:
• people
• location
• activity. **(8 marks)**

Sur la photo, il y a un groupe de jeunes qui sont au cinéma. Je vois deux garçons et quatre filles et un des garçons porte des lunettes. Ils regardent un film et je pense que c'est une comédie car ils sourient. Ils mangent et ils boivent. À mon avis, les gens semblent vraiment contents.

Aiming higher

To get high marks on the picture task, you need to develop ideas and describe relevant aspects of the picture with some variety of vocabulary and grammar. In the worked example, the student has used qui, que and car and the phrase À mon avis as examples of development and variety.

Now try this

LISTENING TRACK 25 | Target grade 2-4 | Listen to the recording

Chloé, Dorian and Camille are talking about going out to the cinema.

What do they say? Listen to the recording and complete the sentences by putting a cross ✗ in the correct box for each question.

1 Chloé likes going to the cinema to …
☐ A watch documentaries.
☐ B meet up with her friends.
☐ C see the latest films.

2 Dorian prefers the cinema because he can …
☐ A watch new films.
☐ B buy food and drink.
☐ C enjoy the atmosphere.

3 Camille says that cinema tickets are …
☐ A very expensive.
☐ B quite expensive.
☐ C too expensive.

(3 marks)

Celebrity culture

Digital resources

Les célébrités

acteur (m)	actor
argent (m)	money
artiste (m/f)	artist
célèbre	famous
célébrité (f)	celebrity
chanteur (m) / chanteuse (f)	singer
fan (m/f)	fan
influenceur (m)	influencer
international(e)	international
médias (mpl)	media
mode (f)	fashion
musique (f)	music
personnalité (f)	personality
riche	rich
succès (m)	success
suivre	to follow
théâtre (m)	theatre
article (m)	article
don (m)	gift, talent
s'identifier à	to relate to

Pronouncing similar words

Track 26

Some French and English words look the same (cognates) or are very similar (near cognates).

International is the same as 'international' in English and théâtre looks very similar to the English 'theatre'.

However, most of these words are pronounced differently. It will be important for speaking tasks, especially the read aloud task, that you can pronounce them properly.

Listen to the audio file to practise some of these words:

acteur	influenceur	riche
article	international	succès
artiste	médias	théâtre
célébrité	musique	
fan	personnalité	

Les célébrités – comme les acteurs, les chanteurs et les artistes – sont souvent riches grâce à leur succès.

Celebrities – like actors, singers and artists – are often rich because of their success.

Worked example

SPEAKING TRACK 27

Target grade 1-9

Listen to the recording

Qui est ta célébrité préférée? Pourquoi?

Ma celébrité préférée est Idris Elba car il est sympa et j'aime ses films. C'est un acteur excellent, et il est aussi très gentil. Je l'ai vu à Birmingham et il m'a parlé!

In the conversation element of the Speaking exam, you can always include personal opinions and events like this. It makes the response more detailed. This is a mid-grade conversation answer.

Gentil is not on the vocabulary list but the student has used it correctly, so would receive equal credit for this.

Now try this

READING

Target grade 7-9

Read this short article about Séverine, a famous singer.

> Séverine est née au Canada et ses parents étaient de célèbres acteurs. Après avoir quitté l'école, elle a commencé à chanter dans la rue avec quelques copines et un jour, elles ont gagné un concours international avec une chanson que Séverine avait écrite à l'âge de quinze ans.
> Elle a décidé d'habiter en France où elle a eu du succès. Elle vient de se marier avec un acteur canadien.

Put a cross ✗ next to each one of the **three** correct statements.

☐	**A** Séverine was not born in France.		☐	**D** She won a competition before she finished school.
☐	**B** Her parents were famous singers.		☐	**E** She wrote a winning song when she was 15.
☐	**C** Séverine started singing in the street.		☐	**F** She is going to marry a Canadian actor.

(3 marks)

Digital resources

Role models

Les modèles

acteur (m)	actor
aider	to help
argent (m)	money
célèbre	famous
célébrité (f)	celebrity
chanteur (m) / chanteuse (f)	singer
fan (m/f)	fan
influenceur (m)	influencer
inspirer	to inspire
international(e)	international
médias (mpl)	media
modèle (m)	role model
personnalité (f)	personality
riche	rich
succès (m)	success
suivre	to follow
théâtre (m)	theatre
don (m)	gift, talent
s'identifier à	to relate to

Pronouncing préféré(e)(s) / préfère

The forms of the verb préférer (to prefer) can be difficult to pronounce and you might sometimes get confused between the pronunciation of préfère and préféré.

Préfère is part of the present tense of préférer and you don't pronounce the final -e.

Préféré is a past participle or an adjective meaning 'favourite' and you pronounce the final -é so it sounds a bit like the e in 'lemon'.

Exam alert

In the conversation part of the Speaking exam, listen carefully to the question. If necessary, ask for it to be repeated: Peux-tu répéter la question, s'il te plaît? Can you repeat the question please?

If you are asked a question starting Tu trouves … ?, you can always begin your answer with Je trouve / Je ne trouve pas …

Worked example

SPEAKING TRACK 28 | Target grade 1-5

Listen to the recording

Tu trouves les célébrités intéressantes? Pourquoi?

Je ne trouve pas les célébrités intéressantes parce que je préfère passer du temps avec mes amis. Ils sont plus importants.

Flexible phrases

C'est surtout parce que / à cause de / grâce à …
It's especially because / because of / thanks to …

Il m'inspire. C'est surtout parce qu'il dit toujours la vérité.
He inspires me. It's especially because he always tells the truth.

Elle est riche. C'est surtout grâce à son succès comme chanteuse célèbre.
She is rich. It is mostly thanks to her success as a famous singer.

Worked example

LISTENING TRACK 29 | Target grade 1-5

Dictation

Listen to the recording

You are going to hear someone talking about role models.

Sentences 1–3: write down the missing words in the gaps provided. In each gap, you will write one word **in French**.

1 Ma ......*sœur*...... est mon ......*modèle*...... .

2 Les ......*célébrités*...... sont ......*généreuses*...... .

3 Je ......*veux*...... être ......*ambitieux*...... .

Sentences 4–6: write down the full sentences that you hear in the spaces provided, **in French**.

4 Ma mère m'inspire.

5 Tous les acteurs célèbres sont riches.

6 Mon ami est sympa.

(10 marks)

Now try this

LISTENING TRACK 30 | Target grade 5-6

Clara is talking about her role model, Rita Ora*.
Listen to the recording and put a cross ✗ in each one of the **two** correct boxes.

Listen to the recording

☐	**A** Clara says that Rita Ora has talent.
☐	**B** Clara thinks that Rita Ora sings well.
☐	**C** Clara gives money to the poor.
☐	**D** Clara needs money to go to Europe.

*Rita Ora is a famous singer.   **(2 marks)**

Places in town

Digital resources

En ville

aéroport (m)	airport	magasin (m)	shop
banque (f)	bank	maison (f)	house
bâtiment (m)	building	marché (m)	market
boulangerie (f)	bakery	métro (m)	underground
bureau (m)	office	musée (m)	museum
café (m)	café	pâtisserie (f)	cake shop
carte (f)	map	pharmacie (f)	pharmacy
centre commercial (m)	shopping centre	piscine (f)	swimming pool
château (m)	castle	poste (f)	post office
école (f)	school	rue (f)	road / street
gare (f)	railway station	théâtre (m)	theatre
		université (f)	university
hôpital (m)	hospital	banlieue (f)	suburb
hôtel (m)	hotel	bibliothèque (f)	library
immeuble (m)	block of flats	gymnase (m)	gymnasium
		industrie (f)	industry

Verb + infinitive

Some verbs are often followed by an infinitive.

* je vais + infinitive I'm going to
  Je vais aller en ville.
  I'm going to go to town.
* j'aime / j'adore + infinitive I like / love
  J'aime visiter le musée.
  I like to visit / visiting the museum.
* je n'aime pas / je déteste + infinitive
  I don't like / hate
  Ma mère n'aime pas aller au bureau.
  My mother doesn't like going to the office.
* vouloir (to want), devoir (to have to) and pouvoir (to be able to)
  Je veux visiter le château.
  I want to visit the castle.

When you have a short extract in Listening, the answer might come quickly, so be alert from the start.

Je peux rencontrer mes amis au café après l'école.
I can meet my friends at the café after school.

Worked example

LISTENING TRACK 31 Target grade 1-2

Diane, Enzo and Gabrielle are talking about their town. What do they say?
Listen to the recording and complete the sentences by putting a cross ✗ in the correct box for each question.

Diane: J'aime bien aller à la pâtisserie. Les gâteaux sont bons.

Enzo: Je déteste le musée en ville car ce n'est pas intéressant.

Gabrielle: Il n'y a pas d'aéroport dans ma ville.

D'aéroport is hard to work out from what you hear as you might think that you are looking for a word starting with d- in French.

1 Diane likes visiting …
☐ A the castle.
☒ B the cake shop.
☐ C the swimming pool.

Listen to the recording

2 Enzo hates the …
☒ A museum.
☐ B market.
☐ C theatre.

3 In Gabrielle's town there is no …
☐ A railway station.
☐ B hospital.
☒ C airport.

(3 marks)

You might have to answer questions about where you live in the Speaking exam. If it comes up in the conversation, remember to add details and opinions (with justifications) and try to include more complex language. This could include adjectives, verb + infinitives and different tenses.

Now try this

SPEAKING Target grade 1-5

Décris-moi ta région.

Digital resources

Things to do

Les choses à faire

améliorer	to improve	piscine (f)	swimming pool
capitale (f)	capital city	place (f)	square
centre (m)	centre	pont (m)	bridge
cinéma (m)	cinema	quartier (m)	neighbourhood
entreprise (f)	company, business	supermarché (m)	supermarket
		terrain (m)	sports pitch, ground
lac (m)	lake		
marché (m)	market	théâtre (m)	theatre
musée (m)	museum	traverser	to cross
parc (m)	park	accueillir	to welcome
pâtisserie (f)	cake shop	vivre	to live

Pouvoir (to be able)

Grammar page 108

You often want to say what you can do in an area. This is done by using a part of pouvoir.

je peux	I can
tu peux	you can
il / elle / on peut	he / she / it / one can
nous pouvons	we can
vous pouvez	you can
ils / elles peuvent	they can

Dans ma région, on peut faire les magasins.
In my region you can go shopping.

Récemment, on a beaucoup amélioré notre ville. Il y a de nouvelles entreprises et on peut visiter un parc énorme.
Recently they have improved our town a lot. There are new businesses and you can visit an enormous park.

Worked example

READING — Target grade 2-3

Read these comments from Emma on an internet forum.

Emma: J'aime bien habiter dans ma région car on peut aller au marché sur la place le vendredi, mais on doit améliorer les transports. Il n'y a pas assez de bus.

Complete the following table **in English**. You do not need to write in full sentences.

1	thing she likes	The market
2	thing she dislikes	The transport / buses

(2 marks)

Worked example

LISTENING TRACK 32 — Target grade 1-2

Clara is talking about her town. What is mentioned? Listen to the recording and put a cross ✗ in each one of the **three** correct boxes.

Listen to the recording

J'adore le vieux quartier de notre ville. Il y a une excellente pâtisserie et un musée intéressant. Ma sœur préfère le nouveau quartier car il y a une piscine et un terrain de sport où elle joue au football chaque semaine. Ce que j'aime le plus, c'est que tout le monde sourit.

☐	A weather	☒	D sport
☒	B food shop	☐	E accommodation
☒	C museum		

(3 marks)

This question targets the past time frames so try to use at least one perfect and one imperfect tense.

Now try this

SPEAKING — Target grade 5-6

Qu'est-ce que tu as fait avec tes amis samedi dernier?

Shopping

Digital resources

Faire les courses

acheter	to buy	jupe (f)	skirt
affaires (fpl)	things	marque (f)	brand
argent (m)	money	monnaie (f)	change
baskets (fpl)	trainers	pull (m)	pullover
cadeau (m)	present	robe (f)	dress
caisse (f)	checkout	sac (m)	bag
chaussette (f)	sock	taille (f)	size
chaussure (f)	shoe	valeur (f)	value
chemise (f)	shirt	vente (f)	sale
client (m)	customer	achat (m)	purchase
courses (fpl)	shopping	chapeau (m)	hat
coûter	to cost	étage (m)	floor
cravate (f)	tie	produit (m)	product
échanger	to exchange	veste (f)	jacket
fermer	to close		

The adjective 'new'

Grammar page 96

Use the irregular adjective **nouveau before** the noun.
- ✓ masculine singular nouveau
  un nouveau pull a new pullover
- ✓ masculine singular before a vowel or silent h nouvel
  un nouvel achat a new purchase
- ✓ feminine singular nouvelle
  une nouvelle chemise a new shirt
- ✓ masculine plural nouveaux
  les nouveaux sacs the new bags
- ✓ feminine plural nouvelles
  les nouvelles baskets the new trainers

Worked example

WRITING · Target grade 1-5

Write a review of a shopping centre for a website.
You **must** include the following points:
- where the shopping centre is
- your opinion of the shopping centre
- when you will next visit the shopping centre.

Write your answer **in French**. You should aim to write between 40 and 50 words. **(14 marks)**

Il y a un centre commercial dans ma ville et c'est excellent. Il y a beaucoup de magasins que j'aime beaucoup. Je vais aller au centre commercial demain car je vais acheter un cadeau pour l'anniversaire de mon petit frère qui va avoir treize ans.

Flexible phrases

… n'est-ce pas?
… isn't it / aren't they?

Si tu veux mon avis …
If you want my opinion …

Cette robe est vraiment belle, n'est-ce pas? Mais si tu veux mon avis, elle est trop chère.
This dress is really beautiful, isn't it? But if you want my opinion, it's too expensive.

Preparing for the role play

The role play may involve a transactional situation like a shop. Make sure you can respond with short phrases.
Practise some key phrases you can draw on in the exam to help give you confidence.

Say what you want to buy. Je voudrais acheter …
Give a detail about the item. Je le / la préfère en bleu(e).
Say why you want it. C'est pour la fête de ma sœur.
Give an opinion. Oui! Ça va bien / C'est trop petit.
Say what size you want. Je voudrais une petite taille.
Ask about the price. C'est combien?
Ask where you can pay. Où est la caisse?

Now try this

LISTENING · TRACK 33 · Target grade 6-7

Listen to the recording

Clara is talking about a recent shopping trip. What does she say? Listen to the recording and complete the sentences by putting a cross ✗ in the correct box for each question.

1 Clara came back from town …
- ☐ **A** an hour ago.
- ☐ **B** at 1 o'clock.
- ☐ **C** yesterday.

2 For herself, she bought …
- ☐ **A** a red dress.
- ☐ **B** a hat.
- ☐ **C** a jacket.

3 She says that the hat is …
- ☐ **A** too small.
- ☐ **B** too big.
- ☐ **C** pink.

(3 marks)

Digital resources

Transport

Les transports

accident (m)	accident	passeport (m)	passport
aller (m)	single ticket	pied (m)	foot
aller-retour (m)	return ticket	rapide	fast
avion (m)	plane	retard (m)	delay
bateau (m)	boat	route (f)	route, way
billet (m)	ticket	station (f)	station
bus (m)	bus	trafic (m)	traffic
car (m)	coach	voiture (f)	car
conduire	to drive	voyager	to travel
feu (m)	traffic light	circulation (f)	traffic
gare (f)	station	louer	to hire
manquer	to miss	véhicule (m)	vehicle
moyen (m)	means of	vol (m)	flight
de transport	transport	voler	to fly

The near future

Grammar page 112

If you want to talk about something which is going to happen in the near future, it is easiest to use a part of aller + the infinitive.

je vais	I'm going
tu vas	you are going
il / elle / on va	he / she / one is going
nous allons	we are going
vous allez	you are going
ils / elles vont	they are going

Nous allons visiter la France.
We are going to visit France.

Worked example

READING **Target grade 5-6**

Manon has written an email about transport.

Je déteste prendre le car parce qu'il y a trop de personnes et je trouve que les cars ne sont jamais propres. À l'avenir, je voudrais bien apprendre à conduire car voyager en voiture est plus pratique. À mon avis, voyager en voiture est assez rapide même s'il y a de la circulation. En voiture, on peut être plus indépendant. Je sais qu'on dit que c'est mauvais pour l'environnement mais je vais aussi essayer d'aller en ville à pied.

Complete the gap in each sentence using a word or phrase from the box below. There are more words than gaps.

(3 marks)

car   coach   plane
to drive   to be more patient   to protect the environment
by bus   on foot   by bike

1 Manon hates travelling by ...*coach*... .
2 She wants to learn ...*to drive*... .
3 She will try to go to town ...*on foot*... .

Worked example

READING **Target grade 7**

Marie writes in her school magazine.

J'aimerais me rendre à l'école à vélo car c'est bon pour l'environnement. Cependant, j'habite trop loin de l'école. Beaucoup de mes amis prennent le train mais ma mère me conduit en voiture. Il y a toujours trop de trafic et d'autres retards comme des accidents. Mais j'aime bien écouter la radio en voiture. Pendant les vacances, je vais visiter Paris et je vais rester chez mon oncle. Je vais y aller en avion, ce qui est rapide mais mauvais pour l'environnement.

Complete the sentences below. Put a cross ✗ in the correct box for each question.

1 Marie goes to school by …
☐ A bike.
☐ B train.
☒ C car.

2 What she likes about travelling by car is …
☐ A it's fast.
☐ B there's lots of traffic to watch.
☒ C she can listen to the radio.

3 She says travelling by plane is …
☐ A necessary.
☒ B fast.
☐ C good for the environment.

(3 marks)

Now try this

SPEAKING

Quel est ton moyen de transport préféré?

Target grade 1-5

You might have to answer questions on transport in the conversation element of the Speaking exam.

Travel and buying tickets

Digital resources

Acheter des billets de transport

à l'heure	on time
aller (m)	single ticket
aller-retour (m)	return ticket
avion (m)	plane
bateau (m)	boat
billet (m)	ticket
bus (m)	bus
car (m)	coach
conduire	to drive
gare (f)	railway station
passeport (m)	passport
pied (m)	foot
port (m)	harbour, port
rapide	fast
retard (m)	delay
route (f)	route, way
station (f)	station
voiture (f)	car
voyager	to travel
quai (m)	platform
valise (f)	suitcase
véhicule (m)	vehicle
vol (m)	flight
voler	to fly

À quelle heure part le train?	What time does the train leave?
Je voudrais un billet pour Paris.	I would like a ticket to Paris.
De quel quai part le train?	Which platform does the train leave from?

En or à?

For most modes of transport you use en, without the le, la or l':

J'y vais **en** car.

J'ai voyagé **en** avion.

J'y suis allé **en** voiture.

However, 'on foot' is **à** pied:

Je suis rentré **à** pied.

'by bike' can use either:

Je suis arrivé **à** vélo / **en** vélo.

Telling the time

You might need to recognise or use times. Remember the 24-hour clock is used much more in France.

Quelle heure est-il? What time is it?

03h00	Il est trois heures.
04h15	Il est quatre heures et quart.
05h30	Il est cinq heures et demie.
06h10	Il est six heures dix.
07h35	Il est huit heures moins vingt-cinq. Il est sept heures trente-cinq.
20h45	Il est neuf heures moins le quart. Il est vingt heures quarante-cinq.

… du matin … in the morning

… de l'après-midi … in the afternoon

… du soir … in the evening

When you are listening for numbers, take care, especially with large numbers such as quatre-vingt-dix-neuf (99).

Worked example

READING
Target grade 1-5

Translate the following sentences **into English**.

1 J'aime voyager en train.
I like travelling by train.

2 Mon frère préfère prendre l'avion.
My brother prefers to take the plane.

3 Je vais en ville à pied.
I go to town on foot.

4 Hier je suis allé à l'école en bus avec mes amis.
Yesterday I went to school by bus with my friends.

5 S'il fait beau, je fais du vélo.
If it's fine / If the weather is fine, I go cycling.

(10 marks)

Now try this

SPEAKING
Target grade 5-9

Read aloud
Read out the text below.

Je suis canadien et je parle deux langues.
Avec mes copains, nous aimons voyager pour découvrir d'autres cultures.
Quand je vais à l'étranger, j'essaie de goûter des plats différents de la région.
Mes parents n'aiment pas prendre l'avion parce qu'ils ont peur de voler et ils pensent que c'est dangereux.

(8 marks)

Digital resources

My region – good and bad

Ma région – du bon et du mauvais

améliorer	to improve
bruit (m)	noise
crime (m)	crime
événement (m)	event
ferme (f)	farm
historique	historic
idéal(e)	ideal
lac (m)	lake
pollution (f)	pollution
public (m)	public
touriste (m)	tourist
zone (f)	zone
attirer	to attract
cité (f)	council estate
déchets (mpl)	rubbish, waste
détruire	to destroy
industrie (f)	industry

Modifiers

You can use modifiers to add detail to a description:

assez	quite	plus	more
très	very	moins	less
beaucoup	a lot	trop	too much
encore	yet, still	vraiment	really
un peu	a little		

Ma ville est vraiment belle.
My town is really beautiful.

Il y a trop de bruit. There's too much noise.

Il y a encore des problèmes.
There are still problems.

Il y a beaucoup moins de crime et de pollution.
There is much less crime and pollution.

Il y a encore plus de touristes.
There are yet more tourists.

Flexible phrases

Pour améliorer … , on pourrait …
To improve … , one could …

D'un côté … , mais de l'autre côté …
On the one hand … , but on the other hand …

C'est une question de point de vue.
It depends on your point of view. / It's a matter of opinion.

Pour améliorer notre ville, on pourrait organiser plus d'événements pour les jeunes.
To improve our town, we could organise more events for young people.

D'un côté, le lac naturel est beau, mais de l'autre côté, il est dangereux pour les très jeunes enfants.
On the one hand, the natural lake is beautiful, but on the other hand, it is dangerous for very young children.

Worked example

WRITING

Target grade 1-5

Write a review of your region for a website.
You **must** include the following points:
- what your area is like
- your opinion of your area
- what you will do in the area next week.

Write your answer **in French**. You should aim to write between 40 and 50 words. (14 marks)

J'habite dans une ville historique et il y a beaucoup de touristes en été. J'aime ma région car c'est belle et il y a beaucoup de choses à faire pour les jeunes. Par exemple, la semaine prochaine je vais aller au cinéma samedi et dimanche je vais jouer au foot au stade avec mes amis.

Now try this

LISTENING TRACK 34

Target grade 4-5

Listen to the recording

Luis is in the tourist office and is asking about tourist attractions.
What does the employee say?
Listen to the recording and complete the following tables **in English**.
You do not need to write in full sentences.

1 The place recommended by the employee	
2 Summer event	
3 A popular site with tourists	
4 Museum opening details	

(4 marks)

Local environment and transport

My area in the past

Digital resources

Ma région dans le passé

appartement (m)	flat
culturel(le)	cultural
entreprise (f)	business
fastfood (m)	fast food restaurant
fermer	to shut down
immeuble (m)	block of flats
rue (f)	road, street
terrain (m)	pitch, sports ground
arbre (m)	tree
construire	to build
situer	to locate, situate

Using two past tenses together

Grammar page 109–111

You will sometimes want to use the perfect and imperfect tenses in the same sentence. The perfect is for simple completed actions in the past, while the imperfect translates the English 'was / were doing' or 'used to do'.

Quand je traversais la rue, j'ai vu mon ami.
When I was crossing the road, I saw my friend.

Worked example

SPEAKING TRACK 35

Target grade 1-9

Qu'est-ce que tu penses de la région où tu habites?

Listen to the recording

J'aime bien la région où j'habite. C'est très historique.

Comment était ta région dans le passé?

Dans le passé, ma ville était plus petite. Il y avait moins de circulation et les rues étaient plus propres. Je pense que la vie était plus simple.

Quand ils construisaient des immeubles, ils ont détruit les arbres.
When they were building the blocks of flats, they destroyed the trees.

This is an example of a first follow-up question after the picture task or read aloud task. It needs a short response.

This is an example of a second follow-up question you might be asked in a conversation task. It needs a more developed answer like this higher-level response.

Now try this

READING

Target grade 5-6

Manon has written this in her diary.

Hier, j'étais en cours d'histoire au collège quand j'ai vu un vieux plan de ma ville. C'était plus petit et il n'y avait pas d'immeubles et il y avait moins d'entreprises. Je pense que je préfère ma ville maintenant car il y a des fastfoods et aussi des terrains de sport!

Put a cross ✗ next to each of the **two** correct statements.

☐	**A** Manon was in school when she saw an old map.
☐	**B** There were no businesses in the past in her town.
☐	**C** Manon prefers her town as it is now.
☐	**D** There used to be more sports grounds in the past.

(2 marks)

Exam alert

- In the **role play**, and in the **follow-up questions to the read aloud task and picture task**, you need to **communicate clearly and accurately**. Therefore, your answer should be **a short sentence or phrase**.
- In the **conversation**, your answers need to be **developed**, giving you the chance to **add variety and complexity**.

Had a look ☐ Nearly there ☐ Nailed it! ☐

Town or country

La ville ou la campagne

animal (m)	animal
bois (m)	wood(s)
campagne (f)	countryside
cheval (m)	horse
ciel (m)	sky
ferme (f)	farm
forêt (f)	forest
poisson (m)	fish
pollution (f)	pollution
village (m)	village
ville (f)	town
arbre (m)	tree
champ (m)	field
chemin (m)	way, path
fleur (f)	flower
rivière (f)	river

Plurals

Normally you can add an -s to a French noun to make the plural form:

la ville the town ➡ les villes the towns

However, many nouns which end in -al don't add -s but change the -al to -aux.

un animal an animal ➡ des animaux some animals

un cheval a horse ➡ des chevaux some horses

Worked example

SPEAKING TRACK 36

Target grade 1-9

Tu préfères la ville ou la campagne?

Moi, je préfère la campagne car il n'y a pas de pollution et on peut marcher dans les champs où tout est calme. Par contre, en ville il y a trop de personnes et trop de bruit.

Listen to the recording

Make sure that you can use negatives like il n'y a pas (there isn't / aren't).

Flexible phrases

Je suis du même avis. I'm of the same opinion.

Ça m'est égal. I don't mind.

Par contre … However …

Aiming higher

In speaking tasks, try to give both sides of an argument if you can as this gives you the chance to compare things and to use connectives.

Mon ami préfère les vacances en ville plutôt qu'à la campagne et moi, je suis du même avis. My friend prefers holidays in towns rather than in the countryside and I'm of the same opinion.

Worked example

SPEAKING TRACK 37

Target grade 1-5

Describe this picture. Your description must cover:
• people
• location
• activity. **(8 marks)**

Je vois des jeunes avec des animaux.

Ils sont à la campagne.
Une fille porte une veste rouge et blanche.

Un garçon a les cheveux roux.
Ils vivent dans une ferme.

Listen to the recording

Now try this

SPEAKING

Target grade 1-5

Read aloud

Read out the text below.

J'aime bien la campagne.
Il n'y a pas de bruit et c'est très calme.
J'adore voir les animaux et la forêt.
Mon frère préfère habiter dans une grande ville.
Il pense que c'est plus intéressant.

(8 marks)

During the holidays

Digital resources

Les vacances

à l'étranger	abroad
à la montagne	in the mountains
au bord de la mer	at the seaside
concert (m)	concert
côte (f)	coast
en été	in summer
en hiver	in winter
mer (f)	sea
neige (f)	snow
plage (f)	beach
souvenir (m)	souvenir
tourisme (m)	tourism
vacances (fpl)	holidays
visite (f)	visit, excursion
voyage (m)	journey
sable (m)	sand

How to say 'to'

Grammar page 95

The word for 'to' is usually à.
However, this changes as follows when saying 'to the'.

- With **masculine** words, use au.
  Je vais au concert. I'm going to the concert.

- With **feminine** words, use à la.
  Je suis allé(e) à la montagne.
  I went to the mountains.

- With **singular** words **which start with a vowel** or **h** use à l'.
  Je voudrais aller à l'étranger.
  I would like to go abroad.

- With **plural** words, use aux.
  On peut aller aux toilettes.
  You can go to the toilet.

📝 Flexible phrases

Pendant les vacances, je …
During the holidays, I …

Aiming higher

When you answer a question in part of the Speaking exam, listen carefully to the question asked, as you can sometimes use what is said to begin your answer. In the worked example, you can repeat pendant les vacances to set you off.

Worked example

SPEAKING TRACK 38 **Target grade 1-5**

Que fais-tu pendant les vacances?

Pendant les vacances, je vais normalement au bord de la mer car j'adore faire de la natation dans la mer s'il fait chaud. S'il pleut, je vais à la piscine. De temps en temps, j'achète des souvenirs pour ma famille.

Listen to the recording

Now try this

LISTENING TRACK 39 **Target grade 1-3**

Listen to the recording

Hugo, Myriam and Clément are talking about holidays.
What do they say?
Listen to the recording and complete the sentences by putting a cross ✗ in the correct box for each question.

1 Hugo often goes …

☐	**A** to the countryside.
☐	**B** to the mountains.
☐	**C** abroad.

2 Myriam buys …

☐	**A** souvenirs.
☐	**B** clothes.
☐	**C** gifts.

3 Clément spends holidays in …

☐	**A** Europe.
☐	**B** Canada.
☐	**C** France.

(3 marks)

Had a look ☐ **Nearly there** ☐ **Nailed it!** ☐

Abroad

Digital resources

À l'étranger

Afrique (f)	Africa
à l'étranger	abroad
Algérie (f)	Algeria
Amérique (f)	America
Angleterre (f)	England
Asie (f)	Asia
Canada (m)	Canada
étonnant(e)	incredible
Europe (f)	Europe
France (f)	France
France d'Outre-Mer (f)	overseas France
Madagascar (m)	Madagascar
Martinique (f)	Martinique
passer	to spend (time)
pays (m)	country
sports d'hiver (mpl)	winter sports
sur la côte	on the coast
visiter	to visit
vue (f)	view
paysage (m)	landscape

How to say 'in' and 'to' with countries

With **feminine** countries, use en.
Je vais en France. I'm going to France.
With **masculine** countries, use au.
Je suis au Canada. I'm in Canada.
With **plural** countries, use aux.
Je vais aux Etats-Unis. I'm going to the USA.

Je n'ai jamais voyagé à l'étranger mais un jour j'aimerais aller en Martinique car le paysage est tellement beau.
I have never travelled abroad but one day I would like to go to Martinique because the landscape is so beautiful.

Worked example

LISTENING TRACK 40 | Target grade 5-6

Listen to the recording

Hugo is talking about holidays. What does he say?

Complete the gap in each sentence using a word or phrase from the box below.

There are more words / phrases than gaps.

winter	spring	summer
the coast	a farm	the beach
the view	the house	a few days

1 Hugo goes to America in ...summer....
2 His aunt and uncle live on ...a farm....
3 At the lake he enjoyed ...the view....

Normalement je passe les vacances d'été en Amérique avec ma tante et mon oncle. Ils habitent dans une ferme à la campagne et c'est différent car j'habite sur la côte. L'année dernière, nous sommes allés à un lac où la vue était étonnante. Le mois prochain, j'irai encore chez eux.

(3 marks)

Listen carefully. For Question 2, the coast (la côte) is mentioned, but Hugo lives there, not his aunt and uncle.

Now try this

READING | Target grade 4-5

Read this comment from Yanis on an internet forum.

Normalement je passe mes vacances en France avec toute ma famille. Mes grands-parents passent les vacances avec nous aussi. Ma mère et ma grand-mère adorent faire des achats en ville mais mon frère préfère faire de la natation et jouer sur la plage avec nos deux chiens. Moi, j'aime bien visiter les musées avec mon grand-père parce que l'histoire m'intéresse.

Answer the following questions **in English**. You do not need to write in full sentences.

1 What does Yanis's brother like to do?
2 What does Yanis like to do?

(2 marks)

42

Types of holiday

Digital resources

Les vacances

à la campagne	in the countryside
à la montagne	in the mountains
au bord de la mer	at the seaside
chaud(e)	hot
choisir	to choose
été (m)	summer
froid(e)	cold
hiver (m)	winter
s'amuser	to enjoy oneself
se reposer	to rest
vacances actives (fpl)	active holidays
vacances culturelles (fpl)	cultural holidays
s'ennuyer	to be bored
se souvenir de	to remember

Reflexive verbs

Grammar page 107

Some verbs need an extra me, te, se, nous, vous:

je + me   nous + nous
tu + te   vous + vous
il(s) / elle(s) + se

Je m'amuse.   I have / am having a good time.

Elle ne s'ennuie pas.
She isn't getting / doesn't get bored.

Reflexive verbs take être in the perfect tense. The past participle has to agree with the subject:

Elles se sont reposées.   They rested.

The **nous**, **vous** and **ils / elles** forms are only needed for Higher tier. **H ONLY**

Worked example

SPEAKING TRACK 41 | **Target grade 1-5**

Quel genre de vacances aimes-tu?

Je préfère les vacances à la campagne.

Je préfère les vacances à la campagne car je peux me reposer et je m'amuse bien avec mes amis ou avec ma famille.

Listen to the recording

Use connectives like **car** to give reasons for your opinion.

Je me demande si je dois partir en vacances sur la côte.
I wonder if I should go on holiday to the coast.

Exam alert

You might be asked this sort of question:

a) as a follow-up to a **picture** or **read aloud** task – in which case your answer should be a simple, clear and accurate sentence.

b) as part of a longer conversation – when your answer should be more developed with reasons.

Now try this

READING | **Target grade 1-3**

Read this extract from a tourist brochure.

La ville est historique et si vous aimez l'histoire, il y a un musée excellent.
On peut visiter la ville en été ou en hiver parce qu'il ne fait jamais froid.

Put a cross ✗ in the correct box for each question.

1 The town is …
- ☐ **A** new.
- ☐ **B** industrial.
- ☐ **C** historic.

2 There is an excellent …
- ☐ **A** museum.
- ☐ **B** market.
- ☐ **C** castle.

3 The weather is …
- ☐ **A** cold.
- ☐ **B** never cold.
- ☐ **C** rarely cold.

(3 marks)

Digital resources

Where to stay

Le logement

appartement (m)	flat
camping (m)	campsite
chambre (f)	bedroom
complet / complète	full
déjeuner (m)	lunch
départ (m)	departure
dormir	to sleep
étage (m)	floor, storey
fenêtre (f)	window
hôtel (m)	hotel
inclus(e)	included
libre	free, available
logement (m)	accommodation
petit-déjeuner (m)	breakfast
privé(e)	private
repas (m)	meal
tente (f)	tent
addition (f)	bill
couverture (f)	blanket
louer	to hire

Time markers

Grammar page 100

Using tenses is important, but time markers can also be very useful.

- **present**
  toujours always
  normalement normally

Je passe **toujours** mes vacances dans un hôtel.
I always spend my holidays in a hotel.

- **past**
  l'été dernier last summer
  il y a deux semaines two weeks ago

L'été dernier, j'ai fait du camping.
Last summer I went camping.

- **future**
  l'année prochaine next year
  dans trois semaines in three weeks' time

L'année prochaine, je vais passer une semaine dans un appartement.
Next year I'm going to spend a week in a flat.

At the hotel

A hotel is one of the possible settings in the role play part of your exam. Practise some short phrases which might be useful to talk about:

- Availability: Avez-vous une chambre libre? Do you have a room available?
- A problem: La télé dans ma chambre ne marche pas. The TV in my room doesn't work.
- Location: Ma chambre est au premier étage. My room is on the first floor.
- Length of time: Je vais passer une semaine ici. I'm spending a week here.
- Opinion: C'est très intéressant. It's very interesting.
- A question: Le petit-déjeuner est inclus? Is breakfast included?
  Où est le restaurant? Where is the restaurant?

Ma chambre est trop froide. J'ai besoin de couvertures.
My room is too cold. I need some blankets.

Worked example

WRITING

Target grade 1-5

Write a review of a holiday flat for a website. You **must** include the following points:
- where the flat is
- your opinion of the flat
- when you will visit the flat again.

Write your answer **in French**. You should aim to write between 40 and 50 words.   **(14 marks)**

Je passe mes vacances dans un grand appartement au centre de Paris avec ma famille. À mon avis, l'appartement est confortable et j'aime bien y dormir. Je vais aller à l'appartement l'année prochaine avec mon oncle et deux amis. On va bien s'amuser.

In English, don't translate the word **les** before **vacances** or **le** before **Canada**.

Now try this

READING

Target grade 5-9

Translate the following paragraph **into English**.

Je crois que les vacances sont très importantes, alors je choisis toujours un hôtel cher. L'été dernier, nous avons passé dix jours intéressants en Amérique. Nous avons trouvé que le logement était assez propre. C'était aussi génial que le petit-déjeuner était inclus! Mes parents visiteront le Canada en août mais ils vont faire du camping, même si ce sera moins confortable.

(10 marks)

Booking accommodation

Digital resources

Les réservations – useful phrases

Je voudrais réserver une chambre avec vue sur la mer pour deux nuits.
I would like to reserve a room with a view of the sea for two nights.

Je veux rester pendant une semaine.
I would like to stay for one week.

Je suis désolé(e), le camping est complet.
I'm sorry, the campsite is full.

J'ai besoin d'une chambre accessible par ascenseur.
I need a room accessible by lift.

Où dois-je poser ma valise / tente?
Where shall I put my suitcase / tent?

J'ai perdu ma clé. I've lost my key.

L'escalier est dangereux. The stairs are dangerous.

Le lit est trop inconfortable pour dormir.
The bed is too uncomfortable to sleep.

Les repas sont inclus dans le prix?
Are meals included in the price?

Je peux louer des vélos? Can I hire bikes?

Ma chambre n'est pas très propre.
My room is not very clean.

L'hôtel est trop cher. The hotel is too expensive.

Emphatic pronouns

Grammar page 103

moi me	nous us
toi you	vous you
lui him / it	eux them (m)
elle her / it	elles them (f)

These pronouns have several uses in French:

- to add **emphasis**

  Moi, je pense que l'hôtel est excellent.
  I think that the hotel is excellent.

- after a **preposition**

  J'ai passé mes vacances avec elle.
  I spent my holidays with her.

- for a **double subject**

  Mon frère et moi sommes allés en France.
  My brother and I went to France.

At Foundation tier, you only need to know the pronouns **moi** and **toi**.

J'ai partagé une tente avec mon père.
I shared a tent with my dad.

Worked example

LISTENING TRACK 42

Target grade 4-5

Listen to the recording

Ahmed, Myriam and Clément are talking about booking accommodation. What do they say?

Listen to the recording and complete the sentences by putting a cross ✗ in the correct box for each question.

1 **Ahmed:** J'ai réservé deux chambres pour mes amis et moi pour sept nuits dans un petit hôtel dans le sud de la France.

2 **Myriam:** Moi, j'ai choisi de passer mes vacances dans un appartement dans un grand immeuble près de la mer.

3 **Clément:** Je vais réserver quatre places pour ma famille dans un petit camping à la montagne.

1 Ahmed booked 2 rooms …

☐	A for two people.
☒	B for seven nights.
☐	C in a big hotel.

2 Myriam's flat was …

☐	A very big.
☐	B in the town centre.
☒	C near the sea.

3 Clément …

☐	A spent four nights on a camp site.
☒	B is going to book a camp site.
☐	C has been camping in the mountains.

(3 marks)

Now try this

SPEAKING

Target grade 4-5

As this is part of a conversation, try to develop your answer with a reason.

Answer this question as part of a conversation:
Quel logement as-tu choisi?

Digital resources

Holiday activities

Les activités

château (m)	castle
durer	to last
entendre	to hear
expérience (f)	experience
extrême	extreme
gratuit(e)	free
île (f)	island
monter	to go up
musée (m)	museum
natation (f)	swimming
parc (m)	park
pont (m)	bridge
recommander	to recommend
rencontrer	to meet (up)
souvenir (m)	memory
critique (f)	review, criticism
foule (f)	crowd
louer	to hire
sable (m)	sand

The perfect tense of regular verbs with avoir

Grammar page 109

The perfect tense is used for completed actions in the past. For many verbs it is formed like this:

① present tense of the verb avoir	+	② a past participle		
		-er verbs - take off -er - add -é	**-ir verbs** - take off -ir - add -i	**-re verbs** - take off -re - add -u
j'ai tu as il / elle / on a nous avons vous avez ils / elles ont		jouer ➡ joué	finir ➡ fini	vendre ➡ vendu
		j'ai joué	j'ai fini	j'ai vendu

There are quite a lot of **irregular** past participles and they are the verbs you probably need most – you simply need to learn them: see page 109 for a list.

Worked example

READING

Target grade 5-6

In the perfect tense, most verbs take **avoir**, but some take **être**; you need to learn these. See page 110.

Lola has written an email about her recent holidays.

> J'ai passé une semaine de vacances à Paris et c'était très agréable. Le premier matin, j'ai acheté un cadeau pour ma meilleure copine avant de passer la journée sur la plage au bord de la rivière au soleil. On est montés en haut de la tour Eiffel, mais il y avait beaucoup de monde. Je vais y aller encore le mois prochain.

Don't assume that words in both the text and options will always be the answer. Here, 'best friend', 'beach' and 'sun' are all mentioned, but they are not correct answers.

Complete the sentences below. Put a cross ✗ in the correct box for each question.

1 Lola spent …

☐	**A** lots of money.
✗	**B** a week in Paris.
☐	**C** two weeks in Paris.

2 She bought a present …

✗	**A** on the first morning.
☐	**B** for her boyfriend.
☐	**C** on the beach.

3 She is going to go back …

✗	**A** next month.
☐	**B** with her best friend.
☐	**C** when the weather is sunny.

(3 marks)

Now try this

LISTENING TRACK 43

Target grade 4-5

Listen to the recording

Emma is talking about activities on holiday. What does she like doing?
Listen to the recording and put a cross ✗ in each one of the **three** correct boxes.

☐	**A** horse riding	☐	**C** visiting museums	☐	**E** cycling
☐	**B** basketball	☐	**D** swimming	☐	**F** trying extreme sports

(3 marks)

Trips and excursions

Digital resources

Faire une excursion

Qu'est-ce qu'on peut voir dans la région?
What is there to see in the area?

Pouvez-vous me recommander une visite?
Could you recommend an excursion?

Le tour dure combien de temps?
How long does the tour last?

Il y a une visite en car à trois heures cet
après-midi.
There is a coach excursion at three
o'clock this afternoon.

La visite en bateau dure deux heures.
The boat tour lasts for two hours.

Je voudrais acheter une carte.
I would like to buy a map.

Ça coûte combien?
How much does it cost?

Le paysage est étonnant.
The landscape is amazing.

Je voyage avec ma sœur.
I am travelling with my sister.

On peut faire une sortie dans la ville?
We could go on an outing to the town?

Expressing likes and dislikes

Likes

- Use aimer / aimer bien (to like)
- Use adorer (to love)
- Use préférer (to prefer)
- Use c'est / c'était +

agréable (pleasant)	extraordinaire
essentiel (essential)	(extraordinary)
étonnant (amazing)	génial (great)
excellent (excellent)	idéal (ideal)
	passionnant (exciting)

Dislikes

- Use détester (to hate)
- Use ne pas aimer (to dislike)
- Use c'est / c'était +

ennuyeux (boring)	inutile (useless)
inquiétant (worrying)	nul (rubbish)
	terrible (terrible)

La vue est extraordinaire et attire des
touristes du monde entier.
The views are extraordinary and attract
tourists from all over the world.

Worked example

SPEAKING TRACK 44   **Target grade 6-7**

Décris une excursion récente.

Pendant mes dernières vacances,
j'ai visité un petit village à la
montagne. Je l'ai trouvé vraiment
génial car il y avait beaucoup de
belles maisons et un musée d'art.

Listen to the recording

Although **décris** is in the present tense,
the word **récente** means that you are being
asked for an answer in the past tense.

Now try this

LISTENING TRACK 45   **Target grade 5-6**

Sarah and Mathis are talking about trips. What do they say?
Listen to the podcast and complete the following tables **in English**. You do not need to write
in full sentences.

Listen to the recording

1 Sarah

Advantage	
Disadvantage	

2 Mathis

Advantage	
Disadvantage	

(4 marks)

Digital resources

Asking for help or directions

Comment demander de l'aide

à côté de	next to
à droite	on the right
à gauche	on the left
aider	to help
chercher	to look for
coin (m)	corner
continuer	to continue
demander	to ask
feu (m)	traffic light
laisser	to leave (something somewhere)
oublier	to forget
perdre	to lose
rendez-vous (m)	appointment, meeting
rue (f)	road, street
tourner	to turn
traverser	to cross

Asking for directions

You can:
- use pour aller + à
  Pour aller au cinéma s'il vous plaît?
  How do I get to the cinema please?
- use Où est / sont … ? Where is / are … ?
  Où est la gare? Where is the station?
- say what you are looking for.
  Je cherche l'hôtel. I'm looking for the hotel.

J'ai perdu mes clés!
I've lost my keys!

Le cinéma n'est pas loin. Continuez – c'est juste après les feux au coin.
The cinema isn't far. Keep going – it's just after the traffic lights on the corner.

Worked example

LISTENING TRACK 46

Target grade 1-3

Emma is asking a passer-by for directions. What do they say?

Listen to the recording and complete the sentences by putting a cross ✗ in the correct box for each question.

Emma: Pour aller au magasin s'il vous plaît?
Passer-by: Prenez la première rue à gauche, ensuite traversez la place et le centre commercial est à droite.

Listen to the recording

1 First, Emma needs to take the …
- ☐ A first right.
- ☐ B second left.
- ☒ C first left.

2 After crossing the square, her destination is …
- ☐ A straight ahead.
- ☐ B on the left.
- ☒ C on the right.

(2 marks)

Now try this

READING

Target grade 4-5

Read these comments from an internet forum.

Eva: Hier, j'ai demandé à mes parents de m'aider avec mon travail scolaire.
Lucas: Je cherchais mon hôtel qui était au coin de la rue et un homme m'a aidé.
Jade: Hier, j'ai laissé mes livres chez moi. Ma mère les a trouvés dans ma chambre!

Complete the sentences below. Put a cross ✗ in the correct box for each question.

1 Eva wanted help with …
- ☐ A directions.
- ☐ B school work.
- ☐ C her family.

2 Lucas's hotel was …
- ☐ A on the street corner.
- ☐ B in the town centre.
- ☐ C closed.

3 Jade's books were …
- ☐ A found by her mother.
- ☐ B in her mother's bedroom.
- ☐ C at school.

(3 marks)

Shopping for gifts

Digital resources

Acheter des cadeaux

à la mode	trendy, fashionable
acheter	to buy
anniversaire (m)	birthday
cadeau (m)	gift, present
centre commercial (m)	shopping centre
échanger	to exchange
jupe (f)	skirt
magasin (m)	shop
marque (f)	brand
mode (f)	fashion
monnaie (f)	change
porter	to wear, carry
robe (f)	dress
souvenir (m)	souvenir
vendre	to sell
achat (m)	purchase
chapeau (m)	hat
produit (m)	product
veste (m)	jacket

Irregular adjectives

Grammar page 96

Normally we add -e to make an adjective feminine and -s to make it plural. However, some are irregular.

	singular		plural	
	masculine	feminine	masculine	feminine
	heureux	heureuse	heureux	heureuses
	sérieux	sérieuse	sérieux	sérieuses

Elles sont heureuses de recevoir ce cadeau.
They (female) are happy to receive the present.

Listen to the recording

Worked example

SPEAKING TRACK 47 • Target grade 5-9

Describe the picture.
Your description must cover:
• people   • location   • activity.

Je peux voir une jeune fille qui porte une veste jaune. Elle achète un cadeau dans un magasin. Il y a une femme à la caisse qui porte un pull noir. Évidemment elle travaille dans le magasin. Elle est plus âgée que la jeune fille. Elles sont toutes les deux à la caisse et la fille est assez contente.

When you have finished your description, listen to two questions relating to the picture. You are expected to say a few words or a short phrase / sentence in response to each question. One-word answers will not be sufficient to gain full marks.

1 Tu aimes acheter des souvenirs?
2 Qu'est-ce que tu as acheté comme cadeau récemment?   (12 marks)

1 J'aime beaucoup acheter des souvenirs.
2 Hier, j'ai acheté une jupe pour ma sœur.

Now try this

READING • Target grade 6-7

Lola writes in her diary.

Ma mère aura quarante ans le mois prochain, donc je suis allée en ville ce matin et je lui ai acheté une belle veste dans un magasin de vêtements. Je crois qu'elle l'aimera car la mode est importante dans sa vie. Mon frère a acheté une robe mais je la trouve nulle car je n'aime pas la couleur.

Complete the gap in each sentence using a word from the box below.
There are more words / phrases than gaps.   (4 marks)

1 Lola's mother is _____ .
2 Lola bought a _____ .
3 Lola's mother likes _____ .
4 Lola's brother has bought a _____ .

40 years old	41 years old	39 years old
dress	jacket	tie
fashion	the colour	shopping
jacket	necklace	dress

49

Tourist information

Digital resources

Les informations pour les touristes

bâtiment (m)	building
carte (f)	map
château (m)	castle
culturel(le)	cultural
demander	to ask
endroit (m)	place
envoyer	to send
fête (f)	festival
office de tourisme (m)	tourist office
plan (m)	plan / map
logement (m)	accommodation
recommander	to recommend
réserver	to book
téléphoner	to telephone
louer	to hire
renseignement (m)	information

Using indirect object pronouns

Grammar page 101

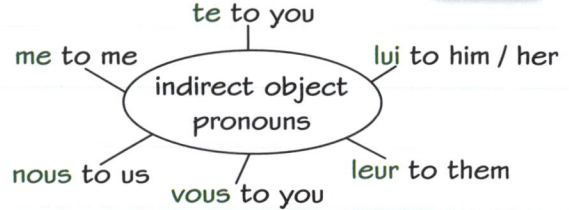

te to you
me to me
lui to him / her
indirect object pronouns
nous to us
leur to them
vous to you

You use these to replace a pronoun (je / moi, tu / toi, etc.) with à in front of it to say 'to me', 'to him', 'to them', etc.

Remember that these words come **before** the verb (and, in the perfect tense, before the part of avoir).

Je lui parle. I'm talking to him / her.

Je leur ai envoyé une carte.
I sent a map to them.

Sometimes English doesn't use 'to', but French does.

Je lui ai posé une question.
I asked him / her a question.

At Foundation tier, you only need to know the indirect pronouns **me**, **te** and **lui**.

Worked example

SPEAKING TRACK 48 | Target grade 5-9

Role play

You are at a tourist information office in Belgium.

Listen to the recording

Bonjour. Je peux vous aider?

1 Say why you are at the tourist information office.

Je voudrais un plan de la ville.

Ah, oui! Vous restez où en ville?

2 Say where you are staying.

Je reste dans un hôtel.

Très bien. Qu'est-ce que vous allez faire le week-end prochain?

3 Say what you will do this weekend.

Je vais faire les magasins.

Intéressant. Vous avez une question?

4 Ask a question about the area.

Est-ce qu'il y a un lac dans la région?

Oui, tout près d'ici. Vous avez une autre question?

5 Ask for a recommendation for a visit.

Pouvez-vous me recommander une visite?

Le château est très populaire.

(10 marks)

Now try this

LISTENING TRACK 49 | Target grade 3-4

Sarah is in the tourist office and is asking about tourist attractions.

Listen to the recording

What does the employee say? Listen to the recording and complete the following table **in English**.

You do not need to write in full sentences.

1 The best place to visit	
2 When shows take place	
3 The problem at the museum	

(3 marks)

Tourist attractions

Digital resources

Les attractions pour les touristes

coûter	to cost
festival (m)	festival
gratuit(e)	free
interdire	to forbid
marcher	to walk
quartier (m)	neighbourhood
religieux / religieuse	religious
risque (m)	risk
sac (m)	bag
se trouver	to be situated
sécurité (f)	security
théâtre (m)	theatre
toilettes (fpl)	toilets
valeur (f)	value
attirer	to attract
voler	to steal

The perfect tense with être

Grammar page 110

Although most verbs use avoir to form the perfect tense, some use être (usually to do with motion).

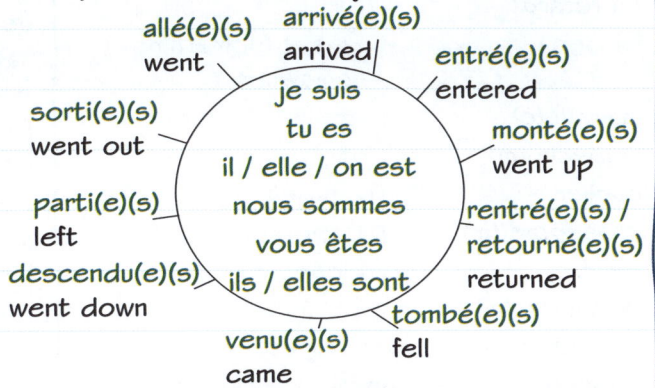

allé(e)(s) went
arrivé(e)(s) arrived
entré(e)(s) entered
sorti(e)(s) went out
monté(e)(s) went up
parti(e)(s) left
rentré(e)(s) / retourné(e)(s) returned
descendu(e)(s) went down
tombé(e)(s) fell
venu(e)(s) came

je suis
tu es
il / elle / on est
nous sommes
vous êtes
ils / elles sont

The past participle must **agree** with the subject: je suis allé I went (1 male) elle est allée she went vous êtes allés you went (2 or more males or males and females)

At the theatre / concert

Je voudrais deux billets pour le spectacle.
I'd like two tickets for the show.

Est-il accessible aux personnes en fauteuil roulant? Is it accessible for a wheelchair?

Il y a des billets assis ou debout?
Are there seated or standing tickets?

Worked example

READING **Target grade 4-9**

Marie writes a school project about her town.

Dans le musée, on peut voir plusieurs objets de valeur, donc il y a beaucoup de sécurité à l'entrée pour les protéger. Il est interdit d'apporter des grands sacs dans le musée pour réduire le risque que quelqu'un vole les objets.

Il y a quelques bâtiments religieux avec des beaux jardins. L'entrée est gratuite mais il est interdit de marcher sur l'herbe*.

*l'herbe – grass

Answer the following questions **in English**. You do not need to write in full sentences.

1 What can you see at the museum?
several valuable objects

2 What is it forbidden to do in the museum?
bring big bags

3 How much is entrance to the religious buildings?
free

(3 marks)

Worked example

READING **Target grade 4-9**

Translate the following paragraph **into English**.

J'aime bien ma ville. Elle attire beaucoup de touristes car on peut visiter le vieux quartier où il y a des maisons anciennes. Le musée d'histoire régionale se trouve aussi dans ce quartier, ce qui est très intéressant.

L'été dernier, je suis allé à un festival qui était vraiment génial. En septembre il y aura une semaine de mode et j'irai là-bas avec mes copines.

(10 marks)

I really like my town. It attracts a lot of tourists because you can visit the old neighbourhood where there are ancient houses. Also, a regional history museum is situated in this neighbourhood which is very interesting.

Last summer I went to a music festival which was really great. In September there will be a fashion week and I'll go (there) with my friends.

Now try this

SPEAKING **Target grade 5-6**

Qu'est-ce qu'il y a dans ta région pour les touristes?

Holiday problems

Digital resources

Les problèmes de vacances

accident (m)	accident
bouger	to move
désolé(e)	sorry
en retard	late
laisser	to leave (something somewhere)
mauvais(e)	bad
médecin (m)	doctor
oublier	to forget
passeport (m)	passport
perdre	to lose
problème (m)	problem
regretter	to regret
repas (m)	meal
route (f)	road, way, route
Quel dommage!	What a pity!
remplacer	to replace
se plaindre	to complain
vol (m)	flight, robbery, theft
voler	to steal, to fly

Aller

Grammar page 108

Aller is a really important verb. As well as meaning 'to go', it can be used to help talk about the future.

Je vais manger. I'm going to eat.

Therefore, it is vital to know all parts in the present tense:

je vais	I go / am going
tu vas	you go / are going
il / elle / on va	he / she / one goes / is going
nous allons	we go / are going
vous allez	you go / are going
ils / elles vont	they go / are going

Remember that **aller** uses **être** in the perfect tense, which means that the past participle has to agree with the subject: see page 110.

Elle est allée chez le médecin.

She went to the doctor's.

Worked example

SPEAKING TRACK 50

Target grade 5-9

Listen to the recording

Je suis désolé! I am sorry!

Parle-moi des problèmes que tu as eus en vacances.

Normalement, nous passons nos vacances en Angleterre mais l'année dernière, nous sommes allés à Paris. Après être arrivé à l'aéroport, mon père a dû rentrer à la maison car il avait laissé son passeport dans sa chambre!

You might be asked a question like this in the conversation part of your exam.

This answer uses a variety of tenses, showing greater complexity and variety of vocabulary and grammar in the response.

Now try this

LISTENING TRACK 51

Target grade 5-6

Thomas is talking about problems on holiday. What does he say?

Complete the gap in each sentence using a word or phrase from the box.

There are more words / phrases than gaps.

with his grandparents	in May	on his own
road accident	car problem	beach accident
nothing	three hours	five hours

Listen to the recording

1 Thomas went on holiday _____ .

2 There was a _____ .

3 The delay was _____ .

(3 marks)

Accommodation problems

Les problèmes de logement

bruit (m)	noise	accès (m)	access
clé (f)	key	ascenseur (m)	lift
désolé(e)	sorry	dommage (m)	damage
fauteuil roulant (m)	wheelchair	étage (m)	floor, storey
fonctionner	to work, function	état (m)	state
laisser	to leave (something somewhere)	Quel dommage!	What a pity!
		remplacer	to replace
logement (m)	accommodation	siège (m)	seat
mauvais(e)	bad	valise (f)	suitcase
oublier	to forget	vol (m)	flight, robbery, theft
perdre	to lose		
problème (m)	problem		
propre	clean	voler	to steal, fly
trop	too, too much		

The negative in different time frames

Grammar page 114

When you use the negative in other time frames, ne ... pas or ne ... jamais etc. still need to go around the verb, just like in the present tense.

Imperfect

L'année dernière, je n'allais pas au collège en bus.
Last year I did not go to school on the bus.

Perfect

ne goes **before** the part of avoir or être and pas goes after it (and before the past participle of the main verb).

Hier, je ne suis pas allé(e) voir ma sœur.
Yesterday I did not go to see my sister.
La semaine dernière, nous n'avons pas monté la montagne.
Last week we did not climb the mountain.

Future

Je n'irai pas chez lui demain.
I will not go to his house tomorrow.
Je ne vais jamais faire de camping!
I'm never going to go camping!

Worked example

SPEAKING TRACK 52 — Target grade 4-6

Listen to the recording

Parle-moi des problèmes de logement que tu as eus en vacances.

L'année dernière, j'ai passé mes vacances dans un hôtel au Canada et c'était horrible parce que ma chambre était trop petite et il n'y avait pas de télé dans la chambre. Je ne vais jamais retourner dans cet hôtel.

In speaking tasks which suggest a past time frame, it is OK to use the past tense and then move on to another tense. Here, the answer starts by referring to a past holiday then talks about the future.

These phrases might be useful in a role play.

Talking about problems

Je peux vous aider? Can I help you?
Il y a un problème avec ma chambre.
There is a problem with my room.
Je suis désolé(e). J'ai perdu ma clé.
I'm sorry. I have lost my key.
Ma chambre est au troisième étage.
My room is on the third floor.
Je reste quatre nuits. I'm staying for four nights.
À quelle heure ouvre le restaurant?
What time does the restaurant open?
Ma chambre n'est pas propre.
My room is not clean.
L'ascenseur ne fonctionne pas.
The lift does not work.
Il n'est pas accessible à mon fauteuil roulant.
It isn't accessible for my wheelchair.
On a volé mon passeport.
My passport has been stolen.

Now try this

LISTENING TRACK 53 — Target grade 1-3

Fatima is talking about accommodation problems. What does she say? Listen to the recording and complete the sentences by putting a cross ✗ in the correct box for each question.

Listen to the recording

1 Fatima's room …
☐ **A** is too small.
☐ **B** is not big enough.
☐ **C** is not clean.

2 The meals in the restaurant are …
☐ **A** rubbish.
☐ **B** nice.
☐ **C** too small.

(2 marks)

Eating out

Au restaurant et au café

allergique	allergic	poisson (m)	fish
baguette (f)	French stick	prendre un repas	to have a meal
café (m)	café	restaurant (m)	restaurant
client (m)	customer	riz (m)	rice
déjeuner (m)	lunch	soir (m)	evening
délicieux / délicieuse	delicious	sortir	to go out
		viande (f)	meat
entrée (f)	starter	addition (f)	bill
frites (fpl)	chips	aigre	sour
fromage (m)	cheese	boisson (f)	drink
gâteau (m)	cake	brûler	to burn
glace (f)	ice cream	goûter	to taste
goût (m)	taste	parfois	sometimes
manger	to eat	plat (m)	dish
pain (m)	bread	savoureux / savoureuse	tasty
pâtes (fpl)	pasta		
petit-déjeuner (m)	breakfast		

Using y

Grammar page 102

- y is used as part of the phrase **il y a** (there is / there are).
  Il y a un bon restaurant en ville.
  There is a good restaurant in town.
- **Il y a** can also mean 'ago' when used with a time phrase.
  il y a deux mois   two months ago
- y can also mean 'there' as a pronoun, when referring back to something. It goes before the verb, including before the part of avoir or être in the perfect tense.
  J'y mange souvent. I often eat there.
  J'y suis allé.   I went there.

H ONLY

> J'y ai mangé il y a trois mois.
> I ate there three months ago.

Worked example

WRITING | **Target grade 1-5**

Describe the photo. Write four short sentences **in French.**   **(8 marks)**

1 Il y a six personnes.
2 Ils mangent.
3 Il y a un restaurant.
4 Je vois une table.

Aiming higher

In writing tasks with a picture, make sure that you only write about what is actually in the picture and don't mention what isn't there!

When you are describing a photo as part of a writing task, keep your answers simple.

Now try this

READING | **Target grade 5-6**

Manon has written this diary entry about eating out.

> Hier, on a fêté l'anniversaire de mon ami dans un restaurant près de chez lui. On y va souvent. J'ai mangé un repas délicieux – des pâtes avec du fromage, mais mon ami m'a dit que la viande qu'il a choisie était brûlée.

Complete the sentences below. Put a cross ✗ in the correct box for each question.

1 Manon went out for a meal …

- ☐ **A** at a restaurant near her house.
- ☐ **B** to celebrate her birthday.
- ☐ **C** at a restaurant she often goes to.

2 She …

- ☐ **A** didn't like her meal.
- ☐ **B** chose pasta.
- ☐ **C** had bread and cheese.

3 Her friend's meal was …

- ☐ **A** tasty.
- ☐ **B** burnt.
- ☐ **C** vegetarian.

(3 marks)

Opinions about food

Les avis sur la nourriture

allergique	allergic
baguette (f)	French stick
café (m)	café
cuisine (f)	cooking, cookery, cuisine
déjeuner (m)	lunch
délicieux / délicieuse	delicious
entrée (f)	starter
faim (f)	hunger
frites (fpl)	chips
fromage (m)	cheese
gâteau (m)	cake
glace (f)	ice cream
goût (m)	taste
légumes (mpl)	vegetables
manger	to eat
œuf (m)	egg
pain (m)	bread

pâtes (fpl)	pasta
petit-déjeuner (m)	breakfast
poisson (m)	fish
prendre un repas	to have a meal
restaurant (m)	restaurant
riz (m)	rice
sortir	to go out
végan	vegan
végétarien / végétarienne	vegetarian
viande (f)	meat
aigre	sour
boisson (f)	drink
goûter	to taste
nourriture (f)	food
plat (m)	dish
savoureux / savoureuse	tasty
sucré(e)	sugary

H ONLY — Using en
Grammar page 102

This important pronoun means 'of' or 'of it / them' and sometimes 'some' or 'any'. It usually replaces de + a noun and comes **before** the verb.

Tu aimes manger de la viande?
Do you like eating meat?
Oui, j'en mange beaucoup.
Yes, I eat a lot of it.
Tu as de l'argent?
Do you have some money?
Non, je n'en ai pas. No. I don't have any.

Saying you like it / them
Grammar page 101

Use le, la or les on its own **before** the verb to say you like / dislike 'it' or 'them'.
Tu aimes bien ce restaurant? Oui, je l'aime bien.
Do you like this restaurant? Yes, I like it.

Tu aimes les omelettes? Non, je ne les aime pas parce que je suis allergique aux œufs.
Do you like omelettes? No, I don't like them because I am allergic to eggs.

Don't be put off by distractors which might lead you to the wrong answers. In the worked example, vegetarian is mentioned but 3A is incorrect.

Worked example
LISTENING TRACK 54 · **Target grade 1-3**

Clara is talking about food. What does she say? Listen to the recording and complete the sentences by putting a cross ✗ in the correct box for each question.

Mon père est allergique au lait, alors il ne mange pas de glaces. Ma mère adore les frites mais elle sait qu'elles sont mauvaises pour la santé. Moi, je suis végétarienne. Je ne mange pas de viande.

Listen to the recording

1 Clara's dad is allergic to …
- [X] **A** milk.
- [ ] **B** fish.
- [ ] **C** fruit.

2 Clara's mum loves …
- [ ] **A** healthy food.
- [X] **B** chips.
- [ ] **C** cheese.

3 Clara doesn't eat …
- [ ] **A** vegetarian food.
- [ ] **B** cheese.
- [X] **C** meat.

(3 marks)

Now try this
SPEAKING · **Target grade 5-6**

You might be asked to give opinions about food in the conversation part of the Speaking exam. Try this question:
Qu'est-ce que tu préfères manger?

Remember that **préfère** and **préféré** are different words and are not pronounced the same!

The weather

Digital resources

Le temps

après-midi (m)	afternoon
beau / belle	beautiful
chaud(e)	hot
ciel (m)	sky
froid(e)	cold
il neige	it's snowing
il pleut	it's raining
jour (m)	day
matin (m)	morning
mauvais(e)	bad
neige (f)	snow
soir (m)	evening
soleil (m)	sun
temps (m)	weather
vent (m)	wind
humide	wet, humid

The weather in the present, past and future

Present

Il fait chaud.	It's hot.
Il pleut.	It's raining.
Il y a du soleil.	It's sunny.

Past

Il a fait chaud. / Il faisait chaud.	It was hot.
Il a plu. / Il pleuvait.	It was raining.
Il y a eu du soleil. / Il y avait du soleil.	It was sunny.

Future   (H ONLY)

Il fera chaud. / Il va faire chaud.	
It will be hot. / It's going to be hot.	
Il pleuvra.	It will rain.
Il y aura du soleil.	It will be sunny.

More weather

Quel temps fait-il?	What's the weather like?
Il y a du brouillard.	It's foggy.
Il fait chaud.	It's hot.
Il fait froid.	It's cold.
Il fait beau.	It's fine / nice weather.
Il fait mauvais.	It's bad weather.

Il y a du brouillard.
It's foggy.

Worked example

WRITING · Target grade 1-5

Describe the photo. Write four short sentences **in French.**   **(8 marks)**

1 Il pleut.
2 Il y a de la neige.
3 Il fait froid.
4 Je vois une personne.

When you describe a picture, don't forget to focus on the background too if you are struggling to find things to write. For example, there are cars in the background of this photo so you could write **Je vois des voitures**.

Some picture tasks have a scene outdoors. Learn your weather vocabulary as this gives you something to talk about!

Now try this

READING · Target grade 1-5

Translate the following sentences **into English.**

1 J'aime quand il fait chaud en vacances.
2 Mon père adore la neige.
3 Quand il fait froid, nous allons à la montagne.
4 S'il y a du vent, mes parents ne sont pas heureux.
5 Hier, il a plu toute la journée.

(10 marks)

Remember that **journée** means 'day', not 'journey'.

Customs and festivals

Les traditions et les fêtes

célèbre	famous
culturel(le)	cultural
événement (m)	event
festival (m)	festival
fête (f)	festival, party
francophonie (f)	French-speaking world
inspirer	to inspire
Nouvel An (m)	New Year
populaire	popular
Saint-Sylvestre (f)	New Year's Eve
Tour de France (m)	Tour de France cycle race
traditionnel(le)	traditional
14 juillet (m)	Bastille Day, national holiday
annuel(le)	annual
fêter	to celebrate
foule (f)	crowd
partout	everywhere
public (m)	audience
scène (f)	scene, stage
son (m)	sound

Adjectives ending -el

Grammar page 96

These are irregular but follow a pattern.

singular		plural	
masculine	feminine	masculine	feminine
annuel	annuelle	annuels	annuelles

La fête traditionnelle se passe aujourd'hui.
The traditional festival takes place today.

J'aime les événements culturels.
I like cultural events.

Flexible phrases

Je m'en souviens clairement.
I can remember it clearly.

Tout le monde s'est tellement amusé.
Everyone had such fun.

Worked example

SPEAKING TRACK 55   Target grade 4-6

As part of some follow-up questions in a conversation you might be asked:
Quel festival français est-ce que tu préfères?

Listen to the recording

J'aime le 14 juillet car tout le monde est content, on mange, on chante et on danse. L'année dernière j'étais en France ce jour-là et c'était excellent.

If you are unsure of any question relating to customs or festivals, stick to something obvious like the French national holiday. You don't need to know every public holiday, but it might help to know one well.

J'aime fêter la Saint-Sylvestre.
I like to celebrate New Year's Eve.

Now try this

READING   Target grade 2-4

Read the extract from a tourist brochure.

Au mois d'août, la ville accueille beaucoup de personnes au festival de la francophonie. Les touristes aiment tous les événements culturels comme la fête du cinéma (le 15 août à 13h) et la fête de la chanson (le 17 août à 17h). Entrée gratuite, mais arrivez tôt!

Complete the sentences below. Put a cross ✗ in the correct box for each question.

1 The festival in August is about …
- ☐ A dancing.
- ☐ B books.
- ☐ C the French-speaking world.

2 The music festival …
- ☐ A starts at 1 pm.
- ☐ B is after the film festival.
- ☐ C costs 17 euros.

3 Visitors are advised to …
- ☐ A bring lots of money.
- ☐ B be early.
- ☐ C speak French.

(3 marks)

57

Visiting a city

Visiter une grande ville

capitale (f)	capital city
centre (m)	centre
chercher	to look for
conduire	to drive
endroit (m)	place
grande ville (f)	city
historique	historic
manquer	to miss (public transport)
quartier (m)	neighbourhood
visiter	to visit
voyager	to travel
banlieue (f)	suburb
industrie (f)	industry
vivre	to live

Alternatives to aller

> Grammar pages 108, 109

Aller (to go) is a very common verb but you might want to try to use visiter (to visit) or voyager (to travel) to avoid repetition.

J'ai visité le centre-ville. I visited the town centre.

J'ai voyagé en ville en bus.

I travelled into town by bus.

> J'aime bien visiter les quartiers historiques.
> I like visiting historical neighbourhoods.

Worked example

READING | Target grade **5-6**

Théo has written a blog about a recent visit.

> Il y a deux semaines, j'ai passé deux jours dans une grande ville qui se trouve dans le sud-est de la France. Je l'ai trouvée géniale. Après avoir manqué le bus, je suis enfin arrivé au centre-ville à pied. Dans la ville il y a des endroits historiques mais il n'y a pas beaucoup d'industries.

> Be careful to look at details in the passage. For example, in the worked example, bus is mentioned, but it is with manquer, so D is not correct.

Put a cross ✗ next to each one of the **three** correct statements.

☐	A	Théo spent two weeks in the town.
☒	B	The town is in southeast France.
☒	C	He found the town excellent.
☐	D	He travelled into town by bus.
☐	E	The town is industrial.
☒	F	The town has historic places.

(3 marks)

Flexible phrases

C'est une question intéressante.
That's an interesting question.

Tu aimes visiter les quartiers historiques?
C'est une question intéressante. J'aime apprendre l'histoire, mais je préfère les bâtiments modernes.
That's an interesting question. I like learning about history, but I prefer modern buildings.

> You might use this when answering one of your questions in the conversation section of your Speaking exam.

Now try this

WRITING | Target grade **2-5**

Write a review of a town / city you know for a website.

You **must** include the following points:

- where the town / city is
- your opinion of the centre
- when you will next visit the town / city.

Write your answer **in French**. You should aim to write between 40 and 50 words.

(14 marks)

School subjects

Digital resources

Les matières scolaires

anglais (m)	English	maths (fpl)	maths
apprendre	to learn	matière (f)	subject
art (m)	art	médias (mpl)	media
classe (f)	classroom, class	musique (f)	music
		note (f)	mark
collège (m)	secondary school	physique	physical
		professeur (m/f)	teacher
cours (m)	lesson, course	sciences (fpl)	science (as a school subject)
cuisine (f)	cooking		
danse (f)	dance	scolaire	school
devoirs (mpl)	homework	sport (m)	sport
école (f)	school	technologie (f)	technology
éducation (f)	education	théâtre (m)	drama
français (m)	French	travail (m)	work
histoire (f)	history	travailler	to work
langue (f)	language	emploi du temps (m)	timetable
lycée (m)	sixth form college		

Depuis + present tense

H ONLY

In English you say 'we have been doing' something for a length of time.

However, in French, you use depuis + **present** tense (because you are still doing it).

J'étudie le français depuis cinq ans.
I have been studying French for five years.

Je suis dans cette école depuis deux ans.
I have been at this school for two years.

Negatives

Grammar page 114

- ne ... pas not
  Je n'étudie pas le théâtre.
  I don't study drama.
- ne ... jamais never
  Je n'ai jamais étudié l'art.
  I've never studied art.
- ne ... plus not any more
  Je n'aime plus l'histoire.
  I don't like history anymore.
- ne ... personne nobody
  Je n'ai vu personne.
  I didn't see anyone.
  Personne n'a reçu une bonne note.
  Nobody received a good mark.
- ne ... rien nothing
  Nous n'avons rien à faire.
  We have nothing to do.

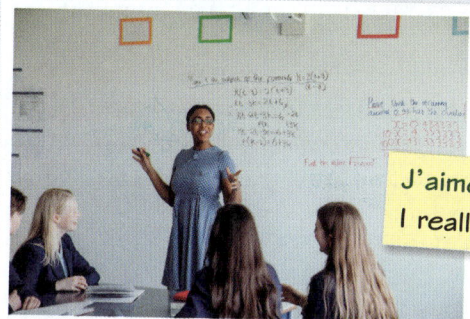

You only need to recognise this form at Higher tier.

J'aime bien les maths.
I really like maths.

Worked example

LISTENING TRACK 56   **Target grade 1-2**

Emma is talking about school subjects.
Which subjects does she mention?
Listen to the recording and put a cross ✗ in each one of the **three** correct boxes.

Listen to the recording

J'étudie beaucoup de matières au collège.
J'apprends l'anglais et j'aime les langues.
J'apprends aussi les sciences et les maths.

☒	**A** English	☒	**D** Science
☐	**B** Music	☒	**E** Maths
☐	**C** P.E.	☐	**F** History

(3 marks)

You can only be asked questions about school subjects which appear in the Edexcel vocabulary list (see page 130), but there's nothing stopping you from mentioning other school subjects in your speaking and writing tasks.

Now try this

SPEAKING   **Target grade 2-5**

Parle-moi de tes matières au collège.

This is the type of question you might be asked in the conversation task of your Speaking exam.

Digital resources

School likes, dislikes and reasons

Ce que j'aime au collège

comprendre	to understand	lecture (f)	reading
cours (m)	lesson	matière (f)	subject
difficile	difficult	note (f)	mark
donner	to give	strict(e)	strict
dur(e)	hard	compétence (f)	skill, ability
effort (m)	effort	encourager	to encourage
facile	easy		
faible	weak	enseigner	to teach
fatigant(e)	tiring, exhausting	épreuve (f)	test
		expliquer	to explain
fort(e)	strong, good at	sévère	severe, strict

Saying 'to be good / bad at'

You might want to give a different reason for liking or disliking a school subject other than using c'est + an adjective.

- To say that you are good at / strong in a subject, use fort en …
  Je suis fort(e) en musique.
  I'm good at music.
- To say that you are bad at / weak in a subject, use faible en …
  Elles sont faibles en histoire.
  They are weak in history.

Les profs nous encouragent.
The teachers encourage us.

Fort and faible need to agree with the subject.

Worked example

READING Target grade 4-5

Read this extract from an email Hugo sent.

J'aime le collège parce que j'ai beaucoup d'amis et je suis assez fort en maths et en sport. L'anglais *m'embête* parce que nous devons beaucoup lire et je n'aime pas les livres.

Which of these is the best translation for *m'embête*?
Put a cross ✗ in the correct box.   **(1 mark)**

☒	**A** annoys me
☐	**B** fascinates me
☐	**C** embarrasses me

In this type of question, you need to work out the meaning of a word you may not be familiar with. Look at the context – the surrounding words. Hugo says he doesn't like books, so what might he think of English lessons?

Worked example

LISTENING TRACK 57 Target grade 6-7

Ahmed is talking about his school subjects.
What does he say?

Listen to the recording

Complete the gap in each sentence using a word or phrase from the box below. There are more words / phrases than gaps.

Ma matière préférée au collège est l'art car je suis fort et mon prof explique bien ses cours. Cependant, la technologie ne m'intéresse pas et le prof nous donne trop de devoirs. La semaine prochaine, nous aurons une épreuve de musique. Je pense que je n'aurai pas de bonnes notes.

interested	good at it	creative
is young	gives too much homework	
is hardworking	test	lesson	teacher

1 Ahmed likes art because he is ...*good at it* .
2 His technology teacher ......*gives too much homework* .
3 Next week, Ahmed will have a music ...*test* .

(3 marks)

In gap-filling tasks, several answers might fit the gap, so check that what you have written makes sense.

Now try this

SPEAKING Target grade 2-5

Quelle est ta matière préférée? Pourquoi?

Your teacher might ask a question like this in the conversation section of your Speaking exam. Make sure you give a reason and extend your answer if you can.

Timetable and school day

Digital resources

La journée scolaire

cahier (m)	exercise book
commencer	to start
cours (m)	lesson
déjeuner (m)	lunch
durer	to last
écouter	to listen to
fatigant(e)	tiring, exhausting
finir	to finish
jour (m)	day
journée (f)	day
matière (f)	subject
pause (f)	break
sac (m)	bag
scolaire	school
se lever	to get up
s'habiller	to get dressed
bibliothèque (f)	library
directeur (m) / directrice (f)	headteacher
emploi du temps (m)	timetable
gymnase (m)	gym
Je vais au collège ...	I go to school ...
... en bus	... by bus
... en car	... by coach
... à pied	... on foot
... en train	... by train
... à vélo	... by bike
... en voiture	... by car

Telling the time

- **o'clock** use heure(s)

Il est une heure.	It is one o'clock.
Il est trois heures.	It is three o'clock.

- minutes **past** the hour

dix heures cinq	five past ten
six heures et quart	quarter past six
huit heures et demie	half past eight

- minutes **to** the hour

onze heures moins dix	ten to eleven
(literally eleven hours minus ten)	
deux heures moins le quart	quarter to two

- midday and midnight

midi	midday
minuit	midnight

Note that demi has no -e after midi or minuit.
midi et demi half past twelve in the afternoon.

> The French often use the 24-hour clock. If you use this, don't use **quart** or **demie**.
> **treize heures quinze** 13.15 (1.15 pm)
> **quinze heures trente** 15.30 (3.30 pm)

> On mange le déjeuner à midi et demi au collège.
> We eat lunch at half past twelve at school.

Worked example

LISTENING   TRACK **58**   Target grade **2-4**

Clara is talking about a school morning. Listen to the recording and put a cross ✗ in each one of the **two** correct boxes.

Listen to the recording

> Je me lève à sept heures et demie et je vais au collège en car avec mon frère. Mon premier cours commence à huit heures vingt-cinq et il y a six cours par jour.

✗	A	Clara gets up at 7.30.
☐	B	She goes to school by car.
☐	C	Her first lesson is at 8.35.
✗	D	There are six lessons a day.

(2 marks)

> Listen carefully for the times to ensure you understand them correctly. For example, Clara's lessons begin at 8.25, not 8.35.

Now try this

SPEAKING   Target grade **4-6**

Quelle est ta journée préférée au collège? Pourquoi?

> Remember that **journée** means 'day', not 'journey'.

61

Digital resources

Equipment and facilities in school

L'équipement scolaire

bâtiment (m)	building
cahier (m)	exercise book
commencer	to start
cour (f)	playground
cours (m)	lesson
équipement (m)	equipment
finir	to finish
ordinateur portable (m)	laptop
projet (m)	project, plan
recherche (f)	research
rentrée (f)	start of school year
sac (m)	bag
salle (f)	room
scolaire	school
spectacle (m)	show
tablette (f)	tablet
terrain (m)	pitch, sports ground
utile	useful
bibliothèque (f)	library
champ (m)	field
directeur (m) / directrice (f)	headteacher
gymnase (m)	gym
profiter de	to take advantage of
s'entraîner	to train

Irregular adjectives ending -if

Grammar page 96

singular		plural	
masculine	feminine	masculine	feminine
actif	active	actifs	actives

On peut faire des activités sportives au collège.
You can do sports activities at school.

Ils sont actifs. They are active.

La journée scolaire est longue.
The school day is long.

> Another irregular adjective, **long**, adds **-ue** for feminine nouns.

> Un aspect négatif de tout l'équipement est qu'il est lourd.
> A negative aspect of all the equipment is that it is heavy.

> This is an example of a question your teacher might ask you in the conversation section of your Speaking exam.

Worked example

SPEAKING TRACK 59   Target grade 4-6

Comment est ton collège?

Mon collège est grand et assez moderne. Nous avons beaucoup de salles avec des ordinateurs où on peut faire des recherches. On a aussi fait construire un nouveau bâtiment de musique que j'adore.

Listen to the recording

> When you have an open-ended question, you can choose what to include. Try to think of lists of connectives or adjectives that you might use. The worked example shows how to use **où** (where) and **que** (which).

Now try this

WRITING   Target grade 1-5

Describe the photo. Write four short sentences **in French**.

(8 marks)

School uniform

Digital resources

L'uniforme scolaire

baskets (fpl)	trainers
chaussette (f)	sock
chaussure (f)	shoe
chemise (f)	shirt
confortable	comfortable
contre	against
cravate (f)	tie
différence (f)	difference
droit (m)	right
interdire de	to ban, forbid
jupe (f)	skirt
pantalon (m)	trousers
pauvre	poor
porter	to wear
pour	for, in favour of
privé(e)	private
propre	own
pull (m)	pullover, jumper
riche	rich
s'habiller	to get dressed
vêtements (mpl)	clothes
cacher	to hide
directeur (m) / directrice (f)	headteacher
se comporter	to behave
veste (f)	jacket

Colours

You may use colours to describe pictures, or in speaking and writing tasks in general.

Here are some colours with their agreements. Note that orange and marron will never change.

	singular		plural	
	masculine	feminine	masculine	feminine
blue	bleu	bleue	bleus	bleues
green	vert	verte	verts	vertes
black	noir	noire	noirs	noires
yellow	jaune	jaune	jaunes	jaunes
white	blanc	blanche	blancs	blanches
brown	marron	marron	marron	marron
orange	orange	orange	orange	orange
grey	gris	grise	gris	grises
pink	rose	rose	roses	roses
red	rouge	rouge	rouges	rouges

une cravate bleue a blue tie

des chaussures noires black shoes

Flexible phrases

Il faut … You have to …

Il est interdit de … It's forbidden to …

Il faut porter une chemise blanche. You have to wear a white shirt.

Propre means 'own' when it's **before** the noun but 'clean' when it's **after** the noun.

mes propres vêtements my own clothes

mes vêtements propres my clean clothes

Worked example

SPEAKING TRACK 60 • Target grade 2-4

Que penses-tu de l'uniforme scolaire?

Je n'aime pas l'uniforme car ce n'est pas confortable. Je voudrais porter mes propres vêtements.

Listen to the recording

In the conversation part of your Speaking exam, you can add a detail which involves a different tense or time frame (here the conditional: 'I would like').

Now try this

WRITING • Target grade 1-5

Describe the photo. Write four short sentences in French. (8 marks)

Digital resources

Class activities

Les activités scolaires

activité (f)	activity
concert (m)	concert
échange (m)	exchange
européen(ne)	European
participer à	to take part in
sortie (f)	outing
visite (f)	visit, excursion
voyager	to travel
concours (m)	competition
directeur (m) / directrice (f)	headteacher

The imperative

Grammar page 116

When you want to tell someone to do something you use the imperative form of the verb. In French this is either the tu or vous form of the verb without the subject.

For most verbs this is easy:

Finis tes devoirs!   Finish your homework!
Allez au college!   Go to school!

However, with -er verbs, the final -s is left off in the tu form:

Va au concert!   Go to the concert!

> You might be asked a question like this in the conversation section of your Speaking exam.

Worked example

SPEAKING TRACK 61 | Target grade 4-6

Décris une visite scolaire récente.

J'aime bien les visites scolaires et il y a deux semaines nous sommes allés au théâtre voir un spectacle intéressant. C'était génial et nous nous sommes bien amusés.

Listen to the recording

Viens avec nous à Londres! Come with us to London!

> Rather than keep using the **je** form of the verb, try to vary the subject. Here the student uses the **nous** (we) form successfully.

> In this type of question, read around the word you are being asked to translate. Here the words **plats**, **délicieux** and **fromage** help give the answer.

Worked example

READING | Target grade 5

Read this message.

Nous avons fait une visite scolaire dans un marché *alimentaire*.

Certains plats étaient délicieux, mais je n'ai pas du tout aimé le fromage!

Which of these is the best translation of the word *alimentaire*?

Put a cross ✗ in the correct box.

✗	A	food
☐	B	clothes
☐	C	craft

(1 mark)

Now try this

READING | Target grade 4-5

Jules has written this diary entry about a school activity.

Aujourd'hui ma classe de français a visité un grand bâtiment moderne au centre-ville où on a vu un concert de musique classique. Moi, je ne joue pas d'instrument, mais j'ai trouvé le concert très passionnant et mes amis l'ont aimé aussi. J'aimerais bien y aller la semaine prochaine pour voir un groupe de musique qui va jouer de la musique pop.

Put a cross ✗ in each one of the **three** correct boxes.

☐	A	Jules went to a music concert with his family.
☐	B	Jules plays a musical instrument.
☐	C	Jules enjoyed the concert.
☐	D	Jules's friends liked the concert.
☐	E	Jules has already been to another music concert.
☐	F	Jules would like to go to another music concert.

(3 marks)

School rules

Les règles de l'école

arriver	to arrive
causer	to cause
classe (f)	class
cours (m)	lesson
en retard	late
heure (f)	hour, time
il est interdit de	it's forbidden to
il faut	you have to
juste	fair
manger	to eat
on doit	you must
on ne peut pas	you can't
on peut	you can
portable (m)	mobile phone
porter	to wear
règle (f)	rule
scolaire	school
tard	late
tôt	early
uniforme (m)	uniform
utiliser	to use
comportement (m)	behaviour
directeur (m) / directrice (f)	headteacher
mener	to lead
se comporter	to behave

Talking about what can and cannot be done

There are many ways of discussing rules. You could use any of the following:

- il faut + infinitive you must, it's necessary to
  Il faut suivre les règles. You must follow the rules.
- on peut / on ne peut pas … you can / can't …
  On ne peut pas manger dans les salles de classe.
  You can't eat in the classrooms.
- on doit … you must …
  On doit bien se comporter. You must behave well.
- il est interdit de + infinitive it's forbidden to

Il est interdit de courir. It's forbidden to run.

Worked example

READING — Target grade 5-6

Clara has written an email about her school rules.

> Dans mon école, il y a beaucoup de règles. Par exemple il faut écouter le professeur tout le temps et il ne faut pas parler en classe. Il est interdit d'avoir un portable en cours et selon moi, ce n'est pas juste. L'année dernière, on pouvait utiliser notre portable pendant la pause, mais maintenant c'est interdit.

Pay careful attention when negatives are involved. In the worked example, there are things which students **must** and **must not** do.

Complete the sentences below. Put a cross ✗ in the correct box for each question.

1 In classes at Clara's school, you cannot …
- ☐ A listen to music.
- ☒ B talk.
- ☐ C leave the room.

2 She thinks that not using mobiles in lessons is …
- ☐ A fair.
- ☒ B unfair.
- ☐ C unhelpful.

3 Last year you could …
- ☐ A use mobiles in lessons.
- ☒ B use mobiles at break.
- ☐ C never use mobiles in school.

(3 marks)

Now try this

LISTENING — TRACK 62 — Target grade 1-3

Listen to the recording

Chloé is discussing rules.
Which things are mentioned? Put a cross ✗ in each one of the **two** correct boxes.

- ☐ A arriving on time
- ☐ B eating
- ☐ C uniform
- ☐ D listening

(2 marks)

Digital resources

Opinions about school

Les avis sur le collège

bon(ne)	good
causer	to cause
contre	against
excellent(e)	excellent
juste	fair
la journée scolaire	school day
mauvais(e)	bad
porter	to wear
pour	for
règle (f)	rule
cesser	to stop
mener	to lead
obliger	to require, force
permettre	to allow, permit
plaire	to please
s'exprimer	to express oneself

Giving a balanced view

You may want to give advantages and disadvantages.

mais	but
même si	even if
par contre	on the other hand
cependant	however
pourtant	yet, nevertheless
sauf	except
au contraire	on the contrary
un avantage	an advantage
un inconvénient	a disadvantage
le pire	the worst
le mieux	the best

H ONLY

Worked example

READING

Target grade 5-6

Read Maxime's blog about her school.

> J'aime bien mon collège. Nous avons d'excellents équipements, mais par contre, les bâtiments sont vieux. Même si les profs sont travailleurs et sympa, il y a trop de devoirs. Je voudrais aller dans une autre école l'année prochaine.

Answer the following questions **in English**.

1 What does Maxime say about the buildings?
They are old.

2 What are the teachers like? (2 details)
hardworking and nice

(2 marks)

When reading a text that mentions good and bad things, make sure that you take extra care to distinguish between them.

Ce qui me plaît, c'est de rencontrer mes amis.
What pleases me is meeting up with my friends.

Le pire, c'est quand on doit passer des examens en été.
The worst is when we have to do exams in the summer.

When you are giving advantages and disadvantages, use the words in the list above to help you structure your sentences.

Now try this

SPEAKING

Target grade 5-6

Quels sont les avantages et les inconvénients de ton école?

This is an example of a question you might be asked in the conversation task in your Speaking exam.

Clubs and activities

Les clubs et activités scolaires

activité (f)	activity
club (m)	club
cuisine (f)	cookery
danse (f)	dance
indépendant(e)	independent
lecture (f)	reading
musique (f)	music
se reposer	to rest, relax
social(e)	social
sport (m)	sport
terrain (m)	sports ground, pitch
théâtre (m)	theatre
athlétisme (m)	athletics
éviter	to avoid
gymnase (m)	gym
s'exprimer	to express oneself
stressé(e)	stressed

Using the infinitive

The infinitive is often used after certain common words like:

- sans without
  Sans attendre … Without waiting …
- avant de before
  Avant de rentrer à la maison …
  Before going home …
- pour / afin de in order to
  Pour se reposer … In order to relax …

Je vais à un club de théâtre pour me reposer.
I go to a theatre club in order to relax.

Worked example

READING   Target grade 1-3

Read Enzo's email about clubs in school.

Il y a beaucoup de clubs scolaires que j'aime. Le mardi, je vais au club de sport où on peut faire des activités sportives. Le jeudi après l'école, je vais au club de danse et je trouve ça intéressant.

Complete the sentences below.
Put a cross ✗ in the correct box for each question.

1 On Tuesdays Enzo goes to …

☐	**A**	music club.
✗	**B**	sports club.
☐	**C**	French club.

2 He goes to dance club …

✗	**A**	on Thursdays.
☐	**B**	with his friends.
☐	**C**	on Fridays.

(2 marks)

Don't forget to revise vocabulary like days of the week that you learned a long time ago!

Flexible phrases

Pour éviter … , il faut …
To avoid … , you must …

Pour éviter le stress, il faut s'amuser et s'exprimer.
To avoid stress, you must have fun and express yourself.

Now try this

SPEAKING   Target grade 5-6

Il y a quels clubs dans ton collège?

It's always a good idea to give specific examples from the past and future if you can, to demonstrate the language that you know.

You might be asked a question like this in the conversation part of your Speaking exam.

Success at school

Réussir au collège

améliorer	to improve
but (m)	aim, goal
comprendre	to understand
effort (m)	effort
espérer	to hope
études (fpl)	studies
examen (m)	exam
inspirer	to inspire
lecture (f)	reading
modèle (m)	role model
notes (fpl)	grades
passer	to take (an exam)
réussir (à)	to succeed in, to pass (an exam)
succès (m)	success
travailleur / travailleuse	hardworking
amitié (f)	friendship
compétence (f)	skill, ability
épreuve (f)	test
objectif (m)	aim
pression (f)	pressure

Using the infinitive after verbs with à and de

Some French verbs are followed by à or de + an infinitive.

Using some of them is useful if you want to show complexity and variety.

- **commencer à** to start / begin to
  Mes amis **ont commencé à faire** du sport.
  My friends (have) started to do sport.

- **réussir à** to succeed in
  J'ai **réussi à** avoir de bonnes notes.
  I succeeded in getting good marks.

- **aider à** to help to
  Mes professeurs m'**ont aidé à améliorer** mes compétences.
  My teachers helped me to improve my skills.

- **décider de** to decide to
  Elle **a décidé d'étudier** l'anglais.
  She decided to study English.

- **essayer de** to try to
  J'ai **essayé de travailler** chaque soir.
  I tried to work every evening.

Worked example

LISTENING TRACK 63 · **Target grade 3-4**

Hugo is talking about success in school in a podcast. What does he say? Complete the gap in each sentence using a word or phrase from the box below. There are more words / phrases than gaps.

Listen to the recording

> Au collège, il faut bien travailler pour avoir de bonnes notes. Moi, je ne suis pas travailleur, mais mon frère travaille beaucoup. Ma soeur, qui est plus jeune que moi, réussit tous ses examens.

Mon objectif est d'aller à l'université. My aim is to go to university.

Words like **travailler** and **travailleur** sound similar, so listen carefully.

stress	happiness	success	happy
hardworking	sporty	younger	
	older	tired	

1 Hugo thinks that hard work leads to …**success**… at school.

2 His brother is **hardworking**.

3 His sister is …**younger**….

(3 marks)

Now try this

WRITING · **Target grade 1-5**

Translate the following five sentences **into French**.

1 I like school.

2 I find all my lessons interesting.

3 My teachers help me every day.

4 Last year I decided to work well in order to succeed.

5 I hope to find a good job.

(10 marks)

Options at 16

Digital resources

Les choix à 16 ans

but (m)	goal, aim, purpose
choisir	to choose
discuter	to discuss
études (fpl)	studies
étudier	to study
formation (f)	training, apprenticeship
lycée (m)	sixth form college
matière (f)	subject
organiser	to organise
professeur (m/f)	teacher
projet (m)	project, plan
s'entendre avec	to get on with
conseiller	to advise
don (m)	skill, talent
objectif (m)	aim, objective

Structuring a sequence

You can make what you say and write in French more interesting by adding a sequence, for example using days of the week.

Le lundi, j'ai parlé avec mes professeurs, le mardi mes parents ont discuté avec moi, le jeudi, j'ai choisi mes matières.

On Monday I talked to my teachers, on Tuesday my parents spoke to me, on Thursday I chose my subjects.

Using different tenses

Remember that you can use different time frames. You can also include phrases like plus tard.

Present: J'étudie les maths tous les jours.
I study maths every day.

Past: Hier, j'ai choisi d'étudier le français.
Yesterday I chose to study French.

Future: Demain, je vais choisir mes matières.
I am going to choose my subjects tomorrow.

Worked example

WRITING   Target grade 1-5

Describe the photo. Write four short sentences **in French**.   **(8 marks)**

1 Il y a une classe.
2 Je vois des élèves.
3 Ils portent un uniforme.
4 Il y a des ordinateurs portables.

Aiming higher

In writing tasks with a picture, make sure that you focus on people, activities, weather (if applicable), descriptions.

Now try this

READING   Target grade 5-6

Manon has written a diary entry about options at 16.

Mes copains n'ont pas encore choisi leurs matières, mais moi, j'ai enfin décidé quelles matières j'allais étudier l'année prochaine. Après avoir parlé avec ma famille et mes profs, j'ai choisi d'étudier les maths et les sciences. J'ai aussi voulu étudier l'anglais mais mon père m'a conseillé de choisir l'art.

Complete the sentences below. Put a cross ✗ in the correct box for each question.

1 Manon spoke to …

☐	**A** her family alone.
☐	**B** both her family and her teachers.
☐	**C** her friends.

2 In the end she didn't choose …

☐	**A** maths.
☐	**B** science.
☐	**C** English.

3 Her father …

☐	**A** likes art.
☐	**B** gave her advice.
☐	**C** is an art teacher.

(3 marks)

69

Digital resources

Schools – France and the UK

Les écoles françaises et britanniques

britannique	British
collège (m)	secondary school
différence (f)	difference
différent(e)	different
études (fpl)	studies
étudier	to study
examen (m)	exam
lycée (m)	sixth form college
matière (f)	subject
passer un examen	to take an exam
privé(e)	private
professeur (m/f)	teacher
rentrée (f)	start of school year
Royaume-Uni (m)	UK
système (m)	system

H ONLY — Comparisons: the superlative

Grammar page 98

In English the superlative often ends in **-est** (e.g. 'tallest', 'best'), but in French a word is added at the start.

adjective	comparative	superlative
grand big	plus grand bigger	le plus grand the biggest
petit small	plus petit smaller	le plus petit the smallest

The adjective agrees with the noun being described.
le collège le plus grand because collège is **masculine**
l'école la plus grande because école is **feminine**
Use que when comparing things.
Mon école est plus grande que ton école.
My school is bigger than your school.
Bon (good) and mauvais (bad) are irregular.

adjective	comparative	superlative
bon	meilleur better	le meilleur the best
mauvais	pire worse	le pire the worst

Worked example

READING — Target grade 4-5

Manon has written a post about French and British schools.

Je pense qu'il y a beaucoup de différences entre les collèges français et britanniques. Mon amie anglaise m'a dit que ses cours commencent à neuf heures moins le quart. Moi, je dois être à l'école avant huit heures, car le premier cours commence plus tôt ici en France. Nous finissons à seize heures trente, mais la journée de mon amie finit à quinze heures! Ce n'est pas juste.

When comparisons are made, make sure you are answering the correct question. Here Manon gives both her details and those of her English friend.

Complete the sentences below. Put a cross ✗ in the correct box for each question.

1 Manon's lessons start at …

☐	A	8.45 am.
☐	B	9.45 am.
✗	C	8.00 am.

2 She finishes school at …

☐	A	3.00 pm.
✗	B	4.30 pm.
☐	C	6.30 pm.

3 She says that things are …

☐	A	fair.
✗	B	unfair.
☐	C	strange.

(3 marks)

Now try this

LISTENING — TRACK 64 — Target grade 5

Dictation

You are going to hear someone talking about French and British schools.
Sentences 1–3: write down the missing words in the gaps provided. In each gap, you will write one word **in French**.

Listen to the recording

1 J'_____ les _____ en France.

2 J'étudie les _____ et l'_____ .

3 Mon _____ adore la _____ .

Sentences 4–6: write down the full sentences that you hear in the spaces provided, **in French**.

4 _____ .

5 _____ .

6 _____ .

(10 marks)

Future study plans

Digital resources

Mes projets d'études

argent (m)	money
études (fpl)	studies
étudiant(e) (m/f)	student
étudier	to study
examen (m)	exam
formation (f)	training, apprenticeship
futur (m) / avenir (m)	future
lycée (m)	sixth form college
passer un examen	to take an exam
projet (m)	plan
réussir (à)	to succeed in, pass an exam
travail (m)	work
université (f)	university
apprenti(e) (m/f)	apprentice
bourse (f)	scholarship, grant
emploi (m)	employment

Je continuerai mes études.
I'll continue my studies.

The future tense: regular verbs

Grammar page 112

When you want to talk about the future, you can use the future tense which translates to the English 'shall' or 'will'.

-er and -ir verbs

Just add the future tense endings to the infinitive:

j'étudierai	I will study
tu étudieras	you will study
il / elle / on étudiera	he / she / one will study
nous étudierons	we will study
vous étudierez	you will study
ils / elles étudieront	they will study

-re verbs

Cross off the final -e and add the same endings:

j'attendrai	I will wait
tu attendras	you will wait
il / elle / on attendra	he / she / one will wait
nous attendrons	we will wait
vous attendrez	you will wait
ils / elles attendront	they will wait

Worked example

LISTENING TRACK 65 **Target grade 4**

Clara is talking to her friend Ahmed about future study plans.
Listen to the recording and complete the sentences below.
Put a cross ✗ in the correct box for each question. **(2 marks)**

Listen to the recording

Clara: Je vais continuer mes études au lycée et après, je voudrais aller à l'université.
Ahmed: Pour étudier la technologie comme moi?
Clara: Non, mais je ne sais pas quoi faire.

When you hear two voices, make sure that you focus carefully on what each one is saying.

1   Clara is going to …
☐ **A** stop studying.
☒ **B** continue her studies.
☐ **C** study technology.

2   At university Clara …
☒ **A** doesn't know what she will study.
☐ **B** will study with Ahmed.
☐ **C** will have a good time.

Now try this

READING **Target grade 5-6**

Sofiane has written this email.

Si je travaille dur, je réussirai à mes examens et j'étudierai les maths à l'université. Mon frère, qui a vingt ans, a décidé de devenir apprenti et il adore ça car il gagne de l'argent.

Answer the questions **in English**.

1   What does Sofiane think will happen if he works hard? **(2 marks)**
2   What has his brother done? **(1 mark)**
3   Why does he like what he did? **(1 mark)**

Digital resources

Future plans

Les projets futurs

ambition (f)	ambition
argent (m)	money
chercher	to look for
devenir	to become
espérer	to hope
gagner	to earn
habiter	to live
poste (m)	job, post
rêve (m)	dream
rêver	to dream
riche	rich
salaire (m)	salary
se marier	to get married
succès (m)	success
trouver	to find
voyager	to travel
désirer	to desire
compagnie (f)	company
employé (m)	employee, worker
métier (m)	job, profession
patron (m) / patronne (f)	boss

H ONLY — The future tense of irregular verbs

Grammar page 112

Here are some irregular verbs to learn. They are only irregular in their stem as the endings are the same as those of regular verbs in the future tense.

je serai	I'll be
j'aurai	I'll have
j'irai	I'll go
je ferai	I'll do / make
je deviendrai	I'll become
je viendrai	I'll come
je verrai	I'll see
je pourrai	I'll be able
je voudrai	I'll want
je saurai	I'll know
je devrai	I'll have to

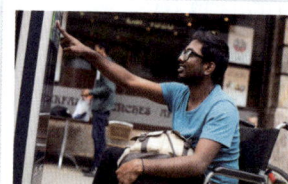

Je verrai de nouveaux endroits. I'll see new places.

J'irai à l'université. I'll go to university.
Je serai riche. I'll be rich.

Worked example

SPEAKING TRACK 66 | Target grade 5-6 | Listen to the recording

You might be asked a question like this in the conversation section of your Speaking exam.

Quelle est ton ambition?

Je voudrais devenir professeur car j'adore aider les jeunes et je crois que c'est un emploi important. J'irai à l'université et je travaillerai dur.

Aiming higher

Even if you are asked a question about the future, you can use a variety of tenses. This student has used present and future tenses, and the conditional.

Now try this

READING | Target grade 2-3

Remember you can use aller + infinitive to express the future. Je vais voyager …

Read these comments from an internet forum about future plans.

Diane: Je vais voyager dans des pays différents et je vais trouver un poste de médecin dans un hôpital.

Jade: J'espère devenir une chanteuse célèbre et être riche.

Nathan: Dans le futur, je vais me marier et je voudrais avoir trois enfants.

Who says what? Choose the correct answers. Put a cross ✗ in the correct column for each question.

	Who …	Diane	Jade	Nathan
1	… wants lots of money?			
2	… wants to have children?			
3	… wants to get married?			
4	… wants to go abroad?			
5	… wants to be famous?			
6	… wants to work in a hospital?			

(6 marks)

Part-time jobs and money

Gagner de l'argent

argent (m)	money
bien payé(e)	well-paid
bureau (m)	office
café (m)	café
chercher	to look for
gagner	to earn
heure (f)	hour
magasin (m)	shop
mal payé(e)	badly paid
payer	to pay
poste (m)	job, position, post
restaurant (m)	restaurant
salaire (m)	salary
supermarché (m)	supermarket
travail (m)	work
dépenser	to spend (money)
désirer	to desire
patron (m) / patronne (f)	boss
petit emploi (m)	part-time job

Saying 'would like'

Grammar page 113

To say 'would like', use the conditional of the verb vouloir.

je voudrais	I would like / I'd like
tu voudrais	you'd like
il / elle / on voudrait	he / she / one would like
nous voudrions	we'd like
vous voudriez	you'd like
ils / elles voudraient	they'd like

H ONLY

Je voudrais trouver un emploi.
I'd like to find a job.

You could also use j'aimerais as an alternative.

J'aimerais gagner de l'argent.
I'd like to earn money.

Je travaille dans un café le week-end.
I work at a café at the weekend.

Worked example

LISTENING TRACK 67   Target grade 1-5   Listen to the recording

Dictation

You are going to hear someone talking about jobs and money.

Sentences 1–3: write down the missing words in the gaps provided. In each gap, you will write one word **in French**.

1 J'aime _travailler_ dans un _café_ .
2 J' _achète_ des _bijoux_ .
3 Mes _collègues_ sont _sympa_ .

Sentences 4–6: write down the full sentences that you hear in the spaces provided, **in French**.

4 Je gagne de l'argent.
5 Le travail est très agréable.
6 Je travaille pendant cinq heures.

(10 marks)

In any Foundation tier dictation task there will be two words not in the vocabulary list (here, **bijoux** and **collègues**) which you will need to try to work out using your knowledge of French words and how they sound.

Try to break down longer words using the sounds you recognise.

Now try this

LISTENING TRACK 68   Target grade 3-4   Listen to the recording

Léa is telling you about her job. What does she say? Listen to the recording and put a cross ✗ in each one of the **three** correct boxes.

☐	**A** Léa works in a market.	☐	**D** She finds the work difficult
☐	**B** She works on Friday evenings.	☐	**E** She likes her job.
☐	**C** She works on Sunday afternoons.	☐	**F** She recently bought a gift.

(3 marks)

Digital resources

Opinions about jobs

Les avis sur les emplois

argent (m)	money
chercher	to look for
client(e) (m/f)	customer
emploi (m)	employment, job
gagner	to earn
heure (f)	hour
payer	to pay
poste (m)	job, position, post
salaire (m)	salary
travail (m)	work
trouver	to find
dépenser	to spend (money)
désirer	to desire

Expressing simple opinions

Make sure that you can express both positive and negative opinions using different tenses.

	positive 🙂	negative 🙁
C'est ... It's ... C'était ... It was ... Ça va être ... It is going to be ... Ce sera ... It will be ...	agréable (pleasant) excellent (excellent) génial (great) facile (easy) utile (useful) bien payé (well paid)	nul (rubbish) difficile (difficult) inutile (useless) mal payé (badly paid)

Remember, the adjectives you use need to agree with the noun.

Les emplois sont bien payés – emplois is masculine and plural.

L'expérience était excellente – expérience is feminine and singular.

Although questions normally follow the order of the text, in this type of question, they are mixed up. Pay particular attention to the vocabulary.

Worked example

READING   Target grade 1-2

Read these comments on jobs from an internet forum.

Patrick: Je trouve mon travail inutile. Je travaille dans une banque.
Richard: Je travaille dans un magasin de mode. C'est amusant.
Sylvie: Je veux travailler dans un bureau car c'est intéressant.

Who says what? Choose the correct answers.
Put a cross ✗ in the correct column for each question.

Who ...	Patrick	Richard	Sylvie
1 ... sells clothes?		✗	
2 ... works in a bank?	✗		
3 ... thinks their work is useless?	✗		
4 ... finds their work fun?		✗	
5 ... wants to work in an office?			✗
6 ... thinks the job is interesting?			✗

(6 marks)

À mon avis, travailler dans un café, c'est nul. Les clients se disputent et ne sont pas sympa.

In my opinion, working in a café is rubbish. The customers argue and are not nice.

Listen carefully to questions you are asked. Here you must give an answer and then a reason to justify your choice.

SPEAKING   Target grade 5-6

Now try this

This is an example of a question you might be asked in the conversation part of your Speaking exam.

À ton avis, quel est l'emploi le plus intéressant et pourquoi?

Job adverts and skills needed

Compétences pour un emploi

argent (m)	money
banque (f)	bank
boulangerie (f)	bakery
bureau (m)	office
chercher	to look for
envoyer	to send
ferme (f)	farm
gagner	to earn
heure (f)	hour
hôpital (m)	hospital
hôtel (m)	hotel
libre	free, available
local(e)	local
magasin (m)	shop
musée (m)	museum

pâtisserie (f)	cake shop
pharmacie (f)	chemist's
piscine (f)	swimming pool
poste (m)	job, position, post
responsable	responsible
salaire (m)	salary
travail (m)	work
travailleur / travailleuse	hardworking
trouver	to find
bibliothèque (f)	library
compétence (f)	skill
disponible	available
gymnase (m)	gym

Feminine form of nouns

Some French nouns have two forms, masculine and feminine.
patron (m) / patronne (f) boss
chef (m) / cheffe (f) boss
chanteur (m) / chanteuse (f) singer

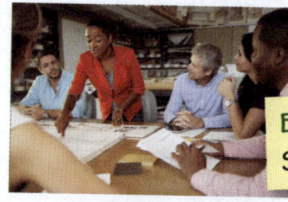

Elle est patronne. She's a boss.

Flexible phrases

Je pense que nous devrions travailler en équipe.
I think we should work as part of a team.

You could use this to talk about work, or improving the environment, or clubs at school.

Worked example

LISTENING TRACK 69   Target grade 1-2

Emma is talking about a job she has seen advertised.

Listen to the recording

Il y a un petit travail dans une boulangerie en ville. C'est bien payé.

Which two aspects of the job does she mention?
Put a cross ✗ in each one of the **two** correct boxes.

☐	A	the hours
✗	B	the salary
☐	C	the qualifications
✗	D	the place of work

(2 marks)

In listening tasks like this, you need to match a general term to a specific item of vocabulary, so place of work = **boulangerie**.

Now try this

READING   Target grade 5-6

You see this advert for a job. Read the advert and then put a cross ✗ in each one of the **three** correct boxes.

Employé recherché pour L'Hôtel de la Gare du centre-ville.
Il faut être responsable et travailleur et on devrait savoir bien travailler en équipe et être disponible trois jours en semaine et le week-end. Si vous pouvez commencer la semaine prochaine, ce serait excellent.
Téléphonez-nous ou envoyez un e-mail.

☐	A	The job is working on the telephone.
☐	B	You need to be able to work well in a team.
☐	C	You must be available in the week and at weekends.
☐	D	The job is at a railway station.
☐	E	You must only contact the place of work by email.
☐	F	Being available soon would be an advantage.

(3 marks)

Digital resources

Applying for jobs

Trouver un poste

chercher	to look for
gagner	to earn
hôtel (m)	hotel
libre	free, available
personnalité (f)	personality
poste (m)	job, position, post
pratique	practical
responsable	responsible
salaire (m)	salary
travail (m)	work
compter sur	to count on
entretien (m)	interview
inquiet / inquiète	worried

Using different tenses

If you are talking about yourself, you'll use je a lot, so try to show variety and complexity by using different tenses.

present	je travaille (I work / am working)
perfect	j'ai travaillé (I worked)
imperfect	je travaillais (I used to work / was working)
future	je travaillerai (I'll work)
immediate future	je vais travailler (I'm going to work)
conditional	je travaillerais (I would work)

You could also say Je voudrais travailler (I would like to work).

Worked example

LISTENING TRACK 70

Target grade 5-6

Clara has an interview for a job. She is talking to a friend, Luis.

What do they say? Listen to the recording and complete the sentences by putting a cross ✗ in the correct box for each question.

Listen to the recording

Clara: Demain, j'aurai un entretien pour un emploi dans un hôtel. Je suis inquiète.

Luis: Il n'y aura pas de problèmes. Tu as déjà travaillé dans un magasin le samedi.

Clara: Ah oui, et mon patron a dit que je m'entendais bien avec les clients.

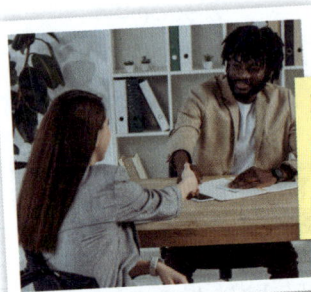

Elle a un entretien pour un emploi. She has an interview for a job.

Flexible phrases

Ça m'inquiète. I'm worried about that.

Listen carefully. Shop is mentioned but it is associated with a past tense not the future. Don't just write a word because you hear it mentioned – try to understand what you hear.

1 Clara has a job interview …

☐	**A** in a shop.
☒	**B** tomorrow.
☐	**C** with her boss.

2 She is …

☐	**A** confident.
☒	**B** worried.
☐	**C** happy.

3 Her boss said that she …

☒	**A** got on well with customers.
☐	**B** was reliable.
☐	**C** wasn't very good.

(3 marks)

Now try this

SPEAKING

Target grade 4-9

Read aloud

Morgan has contributed to a blog about applying for jobs.

Read out the text below.

Je veux travailler dans un magasin ou dans un restaurant en ville.
Ma meilleure copine a un poste dans un petit musée car elle adore l'histoire.
J'ai besoin d'argent et, heureusement, j'ai un entretien avec le patron.
Mon rêve est d'être chanteur parce qu'on peut devenir célèbre.

(8 marks)

Volunteering

Digital resources

Aider les autres

aide (f)	help, aid
animaux (mpl)	animals, pets
association (f)	organisation, charity
catastrophe (f)	catastrophe
comprendre	to understand
difficulté (f)	difficulty
dormir	to sleep
protéger	to protect
rue (f)	street, road
adopter	to adopt
combattre	to fight
lutte (f)	fight
menacer	to threaten
offrir	to offer
se fier à	to rely on
s'occuper de	to look after
soin (m)	care
soutien (m)	support

Ⓗ ONLY Depuis + imperfect tense

To say that you **have been** doing something for a period of time (and are still doing it), use depuis after the present tense.

Je travaille dans l'association depuis deux ans.
I've been working at the organisation for two years.

If you want to say that you **had been** doing something for a period of time, use depuis after the imperfect tense.

Je travaillais dans l'association depuis deux ans.
I had been working at the organisation for two years.

Je travaillais depuis trois ans dans une association qui aide les personnes pauvres.
I had been working for three years in an organisation that helps poor people.

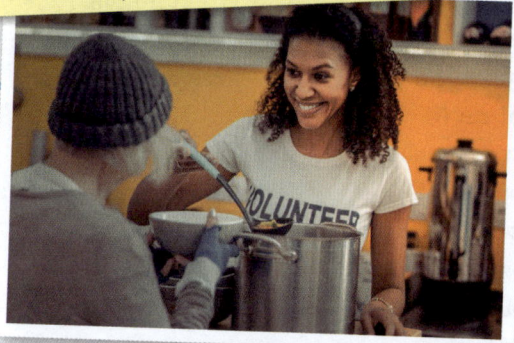

Worked example

READING   Target grade 5-6

Read this extract from an article that your Belgian friend, Clara, has written in her school magazine.

> Avec les autres élèves de mon cours de sciences, on a décidé d'adopter un animal car nous pensons que c'est vraiment important de protéger la nature. Ma meilleure copine adore tout ce qui est naturel et elle voudrait qu'on continue à aider les animaux.

Answer the following questions **in English**.

1 What has Clara's science class done?
adopted an animal

2 Who wants to continue helping animals?
Clara's best friend   (2 marks)

Answer any questions which ask for English responses as briefly as possible and only add the detail you need.

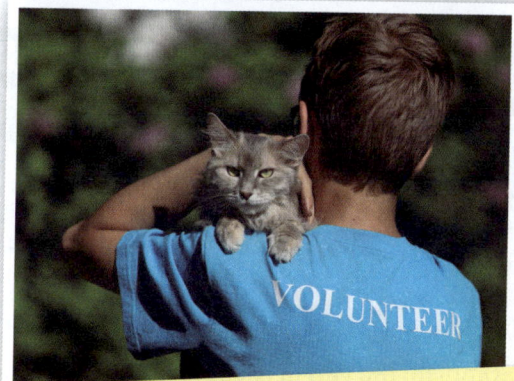

Je travaillais déjà depuis trois heures au centre pour animaux lorsqu'un beau chat est arrivé.
I had already been working for three hours at the animal shelter when a beautiful cat arrived.

You might be asked a question like this in the conversation part of your Speaking exam. In the conversation section, you should try to give reasons and add detail to your answer. It is your chance to show off the French you know!

Now try this

SPEAKING   Target grade 5-6

Dans le futur, tu voudrais travailler pour une association qui aide les gens?

Digital resources

Equality and helping others

L'égalité

aide (f)	help, aid
améliorer	to improve
carrière (f)	career
comprendre	to understand
difficulté (f)	difficulty
droit (m)	right
égal(e)	equal
égalité (f)	equality
femme (f)	woman
handicap (m)	disability
handicapé(e)	disabled
homme (m)	man
juste	fair
sexe (m)	gender
société (f)	society
traiter	to treat
combattre	to fight
discrimination (f)	discrimination
inquiétude (f)	worry
justice (f)	justice
lutte (f)	fight
manifestation (f)	demonstration
s'occuper de	to look after
soin (m)	care
soutien (m)	support
unité (f)	unity

Pronouncing similar words

You will have noticed that many French and English words look the same or similar, but they are pronounced differently. This is important as in your Speaking exam, your teacher will only be able to give you marks for words that would be understandable to a French person.

- **manifestation**: In English, the -tion sounds like *shun*, but in French, it is more like *seeon*.
- **juste, unité**: The u makes an *oo* sound.
- **société**: The i is pronounced a bit like *ee*.
- **carrière**: Careful to sound the i in the right place – a bit like *carry-air*.

Elle manifestait pour l'égalité des femmes.
She was protesting for equality for women.

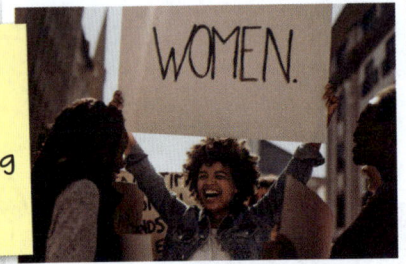

Ils luttent contre l'injustice.
They fight against injustice.

Worked example

LISTENING TRACK 71   Target grade 4-5   Listen to the recording

Lucas is talking about equality.

Je crois qu'il y a des différences entre les salaires des hommes et des femmes, même quand ils font le même travail. À mon avis ce n'est pas juste.

What does he say?
Complete the gap in each sentence using a word or phrase from the box below. There are more words / phrases than gaps.

hours	salaries	uniform
common	fair	ideal

1 Lucas thinks that there are differences in ....salaries.....
2 He says that it's not ......fair...... .   **(2 marks)**

Remember that some of the alternatives will not be needed.

You might be asked a question like this in the conversation section of your Speaking exam. This is a difficult question, so try not to panic. Think of vocabulary you **do** know. You could even tell your teacher that you find the question difficult (**c'est une question difficile**) while you are thinking but then make sure to give an opinion and reasons.

Now try this

SPEAKING   Target grade 5-6

Est-ce que notre société est égale?

The natural world

Digital resources

Le monde naturel

air (m)	air	plage (f)	beach
animal (m)	animal	poisson (m)	fish
bois (m)	wood	pollution (f)	pollution
campagne (f)	countryside	ressource (f)	resource
cheval (m)	horse	sol (m)	ground
ciel (m)	sky	arbre (m)	tree
eau (f)	water	champ (m)	field
environnement (m)	environment	climatique	climate
feu (m)	fire	détruire	to destroy
forêt (f)	forest	espèce (f)	species
fruit (m)	fruit	état (m)	state
habiter	to live	fleur (f)	flower
lapin (m)	rabbit	menace (f)	threat
mer (f)	sea	menacer	to threaten
monde (m)	world	rivière (f)	river
montagne (f)	mountain	sec / sèche	dry
nature (f)	nature		

H ONLY — The passive
Grammar page 116

You might want to use the passive when you want to say that something has been done to / by someone or something.

To form it, use a part of être in the tense you are using plus a past participle which must agree.

Les animaux **sont menacés** par la pollution.
Animals are threatened by pollution.

Les forêts **ont été détruites** par l'homme.
Forests have been destroyed by man.

Worked example

SPEAKING TRACK 72 · Target grade 3-5

Que penses-tu de la nature?

Je crois que la nature est belle. J'adore les animaux car je les trouve très calmes. À l'avenir, je voudrais habiter à la campagne.

Listen to the recording

You might be asked a question like this in the conversation part of your Listening exam. Try to answer it with reasons and different tenses. Here the student has given an answer, then a reason, then said what they would like to do.

Listen carefully to the question asked by your teacher and you can ask them to repeat it if you are unsure.

Now try this

LISTENING TRACK 73 · Target grade 5-6

Listen to the recording

Clément, Yasmina and Mohamed are talking about the natural world.

What do they say? Listen to the recording and complete the sentences by putting a cross ✗ in the correct box for each question.

1 Clément especially likes nature when he is …
☐ A in a field.
☐ B on the ground.
☐ C with friends.

2 Yasmina looks up at the sky when she is …
☐ A unhappy
☐ B in a wood.
☐ C on her bike.

3 She says that the air is …
☐ A polluted.
☐ B fresh.
☐ C free.

4 Mohamed …
☐ A loves the countryside.
☐ B has never been to the countryside.
☐ C will go to the countryside soon.

(4 marks)

Digital resources

Spending time in the countryside

Passer du temps à la campagne

air (m)	air	monde (m)	world
animal (m)	animal	montagne (f)	mountain
bois (m)	wood	nature (f)	nature
campagne (f)	countryside	naturel(le)	natural
cheval (m)	horse	plage (f)	beach
ciel (m)	sky	poisson (m)	fish
eau (f)	water	arbre (m)	tree
feu (m)	fire	champ (m)	field
forêt (f)	forest	espèce (f)	species
fruit (m)	fruit	fleur (f)	flower
habiter	to live	refléter	to reflect
lapin (m)	rabbit	rivière (f)	river
mer (f)	sea		

Using si (if)

Grammar page 113

When you want to use a sentence with 'if' (si) in French, you can use it with the present tense on its own.
Si je peux. If I can.

H ONLY However, if you continue the sentence, you must obey the rules:

- si + the present + the future
  S'il fait beau, j'irai à la campagne.
  If the weather is fine, I'll go to the countryside.

- si + the imperfect + the conditional
  Si je pouvais, j'habiterais à la campagne.
  If I could, I'd live in the countryside.

Si j'étais riche, je vivrais dans une grande maison près de la mer où le ciel se reflète dans l'eau.
If I were rich, I would live in a big house near the sea where the sky reflects in the water.

S'il fait trop chaud, j'irai en vacances à la montagne.
If the weather is too hot, I'll go on holiday to the mountains.

Worked example

READING

Target grade **4-9**

Translate the following paragraph **into English**.   **(10 marks)**

> La nature m'intéresse car je crois qu'il est important de se reposer à la campagne. Hier, j'ai passé une journée au bord d'une rivière dans un petit bois. Les arbres étaient vraiment beaux. Ma famille et moi rêvons de vivre dans une ferme au Canada où il y aurait beaucoup d'animaux.

When you have to translate into English, make sure that what you write reads well and makes sense.

Nature interests me because I think it's important to rest / have a rest in the countryside. Yesterday I spent a day by a river in a little wood. The trees were really beautiful. My family and I dream of living on a farm in Canada where there would be lots of animals.

Now try this

SPEAKING

Target grade **2-5**

Tu aimes la campagne? Pourquoi ou pourquoi pas?

This is a type of question you might be asked in the conversation part of your Speaking exam. Remember to answer the question and give reasons. This is your chance to show your teacher the French you know.

The environment and me

Mon rôle dans l'environnement

air (m)	air	réduire	to reduce
améliorer	to improve	voiture (f)	car
arrêter	to stop	arbre (m)	tree
causer	to cause	bouteille (f)	bottle
eau (f)	water	circulation (f)	traffic
effet (m)	effect	climatique	climate
environnement (m)	environment	déchets (mpl)	rubbish, waste
jeter	to throw away	espèce (f)	species
mer (f)	sea	limiter	to limit
monde (m)	world	manifestation (f)	demonstration, protest
nature (f)	nature		
plastique (m)	plastic	manifester	to protest
pollution (f)	pollution	réutiliser	to reuse
protéger	to protect	verre (m)	glass
recycler	to recycle		

The conditional   Grammar page 113   H ONLY

Use the conditional to say what you would do. It uses the same stem as the future tense (usually the infinitive) but adds the same endings as the imperfect tense.

recycler ➡ je recyclerais I would recycle

manifester ➡ je manifesterais I would protest

La circulation est un problème. Je **devrais** aller au collège à pied. Traffic is a problem. I ought to go to school on foot.

Worked example

SPEAKING TRACK 74   Target grade 4-9   Listen to the recording

Describe the picture.
Your description must cover:
- people
- location
- activity. **(8 marks)**

Sur la photo, je vois qu'il y a trois personnes qui sont en train de recycler. La femme au centre porte une boîte qui contient plusieurs bouteilles en plastique. Elle porte un pull marron et elle sourit. La jeune femme à droite porte un pull aussi et il semble qu'elle recycle les journaux. La troisième jeune femme qui est à gauche porte un pull gris et elle porte une boîte avec des bouteilles en verres pour les recycler. Toutes les femmes sont contentes.

Make sure you learn the words la **femme**, l'**homme**, la **fille** and le **garçon**, but you can also use **personnes**.

When you have finished your description, you will be asked two questions relating to your chosen picture. You are expected to say a few words or a short phrase / sentence in response to each question. One-word answers will not be sufficient to gain full marks.

1 Qu'est-ce que tu recycles à la maison?

Je recycle le papier chaque semaine.

2 Qu'est-ce que tu as fait récemment pour aider l'environnement?

J'ai recyclé le verre et le plastique. **(4 marks)**

Now try this

WRITING

Write to your friend about the environment. You **must** include the following points:

Target grade 4-6

- environmental problems in your area
- your opinion of the environment
- what you have recently done to help the environment
- what you will do in the future to help the environment.

Write your answer **in French**.
You should aim to write between 80 and 90 words. **(18 marks)**

Digital resources

Local environmental issues

Problèmes de l'environnement dans ma région

air (m)	air
améliorer	to improve
arrêter	to stop
boîte (f)	box, tin, can
bus (m)	bus
causer	to cause
eau (f)	water
effet (m)	effect
électrique	electric
énergie (f)	energy
environnement (m)	environment
espace (m)	space
habiter	to live
interdire de	to ban, prohibit
jeter	to throw away
pollution (f)	pollution
propre	clean
protéger	to protect
réduire	to reduce
arbre (m)	tree
bouteille (f)	bottle
circulation (f)	traffic
climatique	climate
concerner	to be relevant to
conserver	to keep, conserve
déchets (mpl)	rubbish, waste
résoudre	to solve
réutiliser	to reuse
véhicule (m)	vehicle

Impersonal verbs

Grammar page 116

Most verbs can be used with je, tu, il, elle etc. Some verbs are only used with il in certain expressions. You can use them to talk about general things.

- il y a there is / there are
  Il y a des véhicules électriques.
  There are some electric vehicles.
- il fait it is (with the weather)
  Il fait chaud. It is hot. (weather)
- il faut it is necessary / you / we must
  Il faut réduire la pollution. We must reduce pollution.
- il est + adjective + de … it is + adjective + to …
  Il est important de résoudre les problèmes de la pollution.
  It's important to resolve pollution problems.

Flexible phrases

H ONLY

Cela en vaut la peine. It's worth it.

Il faut protéger l'environnement pour sauver notre avenir. Cela en vaut la peine.

We need to protect the environment to safeguard our future. It's worth it.

Il vaut la peine is another example of an impersonal verb.

Worked example

WRITING

Target grade 1-5

Describe the photo. Write four short sentences **in French**. **(8 marks)**

1 Il y a des voitures.
2 On peut voir des bus.
3 Il y a beaucoup de personnes.
4 Ils sont dans la rue.

In Writing picture tasks, when you have a lot of words from which to choose, make sure you keep the answers simple and clear.

Now try this

SPEAKING

Target grade 3-5

Quels sont les problèmes d'environnement dans ta région?

You might be asked a question like this in the conversation part of your Speaking exam. You will be given preparation time – use it first to prepare thoroughly for the read aloud, role play and photo tasks before then noting down useful phrases and words to use during the conversation part. You should not write notes to read out, just to prompt your thoughts as you speak in the conversation.

Global environmental issues

Problèmes de l'environnement dans le monde

catastrophe (f)	catastrophe	économie (f)	economy
changement (m)	change	encourager	to encourage
crise (f)	crisis	enseigner	to teach
dépendre de	to depend on	espèce (f)	species
devenir	to become	génération (f)	generation
ensemble	together	gouvernement (m)	government
global(e)	global	inondation (f)	flood
mort(e)	dead	mondial(e)	global
planète (f)	planet	objectif (m)	objective
terre (f)	earth	prévenir	to warn
agir	to act	réfléchir	to think about, reflect
baisser	to lower, turn down		
brûler	to burn	remplacer	to replace
chômage (m)	unemployment	renouvelable	renewable
climatique	climate	se soucier de	to show concern for
conflit (m)	conflict		
construire	to build	soutenir	to support
disparaître	to disappear	véhicule (m)	vehicle
durable	sustainable		

H ONLY Venir de + infinitive

Venir de means 'to have just done something'.

Je viens de lire un article en ligne sur les inondations.
I have just read an internet article about floods.

You can also use the imperfect tense of venir to say 'had just'.

Le gouvernement venait d'annoncer de nouveaux objectifs climatiques.
The government had just announced new climate objectives.

Worked example

READING — Target grade 7-8

Read this article from a school magazine.

> L'avenir de la Terre dépend de nous, les jeunes. Le changement climatique récent est une catastrophe et détruit notre monde. Notre génération doit prévenir les gouvernements que les espèces animales disparaissent à cause des inondations et des feux qui ont détruit les forêts. Il faut remplacer les véhicules par des alternatives durables et renouvelables. Nous devons expliquer à tout le monde pourquoi nous devons essayer de baisser la température des mers. Il faut aussi soutenir des projets qui construisent de nouveaux habitats pour les animaux.

Answer the following questions **in English**.

1 What depends on young people?   **(1 mark)**
the future of the Earth

2 Why have animal species been disappearing?   **(2 marks)**
floods and forest fires

3 What should we try to do regarding the sea?   **(1 mark)**
lower the temperature

4 Which other projects should we support?   **(1 mark)**
building new habitats for animals

Worked example

LISTENING — TRACK 75 — Target grade 2-4

Jade is talking about global issues. Which items does she mention? Listen to the recording and put a cross ✗ in each one of the **two** correct boxes.   **(2 marks)**

Listen to the recording

> Il y a des problèmes sérieux dans le monde. La pollution, c'est nul et il y a trop de personnes qui ont faim.

☐	**A** climate change
☒	**B** pollution
☐	**C** deforestation
☒	**D** hunger

Here **faim** is used for 'hunger' but the passage might have said **pas assez à manger** (not enough to eat).

You might be asked a question like this in the conversation part of your Speaking exam. Try to give reasons and show your teacher the vocabulary you know.

Now try this

SPEAKING — Target grade 5-6

Selon toi, quel est le problème mondial le plus grave? Pourquoi?

Digital resources

Caring for the planet

Prendre soin de la planète

arrêter	to stop
association (f)	organisation, charity
causer	to cause
crise (f)	crisis
danger (m)	danger
environnement (m)	environment
île (f)	island
protéger	to protect
sauver	to save, rescue
terre (f)	earth
agir	to act
climatique	climate
conscient(e)	conscious
détruire	to destroy
disparaître	to disappear
espèce (f)	species
ignorer	to ignore
produire	to produce
résoudre	to solve
se soucier de	to show concern for

Prepositions

Learning these will help you to understand reading and listening tasks. You can also use them in your Speaking and Writing exams.

avec with · sans without · pour for · contre against · vers towards · entre between · par by, for · prepositions · autour around · parmi amongst · dans in, inside · à côté de next to

Il faut se soucier des espèces animales qui disparaissent autour de nous.
We need to show concern for the animal species that are disappearing around us.

Nous allons vers une crise climatique.
We are going towards a climate crisis.

Worked example

READING · Target grade 4-5

Léa has written you an email.

> Nous devons sauver notre planète. La Terre est en danger – il fait plus chaud chaque année et je suis triste. Je vais aider une association qui veut s'occuper de tout le monde.

What does she say? Complete the sentences below.
Put a cross ✗ in the correct box for each question.

1 The Earth is …
☐ A saved.
☐ B cold.
☒ C in danger.

2 The Earth is getting …
☒ A warmer.
☐ B sad.
☐ C better.

3 She is going to …
☐ A be happy.
☐ B work in a school.
☒ C join an organisation.

(3 marks)

Nous devons produire de l'énergie sans détruire notre planète.
We need to produce energy without destroying our planet.

Now try this

LISTENING · TRACK 76 · Target grade 5-6

Listen to the recording

You hear this advert for a programme about caring for the planet. What does it say?
Listen to the podcast and put a cross ✗ in each one of the **three** correct boxes.

☐ A Action is needed to save the planet.	☐ D Animals are safe for the moment.
☐ B Governments are doing enough to help.	☐ E Global temperature is currently stable.
☐ C Some people think there are no problems.	☐ F The programme is next Sunday.

(3 marks)

A greener future

Vers un avenir plus vert

effet (m)	effect
habituel(le)	usual
moyen (m)	means, way
nécessaire	necessary
plusieurs	several
sérieux	serious
voiture electrique (f)	electric car
actuel(le)	current
apparemment	apparently
besoin (m)	need
conscient(e)	conscious, aware
convaincre	to convince
façon (f) / manière (f)	way
ne ... aucun	not one
nombreux / nombreuse	numerous
sinon	otherwise

Introducing your ideas

d'abord	firstly
ensuite	then
enfin	finally
désormais	from now on
au contraire	on the contrary

H ᴼᴺᴸʸ Using être en train de

Use être en train de + infinitive to express being in the middle of doing something.
Use a part of être in the relevant tense, depending on the time frame.

Imperfect

Hier, j'étais en train de lire un article sur la crise climatique quand mon amie m'a téléphoné.

Yesterday I was (in the middle of) reading an article about the climate crisis when my friend phoned me.

Present

Elle se soucie qu'on est en train de détruire la planète.

She is worried that we are (in the middle of) destroying the planet.

Future

Demain à onze heures nous serons en train de manifester contre la pollution.

Tomorrow at 11 am we will be (in the middle of) protesting against pollution.

Worked example

READING   Target grade **7-8**

Read this blog post about the environment.

> Il est évidemment nécessaire de changer l'état actuel de notre planète qui est vraiment terrible. Tout le monde peut aider de plusieurs manières. D'abord, je suis en train de remplacer mes achats habituels par des versions plus vertes car c'est mieux pour l'environnement. Désormais, je n'utiliserai aucun sac en plastique. Apparemment, mon amie est aussi en train de convaincre ses parents d'acheter une voiture électrique. Nous devons tous être plus conscients de nos actions individuelles.

Answer the following questions **in English**.

1   How is the current state of the earth described?
terrible

2   Give one way the writer says they are helping.
buying more environmentally friendly products / will not use plastic bags.

3   Give one way the writer's friend is helping.
convincing her parents to buy an electric car

(3 marks)

Worked example

LISTENING TRACK **77**   Target grade **3-4**

Lucie is talking about school life. What does she mention?

Listen to the recording and put a cross ✗ in in each one of the **three** correct boxes.

Listen to the recording

> À l'avenir, je rêve d'acheter une voiture électrique, si possible. Je vais aussi prendre les transports en commun et mes amis et moi allons devenir végétariens.

☐	**A**	being vegan
✗	**B**	buying an electric car
✗	**C**	using public transport
✗	**D**	being vegetarian
☐	**E**	recycling
☐	**F**	making new friends

(3 marks)

Now try this

SPEAKING   Target grade **5-6**

Comment vas-tu être plus vert à l'avenir?

Had a look ☐   Nearly there ☐   Nailed it! ☐

Digital resources

Paper 1: Speaking

Overview

Task 1: Read aloud

Task 2: Role play

Task 3: Picture

Timing: Preparation – 15 mins before exam; Foundation exam – 7–9 mins; Higher exam – 10–12 mins

Marks: 50 marks; 25% of the exam total

Cans and Cannots

✓ You **can** make notes on an A4 sheet of paper.

✓ You **can** write on the read aloud passage.

✓ You **can** use the notes during the exam.

✓ You **can** use vocabulary not on the prescribed list.

✗ You **cannot** use a dictionary.

✗ You **cannot** write on the role play or picture card.

Task 1: The read aloud task – what to expect

All the assessed words in the read aloud passage come from Edexcel's prescribed lists. In the last one minute of the preparation time, you can read parts or all of it out loud to practise, if you wish.

Your teacher will tell you when the preparation time is up and will ask you to read the card.

After your reading, there are two follow-up questions asking you to give a simple opinion on something related to the passage, usually in the present tense at both Foundation and Higher. These are not printed on the card.

Answers that are relevant and totally clear are awarded 2 marks, those with some ambiguity receive 1 mark. If the message is not communicated – no marks. There are no marks for developing your answer, so keep to a short sentence.

Using the preparation time

- Start with the **role play**. Check the scenario, read the full task and write notes on the paper provided. Just prepare what you are asked for – no extras are needed.

- Next, look at the **picture task**. Decide which photo to talk about. Jot down ideas and vocabulary about the picture, focusing on 'people, location, activity'. Try to add a bit of extra detail where you can.

- Turn to the **read aloud** task. Read it through in your head, getting an understanding of the meaning. Make notes on the card itself of any pauses or tricky pronunciation.

- Think about the **conversation**. Look at the thematic context and jot down notes of vocabulary or phrases you might want to include. Don't write everything down or try to learn something by heart.

This is **one** way to prepare. See what works best for you when you get the chance to practise.

The read aloud task – tips for success

- Take time to understand the passage during the preparation period – your intonation will improve if you know what you are saying.

- You can write on the read aloud text, so make any notes you want to remind you of pauses and particular pronunciations.

- Read the text steadily and clearly. You will not sound 'more French' if you try to read fast – it will just prevent the examiner from hearing your pronunciation.

Answer each follow-up question with a short sentence. Revise phrases like **J'aime / je n'aime pas, J'adore / je déteste, C'est génial / étonnant / terrible / historique** (and other adjectives).

Worked example

twa
J'ai trois frères.
nay   sir
Je n'ai pas de sœur.
famy
Ma famille s'entend bien.
col-air-j
Mon père est professeur dans notre collège.
shee-an
Nous jouons souvent dans le parc avec notre chien.

This student has crossed off some final letters which are not pronounced in French. They have also added notes to remind themselves how to pronounce some words.

Take care with English-looking words like **collège** which are pronounced differently in French.

Paper 1: Speaking

Digital resources

Task 2: Role play – what to expect

- You will be given a card with a setting, a scenario and instructions in English.
- The role play consists of five bullet points (five things to say), with a total of 10 marks.
- Foundation level: you will need to ask one question. Higher level: you will need to ask two.
- All the situations will be 'transactional', e.g. in a café, buying tickets etc.
- At Foundation, all bullet points can be tackled using the present tense or je voudrais. At Higher, one bullet point will refer to a time in the future.
- Each response is awarded 2 marks if the message is relevant and clear, 1 mark if there is some lack of clarity and 0 marks if the message does not come across. Keep your answers short and clear.

> Check that you know question words. You will need to ask one question at Foundation tier and two at Higher tier.

Setting: Train station

Scenario:

- You are at a train station in France.
- The teacher will play the part of an employee and will speak first.
- Your teacher will ask questions in French and you must answer in French.
- You are expected to say a few words or a short phrase / sentence in response to each prompt. One-word answers will not be sufficient to gain full marks.

Task:

1 Say where you want to go.
2 Say why you want to go.
3 Say who you are travelling with.
4 Tell the employee what you think about the town.
5 Ask a question about the next train.

Role play – tips for success

- ✓ You can address your teacher as vous or tu, but don't change between them.
- ✓ If you can't think of a word, think of another way of saying it.
- ✓ Keep to language you know.

Task 3: Picture task – what to expect

Describing the picture – 8 marks

Two weeks before the exam, you will be given a choice of two thematic contexts and you select one. In the exam, you will be given a card with two photos on your chosen theme and you select one to describe.

You always need to describe the **people**, the **location** and the **activity** that you see in the picture. Try to develop your answers with extra detail and opinions and vary your vocabulary, but you must also be accurate.

Two follow-up questions – 4 marks

Answer each question clearly and accurately in a short sentence with a verb. Don't expand your answer for this section. Foundation-level questions are in the present tense and Higher level include one question using a past time frame.

Broader conversation – 16 marks

This has a lot of marks available. Aim to:

- Keep answers relevant – answer the question!
- Demonstrate that you can use past and future tenses as well as the present.
- Develop your answers with detail.
- Use more complex structures and a range of vocabulary. Give opinions and reasons.
- Be as accurate as possible.
- Use what you know. Don't invent words. But you don't have to be truthful – you can make up answers to fit with the French you know.

Describe ONE of these pictures. You will tell your teacher which one you have chosen to describe. Your description must cover:

- people
- location
- activity.

When you have finished your description, your teacher will ask you two questions relating to your chosen picture. You are expected to say a few words or a short phrase / sentence in response to each question. One-word answers will not be sufficient to gain full marks.

You will then move on to a conversation on the broader thematic context of Studying and my future.

During the conversation, your teacher will ask you questions in the present, past and future tenses. Your responses should be as full and detailed as possible.

Digital resources

Paper 2: Listening

Overview

Section A: Listening comprehension
Section B: Dictation
Timing: Foundation – 45 minutes;
Higher – 1 hour
Marks: 50, including 10 marks for the dictation

- There are 11 questions (at Foundation tier) or 9 questions (at Higher tier) in section A, and 6 sentences for dictation in section B.
- You will have a reading time of five minutes before the recording begins. Use it to familiarise yourself with the paper and perhaps jot down the French word for some of the English options. Remember you might hear a related word – perhaps *piscine* instead of *natation*.
- Questions appear in the same order as the recording.
- You will hear the recordings three times. There are pauses to give you time to think and write.
- There is a gradual increase in difficulty throughout the paper.
- Use the marks in brackets on the papers to guide you. One mark usually means one detail.

Multiple choice questions

These are questions where you select one of three given options.

> **(a)** Clara likes
> ☐ **A** swimming
> ☐ **B** dancing
> ☐ **C** tennis   **(1)**

The alternative options will all clearly be wrong. If you make a mistake, put a single line through the box ☒ and put your cross in the correct place.

> Ma meilleure amie Jade est amusante.
>
> Lucie's best friend is …
> ☐ fun
> ☐ sad
> ☐ ill   **(1)**

Some questions test if you know the meaning of a word.

*However, sometimes you may not hear the exact word, but need to work it out, for example if the audio said **Ma meilleure amie Jade me fait rire**.*

Multiple response questions

These are questions where you listen to a slightly longer recording and select three from six options.

You can make notes on the page. Keep your notes away from the answer boxes though! Make sure you write your final answers clearly with a cross in your chosen box(es).

> Le week-end, je travaille au supermarché pendant que mon frère joue au tennis. Ensuite, je promène le chien et je fais mes devoirs. Je n'ai jamais le temps de lire de livres.
>
> **(a)** What does Axelle do at the weekend?
>
> | | |
> |---|---|
> | ☐ | **A** travel to shops |
> | ☒ | **B** work |
> | ☐ | **C** play tennis |
> | ☒ | **D** walk the dog |
> | ☒ | **E** do homework |
> | ☐ | **F** read books |

*Listen out for words which sound like English words, but have different meanings. Here, **travaille** means 'work' not 'travel'.*

Word clouds

These questions require you to complete sentences using a word from a list.

Listen for **negatives** like ne … pas, ne … rien, ne … jamais, and others like sauf as these change the meaning of a sentence.

The possible answers for each question can all be found on the same line.

> Manon is talking about school. What does she say? Complete the gap in each sentence using a word or phrase from the box below.
> There are more words / phrases than gaps.
>
> > bus   train   bike   car
> > tie   jacket   shirt   uniform
> > playing tennis   playing basketball   swimming
>
> **a** Manon goes to school by _____ .   **(1)**
> **b** She dislikes wearing a blue _____ .   **(1)**
> **c** After school she likes _____ with her friends.   **(1)**

All the possible answers for Question (a) are on line 1 of the word cloud.

Paper 2: Listening

Digital resources

Questions to answer in English

These questions require short responses in English. Pauses are inserted into the recording to allow you time to write.

You might need to fill in a table:

> Nous devons y aller demain car le musée ferme à seize heures trente.

Closing time of museum.
16.30

Or answer a question with a short phrase:

> Pour rester en forme, je pense qu'il est plus amusant de pratiquer des sports d'équipe.

(a) What does Camille do to keep fit?

.... play team sports ....

> Answers in the recording come in the same order as the questions.

General Listening tips

- ✓ Ensure you read the question introductions, titles and instructions. They give important information like the context and number of correct answers.
- ✓ You can make notes as you listen (ensuring you leave your answer area clear). For the dictation, you can jot down words in the first listen that you can then check and refine into sentences.
- ✓ Make sure you write a final answer in the correct answer space / box.
- ✓ Do not give two alternative answers when only one is required.
- ✓ Move on when the audio moves on, so you don't miss marks on later questions.
- ✓ When answering in English, don't waste time giving long responses when a short phrase is all that is needed to give a clear answer.

Closing time of museum
16.30

> This answer is quicker to write than **The museum closes at half past four.**

- ✓ If you are not sure, try to work out meanings from the context. If, on the third listen, you still don't know, make a guess. Don't leave blanks.
- ✓ Use the third listen to check your answers.

Dictation

You will listen to a recording and write down what you hear in French.

> There will be an introductory sentence explaining the general subject of the dictation (e.g. music), to help you decide on the words you hear.

> Some sentences will need you to fill in gaps with the words you hear.

> You are going to hear someone talking about school.
> Sentences 1–3: write down the missing words in the gaps provided.
> In each gap, you will write one word **in French**.
>
> 1 Mon _____ est _____.
> 2 Je _____ de la _____.
> 3 Je _____ toujours _____.
>
> Sentences 4–6: write down the full sentences that you hear in the spaces provided, **in French**.
>
> 4 _____.
> 5 _____.
> 6 _____.

> Others will need you to write down whole sentences that you hear.

> There are more whole sentences to write down in Higher tier than Foundation tier.

Dictation – points to remember

The dictation will test your spelling of the typical sounds in the French language. Remember that French words like vous or deux often have silent final consonants. When these are followed by a word starting with a vowel – like vous avez or deux heures – there is **liaison**, which means that the final letter is sounded and the words sound as if they run into each other.

Small errors may not lose you marks unless the meaning of the sentence is lost. For example, if you wrote addore instead of adore, because the sounds are the same and the word is recognisable, it would be accepted.

> There will be two words in Foundation and three in Higher which are not from Edexcel's prescribed list. Don't worry! Try to work out how they might be spelt from your knowledge of other French words.
> All names (people, countries, cities) are taken from the specification and prescribed lists.

Digital resources

Paper 3: Reading

Overview

Section A: Reading comprehension
Section B: Translation
Timing: Foundation – 45 mins; Higher – 1 hour
Marks: 50 (including 10 for the translation into English); 25% exam total

Tips for Reading tasks

- You will write all answers in English or by putting a cross by a letter, so there will be no French to write.
- Pay attention to the number of marks given as this is often a good indicator of how much detail you should give and how long you should spend on that answer.
- Watch out for little words which can modify answers. For example, if a passage says J'ai assez d'argent and you are asked what a person has, you might need to write 'enough money' rather than just 'money'.
- The tasks will include formal contexts like newspaper articles and informal contexts like emails from friends.
- The exam will use only names of people listed in the specification.
- You may meet **cognates** in the Reading paper. These are French words which look the same, or almost the same, in English and have the same meaning in both languages, like le piano.

Questions will increase in difficulty as you work through the paper.

Section A: Reading comprehension

Most questions come in the order of the text, so that if you can find the answer to Questions 1 and 3 and not 2, you should be able to locate the section of the passage in which to try to find the missing answer. These questions are the same format as the Listening questions (pages 88–89).

In Foundation tier, this question type asks you to select one option on each row. This is the only question style where the answers do **not** appear in the same order as the questions.

Hier je suis allé à la piscine mais demain je vais faire du vélo et normalement, je regarde la télé chez moi.

Yesterday he …

☐	**A** watched TV.
☐	**B** went cycling.
☒	**C** went swimming.

(1)

In this case, the tense is important as all three activities are mentioned in the passage, but only one (C swimming) is in the past. The clues here could be **je suis allé** (*I went* in the perfect tense) or even **hier** (yesterday)!

Who says what? Choose the correct answers.

Put a cross ✗ in the correct column for each question.

Eva	Ma matière préférée c'est le français parce que j'aime lire des livres. De temps en temps, on fait des sorties scolaires au théâtre.
Toni	J'aime l'histoire parce que les cours sont intéressants et le professeur est amusant.
Luis	L'art est le meilleur cours car on peut être créatif et parler avec ses amis pendant que l'on travaille.

	Who …	Eva	Toni	Luis
(a)	… goes to the theatre?	✗		
(b)	… finds history interesting?		✗	
(c)	… likes to chat with friends?			✗
(d)	… finds the teacher fun?		✗	
(e)	… likes reading?	✗		
(f)	… likes French?	✗		

(6)

Paper 3: Reading

Digital resources

Section A: Reading comprehension

Glossing may be used for words outside the vocabulary list.

Questions follow the order of the text.

Real exam questions will look slightly different – this one is just to show you some of the features you might meet.

Kite festival in France

Read this online article about a kite festival in France.

Le festival de cerfs-volants* au bord de mer est un événement populaire en France. De nombreux habitants et touristes viennent participer ou observer.

D'habitude, le festival a lieu en avril. Beaucoup de personnes se réunissent sur le sable pour faire voler leurs cerfs-volants qui peuvent prendre des formes étonnantes, comme des animaux et des monstres.

De nombreuses activités gratuites sont proposées aux enfants qui peuvent créer leurs propres cerfs-volants. Le soir, on peut voir un beau spectacle de *feux d'artifice* parfois bruyants dans le ciel.

Images are often used to help you understand the text, but they will not contain clues to the answers!

*cerf-volant = kite

(a) Complete the sentences below. Put a cross ✗ in the correct box for each question.

i. The festival takes place …
- ☐ at the seaside.
- ☐ in the fields.
- ☐ in a local town.

ii. The festival is normally …
- ☐ full of animals.
- ☐ only for adults.
- ☐ in spring.

iii. The activities for children are …
- ☐ free.
- ☐ clean.
- ☐ few.

(b) Which of these is the best translation of the term *feux d'artifice*? Put a cross ✗ in the correct box.
- ☐ windmills
- ☐ fireworks
- ☐ banquets   **(4)**

You will be asked to infer (work out) the meaning of a new term. Look at the context, as there will be clues. Here, the words le soir, beaux, bruyants and ciel are clues to the term feux d'artifice.

Section B: Translation

- This section is a translation from French to English.
- At Foundation tier there are five sentences to translate. At Higher tier, it is a paragraph.
- Read through the text to ensure you understand.
- Make sure you consider each word in your translation, taking care not to miss anything.
- There is often more than one possible correct translation. The key thing is for the same meaning to be communicated into English.
- At Foundation tier, the meaning should be 'appropriately transferred'. So if you do not know an exact translation, you can still get marks for something similar as long as the meaning of your words is not too far from the original. For example, you could put 'I want to go to Africa' for sentence (b) here. However, always try to be as accurate as you can.
- At Higher tier, the meaning should be 'fully and appropriately transferred'. Mes parents et moi rêvons de vivre au Canada could be translated as 'Living in Canada is my parents' and my dream' even though the words vary slightly from the original.
- Read through your work at the end to ensure it makes sense. You may need to amend it to read well in English, but don't change anything that you know is correct.

Although you must consider each word, not every French word will have a direct translation into English. The translation of this sentence is likely to be 'I like adventure holidays', without 'the'.

Translation
Holidays

Translate the following sentences **into English**.

(a) J'aime les vacances d'aventure.

(b) Je veux visiter l'Algérie.

(c) C'est un endroit idéal pour vos vacances en famille.

(d) L'année dernière, je suis allée à Paris avec ma soeur.

(e) L'année prochaine, je vais rester en Angleterre pendant les vacances scolaires.   **(10)**

Make sure you include relevant detail. Translating this as 'It's **the** ideal place for **a** family holiday' misses un and vos, so it is not an exact translation, but would get some credit.

Look out for words which look like English words but mean something different. Here rester means 'to stay', not 'to rest'.

Paper 4: Writing

Overview

Writing tasks: three at Foundation tier, two at Higher tier
Translation task: one at each tier
Timing: Foundation – 1 hour 15 minutes; Higher – 1 hour 20 minutes
Marks: 50; 25% exam total

Foundation tier, Question 1

- This question asks you to describe a photo in four short sentences. It appears only on the Foundation paper.
- Keep your sentences short (but make sure they **are** sentences – include a verb!). Stick to words you know.
- You can use different sentence starters like Il y a and Je vois.
- You can describe the people in the picture by talking about their hair, eyes, height and clothes, including colours.
- If there is more than one person, you can describe just one of them if you prefer to use the il / elle form of the verb. This avoids having to use the ils / elles form. Here you could write La femme boit un café.
- You can write about the weather if it is visible.
- There are only marks for correct communication of relevant information. So make sure your answer is relevant (you are describing something in the photo), correct (your French is accurate) and you communicate a point. There are no marks for elaborating on your answer in this question.

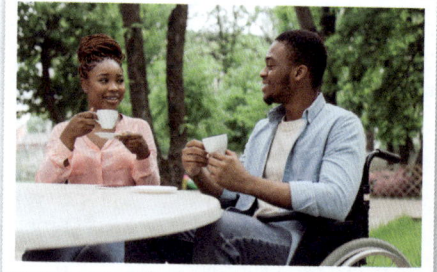

1   Describe the photo. Write four short sentences **in French**.

_____ (2)
_____ (2)
_____ (2)
_____ (2)

Make sure you describe the picture. For example, the sentence **Je vois un chien** in response to this picture would not receive any marks, even though the French is correct, as there is no dog in the photo!

Make sure that your answer is clear. Don't write **Il y a une deux personnes.** ✗ as the number is unclear.

Longer writing tasks

- You **must** write about **all** of the bullet points given in the question, although you can write more about one than another, if you like.
- You are given an expected number of words to write. There is no need to write more than this. Focus on checking that everything you write is correct, since everything will be marked.
- Think hard:
  o What relevant vocabulary do you know?
  o Can you use conjunctions like mais or donc?
  o Can you give an opinion using à mon avis or je pense que?
  o Can you give reasons using car or parce que?
  o Can you use a flexible phrase?
  o Can you use adjectives, adverbs, time phrases and pronouns other than je?

  Revise these beforehand so they come to you more quickly when you are in the exam.
- Even if the context is formal, you can use tu if you prefer.
- You can get full marks by using only words on the Edexcel vocabulary list. However, if you use other words correctly, you will get equal credit for those.
- Check your answer at the end to make sure it is:
  ✓ Accurate – correct any mistakes you see
  ✓ Clear – ensure it makes sense
  ✓ Relevant – check you have covered all bullets – this is very important.
  ✓ Developed – make sure your ideas include a variety of vocabulary and structures.

Paper 4: Writing

Digital resources

Examples of longer writing tasks

You have a choice of two tasks for each question – a or b. Put a cross in the box of the question that you choose.

Read the bullet points carefully. Remember, you **must** cover all of them in your answer.

The bullet points may need you to write in the present, future or past form. Make sure you do this.

Write in French and aim for the number of words stated. Although this is a guideline, and you could write more or less, it helps you achieve enough variety to score highly without making too many errors or running out of time. You could think in terms of writing 4 x 20 words here at Foundation tier, or 4 x 35 words if writing 130–150 words at Higher tier.

Choose either Question 1 (a) or Question 1 (b)

If you answer Question 1 (a) put a cross in the box ☐.

1 (a) Write an email to your exchange partner about school. You must include the following points:

- a description of your school
- your opinion of your school with reasons
- a school event in the past
- what you will do at school next week.

Write your answer **in French**. You should aim to write between 80 and 90 words.

(18)

Use vocabulary, grammar and phrases that you know, but try to vary your language so that you can show off the French that you can use correctly to develop your ideas. Remember – what you write does not need to be true.

This question could appear as Question 1 on a Higher-tier paper or as Question 3 on a Foundation-tier paper. Other longer writing questions look similar, but always read the contexts, bullets and word count guidelines carefully as they vary for different questions.

Always read back your answer to ensure it makes sense.

Translation into French

- At Foundation tier there are sentences to translate; at Higher tier, there is a passage.
- Make sure that you consider each word in your translation and be as accurate as you can when transferring the meaning of the text into French.
- Remember, French may use a different word order to English, especially with adjectives and pronouns. Here, 'the blue sky' is le ciel bleu and 'I am going to help him' is je vais l'aider.
- Remember that a minor error might receive some marks – for example la campagne est beau ✗ (instead of belle ✓) – as the meaning is clear. But using the wrong part of a verb – for example la campagne suis belle ✗ – will lose marks because the meaning is unclear.
- Read through your work at the end to ensure it makes sense. Look out for obvious errors, like missing a plural (son animal instead of ses animaux for example).

Translate the following five sentences **into French**.

(a) I love nature.

_____

(b) The countryside is beautiful.

_____

(c) I run under the blue sky.

_____

(d) Last week I visited my uncle's farm with my sister.

_____

(e) This summer I am going to help him with his animals.

_____ **(10)**

Remember – there is often more than one possible correct translation.

Digital resources

Articles 1

Revise how to say 'the' and 'a' or 'some' in French.

Gender

Every French noun has a gender.
All people, places or things are either masculine (m) or feminine (f).

masculine: le livre (m)   the book
feminine: la table (f)   the table

The words for 'the' and 'a / some' are:

	singular		plural	
	masc	fem	masc	fem
the	le	la	les	les
a / some	un	une	des	des

le livre   the book   un livre   a book
les livres   the books   des livres   some
                                          books

Plurals

Most French nouns make the plural by adding -s but it is not pronounced.

le chat   the cat   ➡   les chats   the cats

- Nouns with the following endings add -x in the plural, and sometimes other letters change too

  -ail   travail   ➡   travaux   works
  -al   animal   ➡   animaux   animals
  -eau   bureau   ➡   bureaux   offices
  -eu   jeu   ➡   jeux   games

- Nouns ending in -x, -z or -s don't change:

  un dos a back   deux dos two backs
  un nez a nose   deux nez two noses

Le and la both become l' if the noun begins with a vowel or silent h:
l'hôpital (m) – hospital
l'éducation (f) – education

Masculine or feminine?

If you don't know the gender of a word, you can look it up in a dictionary or on the internet, but here are some tips.

Masculine nouns

male people: l'homme   the man
male animals: le chat   the cat
days of the week: le lundi Monday
months: juillet   July
seasons: l'été   the summer

Most nouns that end in:

-age   le village   the village
-er   le policier   the police officer
-eau   le bureau   the office

(except eau (f) water)

Feminine nouns

female people: la fille   the girl
female animals: la chatte   the female cat
countries that end in -e: la France

Most nouns that end in:

-e   la voiture   the car
-ée   une entrée   a starter / an entrance

All nouns that end in -sion or -tion:

une émission   a programme
la destination   the destination

All nouns that end in -té:

la quantité   the quantity
une identité   an identity

Forming feminine nouns

Sometimes a masculine word can be made feminine. Sometimes this is done by:

- Adding -e: un ami ➡ une amie But note: no spelling change if the word already ends in -e: un élève ➡ une élève

- Changing -eur to -rice or -euse: un acteur ➡ une actrice, un chanteur ➡ une chanteuse

- Changing -en to -enne: un Canadien ➡ une Canadienne

Now try this

Le, la, l' or **les**? Fill in the missing articles.

_____ garçon   _____ mère   _____ étudiants   _____ printemps

_____ Afrique   _____ France   _____ condition   _____ bleu

_____ décision   _____ père   _____ visage   _____ plage

Always try to learn the le or la when you learn a new noun.

Articles 2

Digital resources

It is crucial that you can use du, de la, de l' or des to say 'some' and au, à la, à l' or aux to say 'to the'.

How to say 'some'

masculine	feminine	beginning with vowel or silent h	plural
du	de la	de l'	des

le lait   milk   ➡ du lait   some milk
la glace   ice cream ➡ de la glace   some ice cream
l'eau   water   ➡ de l'eau   some water
les animaux   animals ➡ des animaux   some animals

But after the negative you only use de / d':
Je n'ai pas de pain.   I haven't any bread.

Il n'a pas d'œufs.
He hasn't got any eggs.

Using 'some' and 'any'

- We don't always need to use 'some' in English. Sometimes we miss it out altogether, but you **have** to use it in French:
  Veux-tu du lait ou du café?
  Do you want milk or coffee?
- And where we use 'any' in a question in English, French uses 'some':
  Avez-vous des boissons?
  Have you got any drinks?
  Avez-vous du pain?
  Have you got any bread?

How to say 'to the'

masculine	feminine	beginning with vowel or silent h	plural
au	à la	à l'	aux

au bureau   to the office
à la gare   to the station
à l'école   to (the) school
aux toilettes   to the toilets

Sometimes the article is included in French where it would not be used in English.
On lutte pour l'égalité. We fight for equality.
Il vient le vendredi. He comes on Fridays.

Nouns from adjectives

You can use le, la or les before an adjective to form a noun.
Il est anglais (adjective) ➡ J'aime l'anglais (noun) au collège.
When the noun becomes a nationality, a capital letter is added.
Je suis français(e) ➡ Je m'entends bien avec les Français.

On va au collège.
We go to school.

Now try this

1 How would you tell someone how to go to these places using **aller**? For example:
Allez au collège.

(a) _____ lycée (m)
(b) _____ toilettes (pl)
(c) _____ gare (f)
(d) _____ aéroport (m)
(e) _____ feux (pl)
(f) _____ supermarché (m)
(g) _____ château (m)
(h) _____ tour Eiffel (f)

2 Translate these phrases **into French**.
(a) I want some bread.
(b) Have you got any milk?
(c) He hasn't got any water.
(d) I'm going to school.
(e) Are you going to the station? (*tu*)
(f) He's going to the toilets.

You have all the vocabulary you need on this page.

Adjectives

When using adjectives, you have to think about **agreement** and **position**.

Regular adjectives

Adjectives must agree with the noun they are describing. Regular adjectives add -e for feminine, -s for masculine plural and -es for feminine plural:

singular		plural	
masc	fem	masc	fem
grand	grande	grands	grandes
petit	petite	petits	petites

Some adjectives already end in -e so don't add another:

masc	fem	masc plural	fem plural
juste	juste	justes	justes

Some adjectives are a little less regular:

masc	fem	masc plural	fem plural	
long	longue	longs	longues	long
blanc	blanche	blancs	blanches	white
sec	sèche	secs	sèches	dry

A few adjectives don't change at all, e.g:
marron chestnut / brown
orange orange

Irregular adjectives

Adjectives that end in -x change their ending to -se in the feminine:

singular		plural	
masc	fem	masc	fem
sérieux	sérieuse	sérieux	sérieuses

Other adjectives like sérieux:
dangereux   dangerous
religieux   religious
heureux   happy

Adjectives that end in -f change to -ve in the feminine:

singular		plural	
masc	fem	masc	fem
actif	active	actifs	actives

Other adjectives like actif:
sportif   sporty   positif   positive

Adjectives that end in -er change to -ère in the feminine:
premier ➡ première   first
dernier ➡ dernière   last

Adjectives that end in -en or -il double the consonant before adding -e in the feminine:
ancien ➡ ancienne   ancient, old, former
pareil ➡ pareille   same

Position of adjectives

Most adjectives come **after** the noun:
les yeux bleus   les cheveux longs
But a few common adjectives come **in front of** the noun:

grand	big	nouveau / nouvelle	new
petit	small	meilleur	best
vieux / vieille	old		

mon meilleur ami
my best friend

ma meilleure amie
my best friend

Now try this

Translate these sentences and phrases **into French**.
1 a little black dog
2 last week
3 My little brother is very active.
4 My best friend (f) is small and happy.
5 Her brother is tall, sporty but a bit serious.

Possessives

Digital resources

Possessives are used to say 'my', 'your', 'our', etc. They change according to gender and number.

Possessive adjectives

In French the possessive adjective ('my', 'your', etc.) changes to agree with the **gender** and **number** of the noun that follows. There are usually three different words, according to whether the noun is masculine or feminine, singular or plural.

mon frère   my brother (masculine)
ma sœur   my sister (feminine)
mes parents   my parents (plural)
Remember, son / sa / ses mean both 'his' and 'her'.

> **Be careful!** You use **mon, ton, son** with a feminine noun if it begins with a vowel. For example: **mon ami, mon amie** – my friend.

masc	fem	plural	
mon	ma	mes	**my**

masc	fem	plural	
son	sa	ses	**his / her**

mon pull   ma veste   mes baskets

son pantalon   sa chemise   ses chaussures

masc	fem	plural	
ton	ta	tes	**your**

ton portable   ta console de jeux   tes jeux

masc	fem	plural	
votre	votre	vos	**your**

votre frère   votre sœur   vos parents

masc	fem	plural	
notre	notre	nos	**our**

notre chat   notre chatte   nos animaux

masc	fem	plural	
leur	leur	leurs	**their**

leur fils   leur fille   leurs enfants

Possessive pronouns (H ONLY)

To say, 'It's mine' or 'They're mine', use the following:

masc singular	C'est le mien.
fem singular	C'est la mienne.

masc plural	Ce sont les miens.
fem plural	Ce sont les miennes.

Now try this

Write these **in French**.

1 my brother _____
2 his friend (m) _____
3 his friends (m and f) _____
4 his bag _____
5 my sister _____
6 her friend (f) _____

7 her friends (m and f) _____
8 her mobile _____
9 my parents _____
10 their friend (m) _____
11 their friends (m and f) _____
12 their car _____

Digital resources

Comparisons

In order to aim for a high grade, you need to be able to use some complex structures such as comparatives and superlatives.

Comparative

You use the **comparative** when you are comparing two things: my house is **taller**.

Form the comparative by putting plus (more) or moins (less) in front of the adjective.
The adjectives have to agree with the noun they are describing.

Mon frère est grand. Alessandro est plus grand. My brother is tall. Alessandro is taller.
Ma sœur est petite. Fathia est plus petite. My sister is small. Fathia is smaller.

To compare two things:
(taller) than = plus (grand) que
Nathan est plus grand que Tom. Nathan is taller than Tom.
(smaller) than = moins (grand) que
Axelle est moins grande que sa sœur. Axelle is smaller than her sister.
as (tall) as = aussi (grand) que
Il est aussi grand que son père. He is as tall as his father.

Nathan est plus grand que Tom.
Nathan is taller than Tom.

Superlative H ONLY

You use the **superlative** when you are comparing more than two things: my house is **the biggest**.

Form the superlative by adding the definite article le / la / les as well as plus:
le plus grand / la plus grande / les plus grand(e)s the biggest
le livre le plus intéressant the most interesting book
la matière la plus ennuyeuse the most boring subject

Exceptions to the rule

adjective		comparative		superlative H ONLY	
bon / bonne	good	meilleur(e)	better	le meilleur / la meilleure	the best
mauvais(e)	bad	pire	worse	le / la pire	the worst

Le film est meilleur que le livre. The film is better than the book.
le meilleur restaurant the best restaurant

Now try this

Complete the sentences with the comparative or superlative.

1 L'Everest* est la montagne _____ du monde. (haut) (*highest*)

2 La jupe est _____ que la robe. (+ cher) (*more expensive*)

3 Demain, il fera _____ qu'aujourd'hui. (+ beau) (*nicer*)

4 _____ solution est de prendre le train. (bon) (*the best*)

5 Julie est _____ qu'Amit. (− amusant) (*less amusing*)

6 Le TGV** est le train _____ . (rapide) (*the quickest*)

*L'Everest – Mount Everest is the highest mountain in the world.

**Le TGV – Le Train à Grande Vitesse is a high-speed train in France.

Other adjectives and pronouns

Digital resources

Here, you will revise demonstrative and interrogative adjectives and pronouns. Like le, la and les, they have to agree with the noun they are referring to.

Demonstrative adjectives

To say 'this / that', 'these / those':

masc sing	fem sing	masc plural	fem plural
ce	cette	ces	ces

ce livre	this / that book
cette fille	this / that girl
ces livres	these / those books
ces filles	these / those girls

Use cet in front of a masculine noun that begins with a vowel or silent h:

cet hôtel   cet espace

Interrogative adjectives

To ask 'which?':

masc sing	fem sing	masc plural	fem plural
quel	quelle	quels	quelles

Quel enfant?	Which child?
Quelle femme?	Which woman?
Quels garçons?	Which boys?
Quelles filles?	Which girls?

Indefinite adjectives

The indefinite adjectives autre (other) and quelque (some) also agree with the word they describe:

mon autre frère	my other brother
ses autres chaussures	her other shoes
pendant quelque temps	for some time
avec quelques amis	with some friends

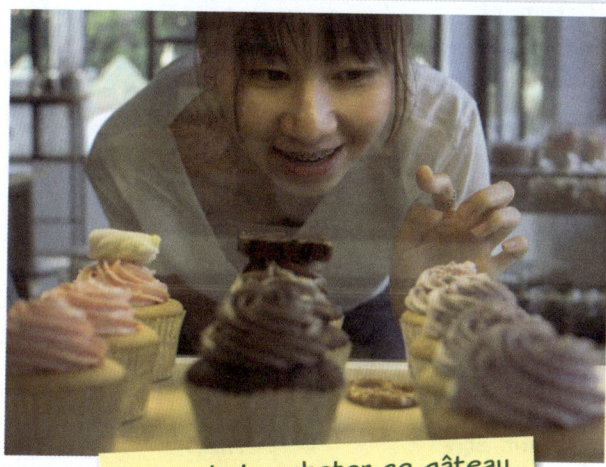

Je voudrais acheter ce gâteau.
I would like to buy this cake.

Regarde ces poissons énormes!
Look at these enormous fish!

Now try this

Fill each gap with the correct word from the four options.

ce   cette   cet   ces

1 _____ stylo
2 _____ homme
3 _____ maison
4 _____ magasin

5 _____ animaux
6 _____ cravate
7 _____ personnes
8 _____ famille

Digital resources

Adverbs

An adverb is a word that 'describes' a verb (hence the name). It tells you **how** an action is done: quickly, slowly, loudly, etc.

Using and forming adverbs

You use an adverb when you want to bring your work to life, give more detail and explain or describe how something is done.

In English, a lot of adverbs end in -ly.

In French, a lot of adverbs end in -ment.

- You can form adverbs by adding -ment to the feminine form of an adjective.

final ➡ finale + ment ➡ finalement finally

- You can form adverbs by dropping -ant(e) / -ent(e) from an adjective and adding -amment / -emment.

indépendant ➡ indépend + -amment ➡ indépendamment independently

Comparative and superlative of adverbs

La voiture va vite, le train va plus vite mais c'est l'avion qui va le plus vite.

The car goes fast, the train goes faster but it's the plane that goes the fastest.

Some adverbs don't follow this pattern:
vrai ➡ vraiment   really
absolu ➡ absolument   absolutely

Adverbs of time

Some adverbs are useful for a time line when narrating a sequence of events:

d'abord / au début	at the beginning
puis / ensuite / alors	then
maintenant	now
finalement	finally
à l'avenir	in the future
aujourd'hui	today
demain	tomorrow

D'abord j'ai joué au basket puis je suis allé à la piscine.

First of all I played basketball, then I went to the pool.

Adverbs of frequency

Other adverbs tell you how often or when:

rarement	rarely
d'habitude	usually
normalement	normally
souvent	often
de temps en temps	from time to time
régulièrement	regularly
quelquefois	sometimes
immédiatement	immediately
toujours	always

Adverbs of position

au-dessus	above	là-bas	over there
au-dessous	below	proche	near
dehors	outside	loin (de)	far (from)
derrière	behind	là	there
en bas	down	partout	everywhere
en haut	up		
ici	here		

Linking adverbs

peut-être	perhaps
par conséquent	as a result
plutôt	rather
probablement	probably
alors	so
seulement	only
toujours	always
clairement	clearly
par contre	however
souvent	often
quelquefois	sometimes

Now try this

Find the **six** adverbs in this passage.

Maintenant, j'aime jouer au tennis. Normalement, je joue avec mes amis. De temps en temps, nous jouons au foot et demain, nous allons faire du vélo ensemble. Ma mère a acheté une nouvelle voiture qui va vite.

Object pronouns

Digital resources

You use a pronoun (e.g. 'it', 'me', 'you', 'them') when you don't want to keep repeating a noun or a name.

> Pronouns make your French sound more natural and will help you achieve a higher grade.

Subject and object

The **subject** is the person or thing that is doing the action (verb).
The **object** is the person or thing that is having the action (verb) done to it.

subject	verb	object
Tracey	sends	the email.

subject pronouns		direct object pronouns		indirect object pronouns	
je	I	me	me	me	(to / for) me
tu	you	te	you	te	(to / for) you
il	he / it	le	him / it	lui	(to / for) him / it
elle	she / it	la	her / it	lui	(to / for) her / it
nous	we	nous	us	nous	(to / for) us
vous	you	vous	you	vous	(to / for) you
ils / elles	they	les	them	leur	(to / for) them

> The plural object pronouns (nous, vous, les, leur) are only needed at Higher tier.

Direct object pronouns

In French, the object pronoun comes in front of the verb.

I send it.	Je l'envoie.
He does it.	Il le fait.
We buy them.	Nous les achetons.
They invite us.	Ils nous invitent.

> In French, the direct object pronoun 'it' or 'them' is the same as the word for 'the'.

Word order

- In a negative sentence, the pronoun goes after the ne:
  Tu ne la regardes pas?
  Aren't you watching it?
- In the perfect tense, the pronoun comes in front of the **auxiliary** verb (avoir or être):
  Je l'ai déjà regardé(e).   I have already seen it.
  Nous les avons acheté(e)s.   We bought them.

The past participle agrees with the object pronoun, so if the object is feminine or plural the past participle must end in -e, -s or -es.

Indirect object pronouns

You use the indirect object pronoun to replace a noun that has à in front of it.
Sarah envoie un e-mail à son ami.
Sarah is sending an email to her boyfriend.
Elle lui envoie un e-mail.
She is sending him an email.

> Elle lui envoie un e-mail.
> She is sending him an email.

Now try this

Rewrite the sentences, replacing the object of each sentence with a pronoun.

1 Il a envoyé un message.

2 Je n'ai pas regardé l'émission.

3 Il n'a pas acheté les chaussures.

4 Tu as vu ce film?

5 Sarah a lu ce livre.

6 Mes parents ont acheté la voiture.

Digital resources

More pronouns: *y* and *en*

H ONLY

Use y and en in your writing and speaking to demonstrate that you can use a wide range of structures.

Y (there)

- You use y to refer to a place which has already been mentioned.

  Tu vas à la gare? Oui, j'y vais.

  Are you going to the station? Yes, I'm going there.

- You also use y with verbs that take à:

  Tu joues au football? Oui, j'y joue.

  Do you play football? Yes, I play it.

- y is also used in some common phrases:

il y a	there is / there are	Vas-y!	Go on!
Il y a beaucoup à faire.	There is a lot to do.	Allons-y!	Let's go!

En (of it / of them)

- You use en to replace a noun (or du / de la / de l' / des + noun) that has already been mentioned:

  Tu veux du café? Oui, j'en veux bien.

  Do you want some coffee? Yes, I'd like some.

- en is not always translated in English, but you have to include it in French:

  Tu manges de la viande? Oui, j'en mange beaucoup.

  Do you eat meat? Yes, I eat a lot (of it).

- en is also used with expressions of quantity:

  Tu as combien de frères? J'en ai deux.

  How many brothers have you got? I've got two (of them).

  Tu as acheté des fruits? Oui, j'en ai acheté un kilo.

  Did you buy some fruit? Yes, I bought a kilo (of it).

- en is also used in the following common phrases:

Qu'est-ce que tu en penses?	What do you think (of it)?
J'en ai marre.	I'm fed up.
Je m'en vais.	I'm going.

Il y a combien d'enfants?
Il y en a trois.
How many children are there?
There are three (of them).

Although these aren't on the Edexcel vocab list, they're great phrases you could use.

Now try this

Rewrite the sentences, replacing the nouns with **y** or **en**.

1 Je suis déjà allé au cinéma.

2 J'ai déjà mangé trop de fromage.

3 Je suis allé à Paris hier.

4 Je vais au cinéma de temps en temps.

5 On va souvent au supermarché.

6 Je ne mange jamais de frites.

Other pronouns

Digital resources

Using pronouns in your writing and speaking tasks helps show that you have mastered a wide range of structures.

Relative pronouns qui and que

These are pronouns that relate back to something or someone you have just mentioned.

- Qui (who / which) replaces the **subject** of the sentence. You know this, as you have been using it from the start:

  J'ai un frère qui s'appelle John.
  I have a brother who is called John.

  Ma sœur est la fille qui porte une robe bleue.
  My sister is the girl who is wearing a blue dress.

- Que (whom / which / that) replaces the **object** of a sentence: **H** ONLY

  L'homme que j'ai vu ne portait pas de lunettes.
  The man (whom) I saw didn't wear glasses.

  J'ai acheté le pantalon que j'ai trouvé sur Internet.
  I bought the trousers (which) I found on the internet.

  C'était la personne que j'avais vue en ville.
  It was the person (that) I had seen in town.

Emphatic / disjunctive pronouns

These are: moi me, toi you, lui him / it, elle her / it, nous us, vous you, eux them (m), elles them (f).

They are used:

At Foundation tier, you only need to know the emphatic pronouns **moi** and **toi**.

- after **prepositions**: avec moi / toi with me / you
  pour lui / elle / nous / vous / eux / elles for him / her / us / you / them / them
- for **emphasis**: Lui, il est travailleur. Him, he's hard-working.
- to form a **double subject**: Ma sœur et moi allons en ville. My sister and I are going to town.

Où and dont   **H** ONLY

- Où (where) refers back to a place that has been mentioned previously or is known:

  La ville où j'ai passé mes vacances est vraiment belle.
  The town where I spent my holiday is really beautiful.

  La maison où il habite est très grande.
  The house where he lives is very big.

- Dont means of 'which' / 'whose' / 'of whom' / 'about whom':

  Le monsieur dont j'ai trouvé les lunettes …
  The gentleman whose glasses I found …

  La fille dont on a déjà parlé …
  The girl whom we have already talked about …

Now try this

Complete these sentences with **qui**, **que**, **où** or **dont**.

1 Mon ami _____ s'appelle Bruno aime le football.

2 L'émission _____ j'ai vue hier n'était pas passionnante.

3 Le quartier _____ ils habitent est vraiment calme.

4 C'est le prof _____ je vous ai déjà parlé.

5 Elle a une sœur _____ est prof.

Digital resources

Present tense: -er verbs

Good news! Most French verbs are -er verbs, and most -er verbs are regular.

Forming the present tense of -er verbs

The endings are:

je	-e	nous	-ons
tu	-es	vous	-ez
il / elle	-e	ils / elles	-ent

> Remember that the endings **-e**, **-es** and **-ent** all sound the same when you say these words.

jouer   to play

I play	je jou**e**	we play	nous jou**ons**
you play	tu jou**es**	you play	vous jou**ez**
he / she / one plays	il / elle / on jou**e**	they play	ils / elles jou**ent**

Some common -er verbs

aider	to help	donner	to give	quitter	to leave
aimer	to like	écouter	to listen	rester	to stay
arriver	to arrive	entrer	to enter	téléphoner	to telephone
parler	to talk	habiter	to live	travailler	to work
décider	to decide	manger	to eat	trouver	to find
détester	to hate	penser	to think	visiter	to visit

Some -er verbs have spelling changes. These are usually to make them easier to pronounce:

• Verbs that end in -ger in the infinitive (manger, nager, plonger)
  add -e in the nous form to keep the g sound soft: nous mang**e**ons.

• Verbs that end in -ler and -ter in the infinitive (appeler and jeter)
  double the l or t in the singular je, tu, il / elle / on and in the third person plural:
  je m'appelle, ils jettent.

• Verbs that end in -yer in the infinitive (payer and envoyer)
  change the y to i in the singular je, tu, il / elle / on and in the third person plural:
  j'envoie, elle paie.

• Some verbs change e or é to è, for example acheter ➡ j'achète; se lever ➡ je me lève;
  préférer ➡ je préfère. The change occurs in the je, tu, il / elle / on and ils / elles forms but the
  nous and vous forms revert to the stem:

je préf**è**re	nous préf**é**rons
tu préf**è**res	vous préf**é**rez
il / elle / on préf**è**re	ils / elles préf**è**rent

Now try this

Complete the passage with the correct parts of the verbs in brackets.

Je (s'appeler) Yasmina. J'ai une sœur qui (s'appeler) Diane et qui (jouer) au tennis. Je (préférer) faire du vélo. Je (chanter) et je (jouer) d'un instrument. Le soir, nous (rentrer) à cinq heures et nous (manger). Ensuite je (parler) avec mes amis et j'(écouter) de la musique. Quelquefois, mon frère et moi (jouer) à des jeux vidéo ou (télécharger) un film à regarder plus tard.

> mon frère et moi = we
> Which form are you going to use?

Present tense: *-ir* and *-re* verbs

There are two groups of -ir verbs: those that take -ss in the plural forms and those that don't.

-ir verbs that take -ss

finir　to finish

je finis	nous finissons
tu finis	vous finissez
il / elle / on finit	ils / elles finissent

Verbs like finir:

choisir　to choose

By now you will have noticed that the je, tu and il / elle forms of most verbs sound the same **but** they are not all spelled the same, so be careful when you are writing!

-ir verbs that don't take -ss

partir　to leave

je pars	nous partons
tu pars	vous partez
il / elle / on part	ils / elles partent

Verbs like partir:

dormir　to sleep (je dors)

sortir　to go out (je sors)

-ir verbs are sometimes referred to as -s -s -t verbs. Can you see why?

-re verbs

répondre　to reply

je réponds	nous répondons
tu réponds	vous répondez
il / elle / on répond	ils / elles répondent

Verbs like répondre:

attendre	to wait
descendre	to go down
entendre	to hear
perdre	to lose
vendre	to sell

Irregular -re verbs

écrire　to write

j'écris	nous écrivons
tu écris	vous écrivez
il / elle / on écrit	ils / elles écrivent

Verbs like écrire:

lire	to read	**but** lisons, lisez, lisent
boire	to drink	**but** buvons, buvez, boivent

H ONLY
You only need to know the plural forms at Higher tier.

H ONLY
To emphasise that you are doing something at this very moment, you can use être en train de.

Je suis en train d'écrire un e-mail. I am in the middle of writing an email.

Exceptions

The verb prendre (to take) and related verbs like comprendre (to understand) and apprendre (to learn) are regular except for the nous, vous and ils / elles forms:

je prends	nous prenons
tu prends	vous prenez
il / elle / on prend	ils / elles prennent

Now try this

Complete these sentences with the correct part of the verb in brackets.

1　Le matin, je (sortir) à sept heures et demie.
2　Le mardi, les cours (finir) à cinq heures.
3　Mon ami ne (boire) pas de café.
4　Le train (partir) à 8h20.
5　Nous (apprendre) le français.
6　Pendant les vacances, nous (dormir) sous la tente.
7　Mes copains (choisir) des frites.

Je dors sous la tente.

Digital resources

Avoir and *être*

To **have** (avoir) and **to be** (être) are two of the most commonly used verbs in French.
They are both irregular, so you need to learn their different parts really carefully.

Avoir

j'ai	I have
tu as	you have (informal)
il / elle a	he / she has
nous avons	we have
vous avez	you have (formal, plural)
ils / elles ont	they have

When to use avoir

In French you use avoir to give your age, or to say that you **have** hunger or fear or cold.

J'ai seize ans.	I am 16 years old.
J'ai faim.	I am hungry.
Il a peur du noir.	He is afraid of the dark.
J'ai froid.	I am cold.

Être

je suis	I am
tu es	you are (informal)
il / elle est	he / she is
nous sommes	we are
vous êtes	you are (formal, plural)
ils / elles sont	they are

The most common mistake with **être** is to add it when you are using other verbs. Don't just replace 'am' with **suis**.

I am talking	je parle
we are going	nous allons

Useful phrases with avoir and être

J'ai trois frères.	I have three brothers.
Vous avez tort.	You're wrong.
J'ai mal à la tête.	I have a headache.
J'ai besoin d'un stylo.	I need a pen.
Je suis anglais(e).	I am English.
La table est marron.	The table is brown.
Nous sommes frères.	We are brothers.
Ils sont étudiants.	They are students.

Auxiliary verbs

Avoir and être are both used as **auxiliary verbs**. This means they are used to make other **tenses**. You can use the present tense of avoir and être to make the perfect tense. Don't forget to make agreements when using être.

J'**ai** mangé.	I have eaten.
Nous **avons** payé.	We have paid.
Elle **est** allée …	She has gone … (or She went …)
Ils **sont** partis.	They have left.

Now try this

1 Complete the sentences with the correct part of the verb **avoir**.

   (a) J' _____ seize ans.
   (b) Nous _____ assez d'argent.
   (c) Elle _____ un frère.
   (d) Ils _____ tort.
   (e) Vous _____ un chien.

2 Complete these sentences with the correct part of the verb **être**.

   (a) Nous _____ en France.
   (b) Elle _____ travailleuse.
   (c) Je _____ en ville.
   (d) Elles _____ dans la maison.
   (e) Vous _____ tristes.

Reflexive verbs

Digital resources

A reflexive verb is a verb used with an extra little pronoun, for example s'appeler (to be called).

Reflexives and their pronouns

To talk about doing something to yourself, you use a reflexive verb. These verbs need a pronoun, which comes between the subject and the verb.

laver – to wash (e.g. the car) ➡ se laver – to get washed (i.e. to wash yourself)

lever – to raise (e.g. hand, finger, feet) ➡ se lever – to get up (i.e. to raise yourself out of bed)

Reflexive pronouns: je + me   nous + nous

tu + te   vous + vous

il / elle / on + se   ils / elles + se

The verb s'appeler

appeler   to call

s'appeler   to call yourself / be called

je m'appelle

tu t'appelles

il / elle / on s'appelle

nous nous appelons

vous vous appelez

ils / elles s'appellent

The verb se lever

lever   to lift

se lever   to get up

je me lève

tu te lèves

il / elle / on se lève

nous nous levons

vous vous levez

ils / elles se lèvent

> You only need to know the plural forms (**nous, vous** and **ils / elles**) of reflexive verbs at Higher tier.

Common reflexive verbs

se lever	to get up
s'amuser	to enjoy oneself
se marier	to get married
se demander	to wonder
se couper	to cut oneself
s'intéresser à	to be interested in
se changer	to get changed
se trouver	to be situated
se reposer	to rest
se rappeler de	to remember
se passer	to happen
Tu t'intéresses au football?	Are you interested in football?
se taire	to be silent
se comporter	to behave
se brûler	to burn oneself
se plaindre	to complain
se concentrer	to concentrate
se cacher	to hide (oneself)
se blesser	to hurt oneself
se présenter	to introduce oneself
se séparer	to separate
se soucier	to worry
se situer	to be situated
se sentir	to feel
se fier à	to rely on
se souvenir de	to remember

Perfect tense reflexive verbs

In the perfect tense, all reflexive verbs take être. So the past participle must **agree** with the subject.

je me suis levé(e) I got up

nous nous sommes amusé(e)s

we enjoyed ourselves

elle s'est mariée

she got married

ils se sont reposés

they rested

Now try this

Complete these sentences with the correct form of the reflexive verbs in brackets in the present tense.

1 Elle (se lever).

2 Ils (s'amuser).

3 Nous (se demander).

4 Elles (se reposer).

5 Je (s'appeler).

Digital resources

Other important verbs

Many common verbs are irregular, so you will need to learn them.

Aller — to go

je vais	nous allons
tu vas	vous allez
il / elle / on va	ils / elles vont

Nous allons à la piscine.

Did you notice the pattern in the ils / elles form?

aller ➡ vont   faire ➡ font
avoir ➡ ont   être ➡ sont

Faire — to do

je fais	nous faisons
tu fais	vous faites
il / elle / on fait	ils / elles font

Using faire

Faire is used in lots of expressions, especially for talking about the weather:

Il fait beau.	It is fine.
Il fait du vent.	It is windy.
Il fait du soleil.	It is sunny.

It is also used for talking about activities:

Je fais de la natation / de la danse / du vélo.
I do swimming / dancing / cycling.

Pouvoir — to be able to

je peux	nous pouvons
tu peux	vous pouvez
il / elle / on peut	ils / elles peuvent

Je peux aller au cinéma.
I can go to the cinema.

Vouloir — to want to

je veux	nous voulons
tu veux	vous voulez
il / elle / on veut	ils / elles veulent

Je veux manger au restaurant.
I want to eat at the restaurant.

Devoir — to have to

je dois	nous devons
tu dois	vous devez
il / elle / on doit	ils / elles doivent

Je dois faire mes devoirs.
I must do my homework.

Savoir — to know how to

je sais	nous savons
tu sais	vous savez
il / elle / on sait	ils / elles savent

Je sais conduire.
I know how to drive.

Now try this

Complete these sentences with the correct parts of the verb and then translate the sentences **into English**.

1 Je (aller) au collège en car.

2 Nous (faire) du vélo en été.

3 On (pouvoir) aller au cinéma en ville.

4 Ils (vouloir) aller en France.

5 Tu (devoir) faire tes devoirs.

6 Elle (savoir) faire de la natation.

The perfect tense 1

Digital resources

The perfect tense is one of the tenses you use to talk about the past. It is called the *passé composé* in French. Many verbs use *avoir* to form the perfect tense.

Formation

The perfect tense of **most** verbs is made up of the verb **to have** (*avoir*) and the **past participle**.

j'ai	nous avons	+ past participle
tu as	vous avez	
il / elle / on a	ils / elles ont	

J'ai joué au tennis.
I have played tennis / I played tennis.

Use of the perfect tense

You use the perfect tense when you are talking about something that happened at a specific time in the past:

Hier soir j'ai regardé un film.
Last night I watched a film.

L'année dernière, mes parents ont acheté une voiture.
Last year my parents bought a car.

Forming the past participle

For -er verbs, take off the -er and add -é:

manger ➡ mangé
regarder ➡ regardé

J'ai mangé une crêpe.

For -ir verbs, take off the -r:

finir ➡ fini
dormir ➡ dormi

For -re verbs, take off the -re and add -u:

répondre ➡ répondu
attendre ➡ attendu

There are quite a lot of **irregular** past participles and they are the verbs you probably need most – you simply need to learn them.

avoir	➡ eu		mettre	➡ mis
boire	➡ bu		ouvrir	➡ ouvert
courir	➡ couru		prendre	➡ pris
dire	➡ dit		recevoir	➡ reçu
écrire	➡ écrit		rire	➡ ri
être	➡ été		devoir	➡ dû
faire	➡ fait		pouvoir	➡ pu
lire	➡ lu		savoir	➡ su
voir	➡ vu		vouloir	➡ voulu

H ONLY

Negative sentences

In a negative sentence, you put the *ne ... pas* round the part of *avoir*:

Je n'ai pas vu le film.
I haven't seen the film.

Il n'a pas joué au foot.
He did not play football.

Useful phrases

Use these with the perfect tense:

samedi dernier	last Saturday
la semaine dernière	last week
le week-end dernier	last weekend
hier	yesterday

Now try this

Put the infinitives in brackets into the perfect tense to complete the text.

> Mercredi dernier, j'(prendre) le bus pour aller en ville. J'y (rencontrer) un ami. Nous (faire) les magasins. J'(vouloir) acheter des baskets rouges mais elles étaient trop chères. Nous (manger) des pâtes et j'(choisir) un café. Mon copain (boire) un thé. J'(laisser) mon sac au café. J'(devoir) y retourner et, par conséquent, j'(rater) le bus et j'(devoir) rentrer à pied.

Digital resources

The perfect tense 2

Most verbs form the perfect tense with avoir **but** some verbs use être instead.
They are mostly verbs to do with movement.

Verbs that take être

The following 14 verbs take être + the past participle in the perfect tense:

aller / venir	to go / to come
arriver / partir	to arrive / to depart
entrer / sortir	to enter / to go out
monter / descendre	to go up / to go down
rester / tomber	to stay / to fall
naître / mourir	to be born / to die
rentrer / revenir	to return

All reflexive verbs also take être.

MRS VAN DER TRAMP spells out the first letters of the 14 verbs listed above and may be useful in helping you to remember them!

naître and mourir are not in the Edexcel vocabulary list, but you may learn them in class.

Formation

être	Past participles
je suis	allé / venu
tu es	arrivé / parti
il / elle / on est	entré / sorti
nous sommes	monté / descendu
vous êtes	né / mort
ils / elles sont	rentré / revenu

Note how the past participle changes according to who is doing the action:

Je suis allé(e).	I went.
Elle est arrivée.	She arrived.
Nous sommes monté(e)s.	We climbed.
Ils sont partis.	They left.

Remember, in the perfect tense, all reflexive verbs also take être and so the participle must agree.

Agreement of the past participle

With verbs that take être, the past participle agrees with the subject of the verb (a bit like adjectives):

Je suis allé(e)
Tu es allé(e)
Il est allé
Elle est allée
Nous sommes allé(e)s
Vous êtes allé(e)(s)
Ils sont allés
Elles sont allées

H ONLY

To emphasise that you have **just** done something, you can use venir de. You use the present tense of venir + de, but it expresses a recent past.
Je viens d'arriver chez moi.
I have just arrived home.

Aiming higher

• You should be able to use the perfect tense if you are aiming at a higher grade.
• Remember, you use the perfect tense when you are talking about one specific time in the past, so you are likely to start the sentence with a time expression referring to the past.
For example:
Samedi dernier …
Hier …
Hier soir …
Il y a deux jours …
Pendant les vacances …

Now try this

Put the infinitives in brackets into the perfect tense to complete the sentences.

1 Samedi dernier, je (partir) tôt.
2 Le matin, je (aller) jouer au football.
3 Je (sortir) à dix heures.
4 L'autre équipe (ne pas venir).
5 Nous y (rester) une heure, puis nous (rentrer).
6 Je (arriver) à la maison juste avant midi.

Je suis allée au match.

The imperfect tense

Digital resources

The imperfect is another verb tense you use to talk about the past.

Forming the imperfect

First, take the nous form of the present tense and remove the -ons ending:

nous habit~~ons~~

Then add the following imperfect endings:

je -ais	nous -ions
tu -ais	vous -iez
il / elle / on -ait	ils / elles -aient

habiter to live

j'habitais	nous habitions
tu habitais	vous habitiez
il / elle / on habitait	ils / elles habitaient

So (for all verbs except être) simply use the stem of the present tense **nous** form and add the endings shown above.

Good news: all verbs except être are regular in the imperfect tense.

For Foundation tier, you only need to know the forms for je, tu, il / elle / on in the imperfect tense.

Using the imperfect

You use the imperfect tense to describe:

- What **was happening**:
  Il pleuvait.   It was raining.
- What **used to** happen:
  Quand j'étais jeune, je jouais au foot.
  When I was young, I used to play football.
- What was **ongoing** when something else happened:
  Je regardais la télévision lorsque mon ami est arrivé.
  I was watching TV when my friend arrived.

The key words to look out for are: 'was / were … ing' and 'used to …'.

Some common verbs

These are a few common verbs you should be able to use in the imperfect.

Present	Imperfect	English
voul~~ons~~	je voul+ais	I wanted
av~~ons~~	j'av+ais	I had
all~~ons~~	j'all+ais	I was going
buv~~ons~~	je buv+ais	I was drinking
mange~~ons~~	je mange+ais	I was eating
achet~~ons~~	j'achet+ais	I was buying
finiss~~ons~~	je finiss+ais	I was finishing
dorm~~ons~~	je dorm+ais	I was sleeping

Être in the imperfect

The **only** irregular verb in the imperfect tense is être. The stem is ét- and you add the normal imperfect endings to this stem:

j'étais	I was
tu étais	you were
il / elle / on était	he / she / one was
nous étions	we were
vous étiez	you were
ils / elles étaient	they were

Now try this

Complete the text with the imperfect tense of the verbs in the box, then translate it **into English**. Why is it written in the imperfect tense?

> avoir   être   habiter   jouer   aller   acheter   manger   boire   rentrer

Quand j'_____ jeune, j' _____ à la campagne.
Nous _____ un grand jardin où je _____ au foot avec mes frères.
Le samedi, on _____ au marché en ville. Il y _____ beaucoup de magasins où j'_____ des cadeaux. Nous _____ des pâtes et nous _____ du café. On _____ en bus avec tous nos voisins et nos achats!

111

Digital resources

The future tense

To aim for a high grade you need to use the future tense as well as the present and past!

Near future tense (futur proche)

When you are talking about what you are **going** to do, use the verb to go (aller) + an infinitive, just as in English:

Je vais aller …   I am going to go …
Ils vont jouer au tennis.
They are going to play tennis.
Mon copain va rentrer à 21h00.
My friend is going to go home at 9 o'clock.
On va manger en ville.
We are going to eat in town.

Remember all the parts of aller (to go):

je vais	nous allons	
tu vas	vous allez	+ infinitive
il / elle / on va	ils / elles vont	

Remember, the **infinitive** is the part of the verb you will find in the dictionary – usually ending in -er, -ir or -re.
For example:
-er: jouer / manger
-ir: finir / choisir / sortir
-re: lire / dire

Future tense (futur simple)

If you are aiming for a top grade, you will need to be able to understand and use the 'proper' future. It is used to say what you **will** do. The future is made from the **infinitive** + **future tense endings**:

-er verbs:	manger	➡ je mangerai	I will eat
-ir verbs:	finir	➡ je finirai	I will finish
-re verbs:	répondre	➡ je répondrai	I will reply

Remember, -re verbs drop the final -e.
The future tense **endings** are the same as the present tense forms of avoir, except for the nous and vous forms:

je mangerai	nous mangerons
tu mangeras	vous mangerez
il / elle / on mangera	ils / elles mangeront

In the exam, it is fine to use the near future tense if saying or writing anything about the future.

Which future to use?

Near future (futur proche):
I am going to play football tonight.
This is a simple fact.
Proper future (futur simple):
I will play football tonight.
You might be:
• expressing an intention.
• responding to a suggestion that you might **not** do something.

Je jouerai au foot dans le parc.

Sometimes you can even use a present tense as long as you make sure to use a future time indicator.
Ce week-end, je fête l'anniversaire de mon frère. This weekend I am celebrating my brother's birthday.

Irregular verbs

Be careful! There are a few common verbs that don't use the infinitive as the stem, but have an irregular stem. The good news is the endings are always the same.

aller	j'irai	I will go
avoir	j'aurai	I will have
être	je serai	I will be
faire	je ferai	I will do
pouvoir	je pourrai	I will be able to
venir	je viendrai	I will come
voir	je verrai	I will see
vouloir	je voudrai	I will want

Now try this

Put all the infinitives in brackets into the correct form of the future tense.

1 Je (manger) au restaurant.
2 Elle (aller) en France.
3 Il (faire) du vélo.
4 Ils (partager) le gâteau.
5 Tu (avoir) seize ans demain.
6 Il (être) triste.

The conditional tense

Digital resources

You should know a few verbs in the conditional and be able to use them in your writing and speaking in order to aim for a higher mark.

The conditional (H ONLY)

The conditional is used to say what you **would** do:

| je voudrais | I would like |
| je jouerais | I would play |

It is also used for making suggestions:

on pourrait …   we could …

The conditional is formed in a similar way to the future. It uses the same stem (usually the infinitive) but then adds the same endings as the imperfect tense:

manger	➡ je mangerais	I would eat
finir	➡ je finirais	I would finish
vendre	➡ je vendrais	I would sell

You may meet the conditional after si (if):

Si + imperfect tense + conditional

Si tu mangeais correctement, tu n'aurais pas faim.

If you ate properly, you wouldn't be hungry.

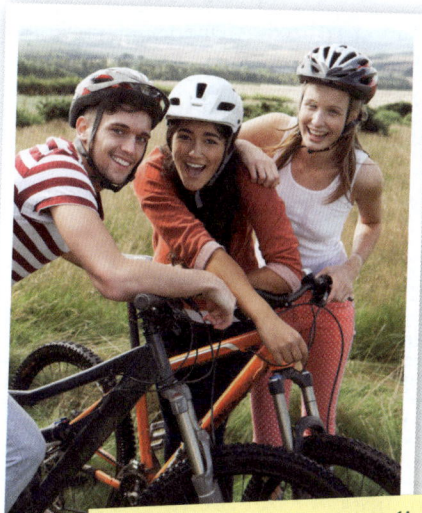

On pourrait faire du vélo?
We could go cycling?

Vouloir

At Foundation tier, you only need to learn the following instances of the conditional:

je voudrais	I would like
tu voudrais	you would like
il / elle / on voudrait	he / she / one would like

However, if you want to use other examples of the conditional you can!

Foundation tier: this is all you need to learn for the conditional.

Irregular conditionals (H ONLY)

Irregular conditionals use the same stems as the irregular future:

infinitive	conditional	English
aller	j'irais	I would go
avoir	j'aurais	I would have
être	je serais	I would be
faire	je ferais	I would do

The endings are always the same, whether the verb is regular or irregular:

je serais	nous serions
tu serais	vous seriez
il / elle serait	ils / elles seraient

Je voudrais aller au concert ce soir.
I'd like to go to the concert this evening.

Now try this

Put the infinitives in the following sentences in the conditional.

1 Je (vouloir) aller en France.

2 Si j'avais assez d'argent, j'(aller) au Canada.

3 Il (faire) un long voyage.

4 Tu (aimer) voir ce film?

5 Je (préférer) manger au restaurant.

6 Si j'avais faim, je (manger) du fromage.

7 Il (vouloir) aller en ville samedi.

8 On (aller) à la plage s'il faisait beau?

9 Tu (aller) au match si tu restais encore deux jours.

10 Elle (vouloir) quelque chose a boire?

Digital resources

Negatives

You need to be able to understand and use a variety of negatives to aim for a higher grade in all parts of your exam.

Negative expressions

ne ... pas	not
ne ... jamais	never
ne ... plus	no longer, not any more
ne ... rien	nothing, not anything
ne ... personne	nobody, not anybody
ne ... aucun(e)	not any
ne ... que	only
ne ... ni ... ni ...	neither ... nor

Formation

You know that negatives are made by making a ne ... pas sandwich around the verb.

The ne is a marker to tell you that a negative is coming ...

ne	verb	pas

Word order

- Personne can also come in front of the verb:
Personne n'est venu. No one came.
- When the verb has two parts, the negative forms the sandwich around the auxiliary:
Je ne suis jamais allé(e) en France.
I have never been to France.
- If there is a pronoun before the auxiliary, it is included in the sandwich:
Je n'y suis jamais allé(e).
I've never been there.

- If there are two verbs, the sandwich goes around the first verb:
Je ne veux pas y aller.
I don't want to go there.
Nous ne pouvons pas télécharger l'appli sans mot de passe. We can't download the app without a password.
- If there is a reflexive pronoun, that is included in the sandwich, too:
Ils ne s'entendent pas bien.
They don't get on well.

Now try this

1 Match the French negative sentences with the English ones on the right.

1 Il ne mange pas de viande.	**A** We don't want anything else.
2 On m'a dit que tu ne joues plus au tennis.	**B** Manon has never eaten eggs.
3 Manon n'a jamais mangé d'œufs.	**C** I didn't see anyone.
4 Nous ne voulons plus rien.	**D** He's only ten.
5 Je n'ai vu personne.	**E** She has no doubts.
6 Elle n'a aucun doute.	**F** Someone told me you don't play tennis any more.
7 Il n'a que dix ans.	**G** Where's she from? She's neither French nor English.
8 D'où vient-elle? Elle n'est ni française ni anglaise.	**H** He doesn't eat meat.

2 Make negative sentences with the expressions provided.
- **(a)** Tu fais (ne ... rien).
- **(b)** Tu m'as aidé à la maison (ne ... jamais).
- **(c)** Tu fais tes devoirs (ne ... plus).
- **(d)** Tu respectes (ne ... personne).
- **(e)** Tu fais le nécessaire (ne ... que).
- **(f)** Tu peux aller au football ou au restaurant ce soir (ne ... ni ... ni).

H ONLY

The perfect infinitive and the present participle

Digital resources

If you can use the perfect infinitive or a present participle, you will show greater complexity in your speaking and writing.

Après avoir (the perfect infinitive)

This is used to translate 'after doing something'.
It is formed by using
après avoir + past participle.

> Après avoir joué au foot, nous sommes rentrés chez nous. After playing football, we went home.

For verbs which take être in the perfect tense, you would use après être + past participle which would have to agree with the subject. For example, après être arrivé(e)(s).

Although you may see this in your books or real French texts, après être + past participle is not required for the Edexcel GCSE exams from 2024.

Avant de

This is used to mean 'before doing something'.
It is followed by the infinitive of the verb.
Avant de rentrer à la maison, nous avons joué au football. Before going home, we played football.

The present participle

The English present participle ends in -ing and is used frequently. The French present participle ends in -ant and is far less common. You will, however, often see the present participle used after the word en. In such cases it translates the idea of 'by', 'in', 'on' or 'while doing something'.
Il travaille en écoutant de la musique.
He works while listening to music.

To form the present participle, take the -ons off the nous part of the present tense of the verb and simply add -ant:
travailler ➡ travaillons ➡ travaillant
  working
aller ➡ allons ➡ allant going
There are three exceptions:
avoir ➡ ayant having
être ➡ étant being

> Another way of saying -ing is to use an infinitive as a noun in French. This is part of the course at Foundation tier.
> Regarder des films d'action c'est passionnant.
> Watching action films is exciting.

Now try this

1 Translate these sentences:
   (a) After watching TV, I played football.
   (b) After finishing his homework, he went into town.
   (c) After listening to some music, they went to school.

2 Put these verbs into the correct form of the present participle.
   (a) manger
   (b) avoir
   (c) travailler
   (d) finir
   (e) faire

Digital resources

The passive, the imperative and impersonal verbs

The passive

The passive is used to say what is done to someone or something.

It is formed from a part of être and a past participle. The past participle must agree with the noun.

La maison a été construite en 1930.

The house was built in 1930.

Les appartements sont vendus.

The flats are sold.

If you want to add who or what did the action, you use par.

La meilleure histoire a été racontée par le plus jeune enfant. The best story was told by the youngest child.

To avoid the passive in French, you can turn the sentence round by using on.

On m'a invité(e).

I was invited (someone invited me).

The imperative

The imperative is used to tell someone to do something, for example, in a recipe or to give directions. In French this is either the tu or vous form of the verb **without** the subject.

Finis tes devoirs!   Finish your homework!

Tournez à gauche.   Turn left.

However, with -er verbs, the final -s is left off in the tu form:

Ferme la porte, s'il te plaît.

Shut the door, please.

> To suggest doing something together, such as in the English expression 'Let's … ', use the nous form of the verb in the present tense without the subject.
> Regardons ce film! Let's watch this film!
> Partons ensemble. Let's leave together.
> Prenons le prochain bus.
> Let's get the next bus.

Impersonal verbs

Impersonal verbs are verbs that are only used with il, or verbs which can be used in this way. You can use them to talk about general things.

- il y a there is / there are
  Il y a des voitures électriques.
  There are some electric cars.
- il fait it is (with the weather)
  Il fait froid. It is cold (weather).
- il + weather expressions
  Il neige. It is snowing.
- il faut it is necessary / you / we must
  Il faut réduire la pollution.
  We must reduce pollution.

- il est + adjective + de … it is + adjective + to …
  Il est important de résoudre les problèmes de la pollution.
  It's important to resolve pollution problems.
- il manque + noun … is missing
  Il nous manque trois personnes.
  We are missing three people.
- il vaut mieux + infinitive it's better …
  Il vaut mieux y aller en train.
  It's better to go by train.
- il vaut la peine de + infinitive it's worth …
  Il vaut la peine d'arriver tôt. It's worth arriving early.

Now try this

Match the French sentence with the English ones on the right.

1 J'ai été invité.	A My house will be sold.
2 Ma maison sera vendue.	B The story is written.
3 Le professeur est très bien aimé.	C I have been / was invited.
4 L'histoire est écrite.	D The song has been / was sung.
5 La chanson a été chantée.	E The teacher is very well liked.

Questions, prefixes, suffixes, prepositions

Digital resources

Ways of asking yes / no questions

- Change a statement into a question by raising your voice at the end.

  Tu vas en ville?

- Put est-ce que at the start.
  Est-ce que tu vas en ville?

- Swap the subject and verb.
  Vas-tu en ville? Va-t-il en ville?

Question words

Qui?	Who?	A quelle heure?
Quand?	When?	At what time?
Où?	Where?	Pourquoi? Why?
Comment?	How?	Que? What?
Combien de? How many?		Depuis quand? Since when?

Question words can be followed by est-ce que:
Où est-ce que tu habites? Where do you live?

Prefixes

You can make some words into their 'opposite' by adding im- or in-.

sécurité ➡ insécurité security ➡ insecurity

possible ➡ impossible possible ➡ impossible

Prepositions

- **After verbs**
  Some verbs need to be followed by à or de.
  décider de (sortir) to decide to (go out)
  réussir à (faire) to succeed in (doing), pass (an exam)
  Jouer à is used for sport.
  Je joue au tennis.
  Jouer de is used for instruments.
  Je joue du piano.

  > faire de can also be used for sports which you don't 'play'. Je fais de la danse.

- **Showing possession**
  C'est le stylo de ma mère.
  It's my mother's pen.
  C'est le livre de Manon. It's Manon's book.

- **With places**
  Use en with feminine countries.
  Je suis allé(e) en France. I went to France.
  Use au with masculine countries.
  Je veux aller au Canada. I want to go to Canada.

- **Before infinitives**
  Pour can be used to mean 'in order to …'
  pour sauver la planète in order to save the planet
  Sans can be used to mean 'without'.
  sans détruire les forêts without destroying forests

Suffixes

- **Adding -ième**
  You may use this with dates or positions.
  Deux ➡ deuxième two ➡ second
  Trois ➡ troisième three ➡ third
  When the number ends in -e, drop that -e.
  Quatre ➡ quatrième four ➡ fourth
  Sometimes a minor change is needed.
  Cinq ➡ cinquième five ➡ fifth

- **Adding -able or -eable**
  Add to some verb stems to make an adjective indicating possibility.
  réutiliser ➡ réutilisable
  to reuse ➡ reusable

- **Adding -ation**
  Add to some verb stems to make a noun.
  préparer ➡ préparation
  to prepare ➡ preparation

- **Adding -eur**
  Add to some verb stems to make a noun for the person who does the verb.
  chanter ➡ chanteur to sing ➡ singer

H ONLY

Now try this

Match up the two parts of each question.
Then translate the questions **into English**.

1	Où	apprends-tu le français?
2	Qui	rentrent tes parents?
3	Comment	voulez-vous faire?
4	Combien	allez-vous?
5	À quelle heure	travaille ton père?
6	Pourquoi	as-tu pris le bus?
7	Que	d'amis as-tu sur Facebook?
8	Depuis quand	va à la fête?

Vocabulary

This vocabulary section contains a comprehensive list of words that are in the Edexcel GCSE French vocabulary list. Verbs are included in their infinitive form only; please refer to the specification for more on the forms and tenses required.

To help you learn the words, they have been divided into subjects. However, words are flexible and you can use them for a variety of subjects. Remember, any vocabulary could appear in any of Edexcel's thematic contexts in the exam. Words that are shaded purple are Higher tier only.

1 Basic vocabulary

Greetings

au revoir	bye, goodbye
bonsoir	good evening
bonjour	hello
salut	hi, bye
madame	madam, Mrs
non	no, not
d'accord(?)	ok(?)
s'il te / vous plaît	please
monsieur	sir, mister, Mr
désolé	sorry
merci	thank you
ouais / oui	yeah / yes
à bientôt	see you soon
si	yes (response to a negative)

Days, months and seasons

lundi (m)	Monday
mardi (m)	Tuesday
mercredi (m)	Wednesday
jeudi (m)	Thursday
vendredi (m)	Friday
samedi (m)	Saturday
dimanche (m)	Sunday
janvier (m)	January
février (m)	February
mars (m)	March
avril (m)	April
mai (m)	May
juin (m)	June
juillet (m)	July
août (m)	August
septembre (m)	September
octobre (m)	October
novembre (m)	November
décembre (m)	December
saison (f)	season
automne (m)	autumn
printemps (m)	spring
été (m)	summer
hiver (m)	winter

Numbers

zéro	zero
un	one
deux	two
trois	three
quatre	four
cinq	five
six	six
sept	seven
huit	eight
neuf	nine
dix	ten
onze	eleven
douze	twelve
treize	thirteen
quatorze	fourteen
quinze	fifteen
seize	sixteen
dix-sept	seventeen
dix-huit	eighteen
dix-neuf	nineteen
vingt	twenty
trente	thirty
quarante	forty
cinquante	fifty
soixante	sixty
soixante-dix	seventy
quatre-vingts	eighty
quatre-vingt-dix	ninety
cent	a hundred
mille	a thousand
million (m)	a million
premier	first
deuxième	second
seconde	second, year 11
troisième	third, year 10
quatrième	fourth, year 9
dernier	last
centaine (f)	about 100
dizaine (f)	about 10

Times of day

après-midi (m)	afternoon
jour (m)	day
journée (f)	day
fin (f)	end
soir (m)	evening
et demie	half past
heure (f)	hour, o'clock
midi (m)	midday
minuit (m)	midnight
minute (f)	minute
matin (m)	morning
nuit (f)	night
début (m)	start, beginning
fois (f)	time
semaine (f)	week
week-end (m)	weekend
mois (m)	month
année (f)	year
an (m)	year
siècle (m)	century
soirée (f)	evening
moment (m)	moment
lendemain (m)	the next day
veille (f)	the night before

Colours

noir	black
bleu	blue
châtain	brown
marron	brown
couleur (f)	colour
vert	green
gris	grey
orange	orange
rose	pink
rouge	red
blanc (m) / blanche (f)	white
jaune	yellow

Now try this

Look around you. Describe what you can see, using as many colours and numbers as possible.

Had a look ☐   Nearly there ☐   Nailed it! ☐

② Basic vocabulary

Cultural and geographical words

Algérie (f)	Algeria
Canada (m)	Canada
Angleterre (f)	England
France (f)	France
Madagascar (m)	Madagascar
Martinique (f)	Martinique
Royaume-Uni (m)	United Kingdom
Afrique (f)	Africa
Amérique (f)	America
Asie (f)	Asia
Europe (f)	Europe
14 juillet (m)	Bastille Day
francophonie (f)	French-speaking world
Nouvel An (m)	New Year
Saint-Sylvestre (f)	New Year's Eve
France d'Outremer (f)	overseas France
Paris (m)	Paris
Tour Eiffel (f)	the Eiffel Tower
Tour de France (m)	the Tour de France
Fête de la Musique (f)	World Music Day

Names used in assessments

Girls

Ana	Fatima	Maria
Chloé	Inès	Marie
Clara	Jade	Myriam
Diane	Léa	Nadia
Emma	Lola	Sarah
Eva	Lucie	Yasmina
Fathia	Manon	Zoé

Boys

Ahmed	Louis	Rachid
Alessandro	Lucas	Raphaël
Clément	Luis	Sofiane
Dorian	Mathis	Théo
Enzo	Mehdi	Thomas
Hugo	Mohamed	Tom
Jules	Nathan	Yanis

Short phrases and names

aussi … que	as … as
en ce moment	at the moment
bon appétit!	enjoy your meal!
de temps en temps	from time to time
(comment) ça va?	how are you?
je suis d'accord avec	I agree with
ça va bien	I am good / well, it fits
ça m'est égal	I don't mind, I'm not bothered
à l'arrière plan	in the background
au premier plan	in the foreground
il est (+ time)	it is / it's (+ time)
il faut + infinitive	it is / it's necessary + verb, must + verb
il fait (beau)	it is / it's (nice)
il pleut	it rains / it's raining
il neige	it snows / it's snowing
il y a du (brouillard)	it's (foggy)
à côté de	next to
bien sûr	of course
est-ce que / est-ce qu'?	(questioning device)
il y a | il y avait | il y aura	there is, there are, ago | there was, there were, there used to be | there is going to be, there will be
qu'est-ce qui ne va pas?	what's wrong?
de rien	you are welcome
être en train de + infinitive	(to) be in the middle of + verb
venir de + infinitive	(to) have just + past participle
il manque …	… is missing
il est (difficile) de + infinitive	it is (difficult) + verb
il vaut mieux + infinitive	it is better + verb
il vaut la peine de + infinitive	it is / it's worth + verb
d'un côté, de l'autre côté	on the one hand, on the other hand
c'est-à-dire	in other words

Boys and Girls

Alex	Louis(e)
Axel / Axelle	Maxime
Camille	Morgan(e)
Charlie	Sacha
Gabriel / Gabrielle	Toni

Female adults

Sabrina
Sylvie

Male adults

Patrick
Richard

Now try this

Choose five of the short phrases and write a sentence that includes each one.

❸ Basic vocabulary

Articles and pronouns

on	one, you, we
tous	everyone, all
tout le monde	everybody
tout	everything, all
quelqu'un	someone
ça, cela	that, it
que (?)	what (?), that

Question words

combien (?)	how much (?), how many (?), how long (time) (?)
comment (?)	how (?)
quand (?)	when (?)
où (?)	where (?)
qui (?)	who (?)
pourquoi (?)	why (?)

Negatives

ne … jamais	never
ne … personne	no one, not anyone
ne … rien	nothing, not anything
ne … aucun	not one
ne … plus	no longer
ne … ni … ni	neither … nor
ne … pas encore	not yet
ne…que	only, nothing but

Conjunctions

et	and
comme	as, like, in terms of
car	because
parce que	because
mais	but
si	if
ou	or
donc	therefore, so
quoique	although
cependant	however
sinon	otherwise
puisque	since
lorsque	when, while
pourtant	yet, nonetheless

Prepositions

contre	against
à	at, to, in, on
chez	at / to (the house of)
avant; avant de + inf	before; before + verb
derrière	behind, at the back
entre	between
pendant	during
pour	for, in order to
voici	here is
dans	in, inside
en	in, by, to
devant	in front of
près (de)	near, nearby
de	of, from
sur	on, upon
voilà	there, there you are
sous	under
avec	with
sans	without
selon	according to
après avoir + past participle	after having + past participle
parmi	amongst
autour	around
dès	as soon as
par	by, for
malgré	despite
sauf	except
depuis	for, since
afin de	in order to
grâce à	thanks to
vers	towards
envers	towards
jusque	until

Parts of the body

bras (m)	arm
cœur (m)	heart
corps (m)	body
doigt (m)	finger
dos (m)	back
gorge (f)	throat
jambe (f)	leg
main (f)	hand
nez (m)	nose
oreille (f)	ear
pied (m)	foot
tête (f)	head
ventre (m)	stomach
visage (m)	face
yeux (mpl)	eyes
peau (m)	skin
voix (f)	voice

Now try this

To learn the parts of the body, draw a picture of a person and label the different parts.

④ General vocabulary

accepter	to accept	chercher	to look for, search	donner	to give
action (f)	action	choc (m)	shock, clash	droit (m)	right
adolescent (m)	teenager	choisir	to choose	droite (f)	right
adorer	to love	choix (m)	choice	dur	hard, difficult
adulte (m)	adult	chose (f)	thing	durer	to last
âge (m)	age	clair	light, bright, clear	écouter	to listen
aider (à)	to help (to)			écrire	to write
aimer	to like	coin (m)	corner	égal	equal
aller	to go	commencer (à)	to start / begin (to)	emporter; à emporter	to take, remove; to take away
alors	so				
ancien (m) / ancienne (f)	ancient, former	comparer	to compare	ennuyeux (m) / ennuyeuse (f)	boring
anglais	English	comprendre	to understand		
année (f)	year	condition (f)	condition	énorme	enormous, big
annoncer	to announce	confortable	comfortable	entrer	to enter, go in
appeler; s'appeler	to call; to be called	connaître	to know	erreur (f)	error, mistake
		contact (m)	contact	espace (m)	space, room
après-midi (m)	afternoon	continuer (de)	to continue	espérer	to hope
arriver; arriver à	to arrive; to manage	couleur (f)	colour	essayer de; essayer	to try; to try on (clothes)
		courir	to run		
attention (f)	attention	court	short	essentiel (m) / essentielle (f)	essential
aussi	also	création (f)	creation		
autre	other	croire	to believe	étonnant	surprising, amazing
avenir (m)	future	culturel (m) / culturelle (f)	cultural		
avis (m)	opinion			être	to be
avoir	to have	date (f)	date	euro (m)	euro
avoir ... ans	to be ... years old	début (m)	start, beginning	européen	European
		décider (de)	to decide (to)	événement (m)	event
bas (m) / basse (f)	low	décision (f)	decision	exact	exact
beau (m) / bel; beau-beaux (mpl) belle (f); belle-	beautiful, handsome, nice (weather); step-	décrire	to describe	excellent	excellent
		définition (f)	definition	exemple (m)	example
		demander (à ... de + infinitive); se demander	to ask (someone to + verb); to wonder, ask oneself	extraordinaire	extraordinary
				face (f)	front, face, side
boire	to drink			facile	easy
bon (m) / bonne (f)	good			faire	to do, make, go
		dépendre (de)	to depend (on)	fatigant	tiring
bord (m)	edge, side	descendre	to go down	fausse (f)	false
britannique	British	désolé	sorry	faux (m)	false
canadien	Canadian	détail (m)	detail	faveur (f)	favour
cas (m)	case	détester	to hate	fermé	closed
cause (f)	cause	devenir	to become	fermer	to close, shut (down)
causer	to cause	devoir	to have to, must		
certain	certain	différence (f)	difference	fin (f)	end
chance (f)	luck	différent	different	final	final
changement (m)	change	difficile	difficult	finir	to finish
changer; se changer	to change; to get changed	difficulté (f)	difficulty, issue, problem	fois (f)	time
				folle (f)	crazy, wild
chaque	each, every	dire	to say	fonctionner	to function, work
chaud	hot	discuter	to discuss		
cher (m) / chère (f)	expensive, dear	divers	various	fond (m)	bottom, back
				former	to form

Now try this

Choose five words from the list on this page that you find difficult to remember. Write a sentence using each one.

⑤ General vocabulary

fou (m) / folle (f)	crazy, wild	mal	bad, badly	parfait	perfect		
français	French	marcher	to walk,	parler	to speak, talk		
francophone	francophone		function	partie (f)	part		
froid	cold	matin (m)	morning	partir	to leave		
gauche (f)	left	mauvais	bad	passé (m)	past		
général	general	maximum (m)	maximum	passer; se	to spend		
génial	great	meilleur	better	passer	(time), take		
gens (mpl)	people	même	same		(an exam); to		
grâce (f); grâce à	grace, thanks	mètre (m)	metre		happen		
	to	mettre	to put (in, on)	passion (f)	passion		
grand; grand-	great, big,	minimum (m)	minimum	passionnant	exciting		
	tall; grand-	minute (f)	minute	pauvre	poor		
gratuit	free	moderne	modern	pays (m)	country		
gros (m) /	big, large,	moins (... que)	less / fewer	penser (à)	to think (of)		
grosse (f)	lots of		(than)	perdre	to lose		
groupe (m)	group, band	mois (m)	month	période (f)	period		
habituel (m) /	usual	moitié (f)	half	personne (f)	person		
habituelle (f)		monter	to go up	petit	small, little		
heure (f)	hour, o'clock	mot (m)	word	photo (f)	photo		
histoire (f)	story, history	mouvement (m)	movement	pire	worse		
idéal	ideal	moyen (m)	means, way	place (f)	room, space,		
idée (f)	idea	mur (m)	wall		square, place		
image (f)	image, picture	national	national	plaisir (m)	pleasure		
importance (f)	importance	nécessaire	necessary	plus (... que)	more (... than)		
important	important	nécessité (f)	necessity	plusieurs	several, many		
impossible	impossible	négatif (m) /	negative	point (m)	point		
indépendance (f)	independence	négative (f)		populaire	popular		
inspirer	to inspire	niveau (m)	level	population (f)	population		
intéressant	interesting	nombre (m)	number	porte (f)	door		
international	international	nord (m)	north	poser	to ask (a		
inutile	useless	normal	normal, usual		question)		
jardin (m)	garden	nouveau (m) /	new	positif	positive		
jour (m)	day	nouveaux (mpl) /		possibilité (f)	possibility		
journal (m)	newspaper	nouvelle (f)		possible	possible		
journée (f)	day	nuit (f)	night	pouvoir	to be able to		
juste	fair, just, only	nul (m) / nulle (f)	rubbish, bad	pratique	practical		
laisser	to let, leave	numéro (m)	number	préféré	favourite		
large	large, wide,	occupé	busy	préférer	to prefer		
	big	offre (f)	offer	premier (m) /	first		
léger (m) /	light	opinion (f)	opinion	première (f)			
légère (f)		ordinaire	ordinary	prendre	to take		
lent	slow	ordre (m)	order	préparer	to prepare		
libre	free, available	organiser	to organise	présent (m)	present		
lien (m)	link	original	original	présentation (f)	presentation		
lire	to read	oublier	to forget	président (m)	president		
liste (f)	list	ouest (m)	west	principal	main, principal		
long (m) /	long	ouvert	open, opened	problème (m)	problem, issue		
longue (f)		ouvrir	to open				
majorité (f)	majority						

Now try this

Test yourself by covering the French words and saying the French word. Then cover the English words and say the English word.

⑥ General vocabulary

prochain	next	rester	to stay
progrès (m)	progress	retourner	to return
promesse (f)	promise	revenir	to come back
prononcer	to pronounce	rire	to laugh
propre	clean, proper, own	saison (f)	season
protection (f)	protection	savoir	to know how to
public (m) / publique (f)	public	semaine (f)	week
qualité (f)	quality	sens (m)	sense, meaning
quantité (f)	quantity	sérieux (m) / sérieuse (f)	serious, important
quart (m); et quart; moins le quart	quarter; quarter past; quarter to	seul	alone, only, lonely
quelque	some	silence (m)	silence
question (f)	question	simple	simple, plain
quitter	to leave	s'intéresser à	to be interested in
rappeler; se rappeler de	to recall, remind; to remember	situation (f)	situation
réalité (f)	reality	société (f)	society
récent	recent	soir (m)	evening
recevoir	to receive	solution (f)	solution
recherche (f)	research	sorte (f)	sort, kind, type
rechercher	to look for, search, collect	sortie (f)	exit, outing
reconnaître	to recognise	sortir	to go out
réel (m) / réelle (f)	real	sourire	to smile
regarder	to watch, to look	spécial	special
regretter	to regret	sud (m)	south
régulier	regular	suivant	next, following
rendez-vous (m)	appointment	suivre	to follow
rendre	to return, give back	sujet (m)	subject, topic
rentrer	to go back in, return	sûr	sure, safe, certain
répéter	to repeat	surprise (f)	surprise
répondre (à)	to reply (to)	symbole (m)	symbol
réponse (f)	answer, reply	système (m)	system
respect (m)	respect	tableau (m)	board, painting
respecter	to respect, follow	téléphone (m)	telephone
reste (m); restes (mpl)	rest, remainder; leftovers	temps (m)	time, weather
		tendance	fashionable, trendy
		tendance (f)	trend, tendency
		tenir	to hold
		terrible	terrible
		thème (m)	theme, topic
		toilettes (fpl)	toilet(s)
		tort (m)	wrong, incorrect
		tout (m), tous (mpl)	all, the whole

tradition (f)	tradition
traditionnel (m) / traditionnelle (f)	traditional
traduire	to translate
traitement (m)	treatment
traiter	to treat, handle, deal with
truc (m)	thing
type (m)	type, kind, sort
utile	useful
utiliser	to use
valeur (f)	value, worth
venir	to come
vérité (f)	truth
version (f)	version
victime (f)	victim
vide	empty
vieux (m) / vieille (f)	old
visiter	to visit
voir	to see
volume (m)	volume
vrai	true, correct
week-end (m)	weekend

Now try this

When you learn nouns, learn them with le or la, to help you remember whether they are masculine or feminine: le volume, la victime.

7 General vocabulary H

accent (m)	accent	évident	obvious
accord (m)	agreement	éviter	to avoid
actuel (m) /	current,	exceptionnel (m)	exceptional
actuelle (f)	present	/ exceptionnelle (f)	
adapter	to adapt	excuse (f)	excuse
apercevoir	to see, notice	exister	to exist
appartenir (à)	to belong (to)	explication (f)	explanation
apporter	to bring	expliquer	to explain
aspect (m)	aspect	expression (f)	expression
augmenter	to increase	façon (f)	way
besoin (m)	need	fournir	to provide, supply
bonheur (m)	happiness	frontière (f)	border
bref (m) /	brief	garder	to keep
brève (f)		grave	serious, grave
capable	capable	honte (f)	shame
cesser	to stop	humain	human
civil	civil	ignorer	to ignore, not
colère (f)	anger		know
communiquer	to communicate	imaginer	to imagine
complexe	complex,	immédiat	immediate
	difficult	impression (f)	impression
concerner	to be relevant	inconnu	unknown
	to	inconvénient (m)	disadvantage
conseil (m)	advice	indispensable	essential
conseiller	to advise	joie (f)	joy
conséquence (f)	consequence	maintenir	to maintain
considérer	to consider	majeur	major, main
contenir	to contain	manque (m)	lack
contraire	contrary	nombreux (m) /	numerous, many
contribuer	to contribute	nombreuse (f)	
convaincre	to convince	nommer	to call, name
créer	to create	noter	to note, notice
crier	to shout	objet (m)	object
décevoir	to disappoint	obliger	to require, oblige,
découvrir	to discover	observer	to observe, watch
défendre;	to defend; to	obtenir	to get, obtain
défendre de	forbid, ban	occasion (f)	occasion, chance
désirer	to desire	offrir	to offer
développer	to develop	or (m)	gold
discussion (f)	discussion	origine (f)	origin
dommage (m)	(what a) pity	oser	to dare
doute (m)	doubt	pareil (m) /	same
écart (m)	gap	pareille (f)	
efficace	efficient	pensée (f)	thought
entier (m) /	entire, full,	permanent	permanent
entière (f)	whole	peur (f)	fear, fright
envie (f)	wish, desire,	plaire	to please
	want		
esprit (m)	spirit		
étroit	narrow		

plein	full
plupart	most
posséder	to own, possess
pouvoir (m)	power
précédent	previous
prêt	ready
principe (m)	principle
produire	to produce
profond	deep
public (m)	public, audience
quotidien (m) /	daily
quotidienne (f)	
rare	rare
refuser de	to refuse
régler	to settle, set
remplacer	to replace
remplir	to fill
responsabilité (f)	responsibility
risquer	to risk
s'asseoir	to sit
se taire	to be quiet
sembler	to seem
s'exprimer	to express
	oneself
siècle (m)	century
signifier	to mean
souhaiter	to wish
sourire (m)	smile
suffisant	enough
taux (m)	rate
tenter de	to try, attempt
terminer	to finish, end
toucher	to touch, affect
vérifier	to check
vivre	to live
volonté (f)	will, desire

Now try this

Choose five verbs from this page and say the past, present and future forms.

8 Adverbs; Family, friends, identity and equality

When a verb was done

longtemps	a long time
après	after
encore	again, still, yet
déjà	already
toujours	always
avant	before
directement	straightaway
tôt	early
finalement	finally
en retard	late
tard	late
normalement	normally
maintenant	now
souvent	often
récemment	recently
quelquefois	sometimes
bientôt	soon
ensuite	then
aujourd'hui	today
demain	tomorrow
hier	yesterday
actuellement	currently
enfin	finally
d'abord	firstly
désormais	from now on
immédiatement	immediately
auparavant	previously
parfois	sometimes
puis	then, next
d'habitude	usually
toutefois	yet

Where a verb was done

à l'étranger	abroad
loin (de)	far (from)
ici	here
près de	near
dessus	on top
dehors	outside
là-bas	over there
là	there
dessous	underneath
ailleurs	elsewhere
partout	everywhere

How a verb was done

beaucoup	a lot
absolument	absolutely
mieux	better
certainement	certainly
clairement	clearly
complètement	completely
facilement	easily
assez	enough, quite
même	even
exactement	exactly
extrêmement	extremely
généralement	generally
par contre	however
peu	few, little
seulement	only
parfaitement	perfectly
probablement	probably
rapidement / vite	quickly, fast
vraiment	really
réellement	really
simplement	simply
ensemble	together
trop	too much / many
totalement	totally
malheureusement	unfortunately
très	very
bien	well, a lot
environ	approximately
également	as well, equally
apparemment	apparently
différemment	differently
soit	either
entièrement	entirely
surtout	especially
peut-être	perhaps
presque	nearly
évidemment	obviously
uniquement	only
autrement	otherwise
particulièrement	particularly
plutôt	rather
sérieusement	seriously
tellement	so much
tant	so much / many
ainsi	so, thus

Family, friends, identity, equality

agréable	nice, pleasant
ami (m)	friend
amusant	funny, fun
anniversaire (m)	birthday
beau-père (m)	step-father, father-in-law
belle-mère (f)	step-mother, mother-in-law
bisexuel (m) / bisexuelle (f)	bisexual
blond	blond
chat (m)	cat
cheveux (mpl)	hair
chien (m)	dog
commun	common
communication (f)	communication
content	glad, happy
conversation (f)	conversation
couper, se couper	to cut / switch off
couple (m)	couple
demi-frère (m)	step- / half-brother
demi-sœur (f)	step- / half-sister
droit (m)	right, law
égalité (f)	equality
enfant (mf)	child
entendre; s'entendre (avec)	to hear; to get on (with)
faire la fête	to party
familial	family
famille (f)	family
fauteuil roulant (m)	wheelchair
femme (f)	woman, wife
fête (f)	festival, party
fille (f)	girl, daughter
fils (m)	son
frère (m)	brother
gay	gay
grand-mère (f)	grandmother
grand-père (m)	grandfather
grands-parents (mpl)	grandparents
habiter	to live

Now try this

To help you learn family words, draw a family tree and label the relationships in French.

9 Family, friends, identity, equality continued

handicap (m)	disability
handicapé	disabled
hétéro(sexuel) (m) / hétéro(sexuelle) (f)	straight
heureux (m) / heureuse (f)	happy, lucky
homme (m)	man
identité (f)	identity
indépendant	independent
influence (f)	influence
inviter	to invite
jeune; jeune (m)	young; young person
lapin (m)	rabbit
lesbien	lesbian
lettre (f)	letter
lunettes (fpl)	glasses
maison (f)	house, home
mari (m)	husband
mariage (m)	marriage
mère (f)	mother, mum
modèle (m)	role model
mort	dead
né	born
nom (m)	name, surname
non-binaire	non-binary
oncle (m)	uncle
parent (m)	parent
partager	to share
partenaire (mf)	partner
patient	patient
père (m)	father, dad
personnel	personal
pleurer	to cry
racisme (m)	racism
relation (f)	relationship
religieux (m) / religieuse (f)	religious
religion (f)	religion
rencontrer	to meet (up)
responsable	responsible
réunir	to gather, meet
riche	rich
salle (f)	room
s'amuser	to enjoy oneself
s'habiller	to get dressed
se marier	to get married
secret (m)	secret
sexe (m)	gender, sex
sexisme (m)	sexism
sœur (f)	sister
sportif (m) / sportive (f)	sporty
sympa	nice, kind
tante (f)	aunt
transgenre	transgender
travailleur (m) / travailleuse (f)	hardworking
triste	sad
unique	unique, only (child)
voisin (m)	neighbour
adopter	to adopt
âgé	old
aîné	older, oldest
allié (m)	ally
amitié (f)	friendship
apprécier	to appreciate
citoyen (m) / citoyenne (f)	citizen
combattre	to fight
compagnie (f)	company
compter (sur)	to count (on), intend
confiance (f)	trust
conflit (m)	conflict
copain (m) / copine (f)	friend, mate
courage (m)	courage, bravery
courrier (m)	mail
discrimination (f)	discrimination
don (m)	gift, talent, donation
emprunter	to borrow
encourager	to encourage
fêter	to celebrate
fidèle	loyal, faithful
fier (m) / fière (f)	proud
fierté (f)	pride
foi (f)	faith
foyer (m)	home
génération (f)	generation
inquiet (m) / inquiète (f)	worried, anxious
inquiétant	worrying
inquiétude (f)	worry
introduire	to introduce
jeunesse (f)	youth
jugement (m)	judgement
juger	to judge
jumeau (m) / jumelle (f)	twin
jumeaux (mpl)	twins
naissance (f)	birth
présenter; se présenter	to present; to introduce oneself
prêter	to lend
promettre	to promise
proposer	to propose
prudent	careful
raconter	to tell
rapport (m)	relationship
remercier	to thank
ressembler à	to look like
se fier à	to rely on
se séparer	to separate
s'ennuyer	to be bored
sentiment (m)	feeling
sentir; se sentir	to smell; to feel
séparation (f)	separation
s'excuser	to apologise
s'identifier (à)	to identify (with), relate (to)
s'inquiéter	to worry
s'occuper de	to look after
soirée (f)	evening, dinner party
soutenir	to support
soutien (m)	support
surprendre	to surprise

Now try this

Write sentences to describe people you know using some of the adjectives on this page.

Had a look ☐ **Nearly there** ☐ **Nailed it!** ☐

10 Interests, wellbeing and technology

Interests

basket (m)	basketball
chanson (f)	song
chanter	to sing
classique	classic, classical
concert (m)	concert, gig
danse (f)	dance
danser	to dance
équipe (f)	team
foot(ball) (m)	football
handball (m)	handball
instrument (m)	instrument
jeu (m)	game
jouer (à / de)	to play (sport / instrument)
match (m)	match
membre (m)	member
musique (f)	music
natation (f)	swimming
participer	to participate
piscine (f)	swimming pool
pratiquer	to practise
résultat (m)	result
rythme (m)	rhythm
spectacle (m)	show
sport (m)	sport
stade (m)	stadium
style (m)	style
tennis (m)	tennis
terrain (m)	pitch (sports)
théâtre (m)	theatre, drama
vélo (m)	bike, bicycle, cycling
athlétisme (m)	athletics
concours (m)	competition
épreuve (f)	test
gymnase (m)	gym
pièce (f)	play, coin, room
roman (m)	novel
scène (f)	scene, stage
s'entraîner	to train

Wellbeing

actif (m) / active (f)	active
avoir mal à la / au / aux	to ache, hurt
bouger	to move
courir	to run
danger (m)	danger
doigt (m)	finger
dormir	to sleep
drogue (f)	drug
émotion (f)	emotion, feelings
exercice (m)	exercise
forme (f); en forme	shape; in shape, fit, healthy
hôpital (m)	hospital
loisir (m)	leisure, hobby
malade	ill
maladie (f)	illness
malsain	unhealthy
médecin (m)	doctor
médical	medical
médicament (m)	medicine, pill
mental	mental
physique	physical
risque (m)	risk
sain	healthy
santé (f)	health
tomber	to fall
virus (m)	virus
fièvre (f)	fever
intégrer, s'intégrer	to integrate, to fit in
limiter	to limit
poids (m)	weight
sang (m)	blood
se blesser	to hurt oneself
se brûler	to burn oneself
se cacher	to hide
secours (m)	help (in an emergency)
soin (m)	care
souci (m)	worry
souffrir	to suffer
urgence (f)	emergency

Technology

appli(cation) (f)	app
célébrité (f)	celebrity, star
charger	to load, charge
commentaire (m)	comment
console (f)	console
e-mail (m)	email
envoyer	to send
influence (f)	influence
influenceur (m) / influenceuse (f)	influencer
Internet (m)	internet, web
joueur (m) / joueuse (f)	player
message (m)	message
mot de passe (m)	password
ordinateur portable (m)	laptop
personnage (m)	character
portable (m)	mobile phone
réseau (m)	network
sécurité (f)	security, safety
social	social
streaming (m)	streaming
tablette (f)	tablet
technologie (f)	technology
télécharger	to download
téléphoner	to phone
victoire (f)	victory, winning
vidéo (f)	video
violence (f)	violence
virus (m)	virus
appareil (m)	device
code (m)	code
cybercriminalité (f)	cyber crime
données (fpl)	data
écouteurs (m)	headphones, earbuds
écran (m)	screen
enregistrer	to record
virtuel	virtual

Now try this

List five activities you like doing and five that you don't like doing. Then try to memorise them all!

11 Food and drink and shopping

Food and drink

allergique	allergic	restaurant (m)	restaurant
baguette (f)	French stick	riz (m)	rice
boire	to drink	service (m)	service
boîte (f)	box, tin	servir	to serve
bouche (f)	mouth	soif (f)	thirst
café (m)	coffee, café	sucre (m)	sugar
carte (f)	card, map, credit card, menu	table (f)	table
		thé (m)	tea
		végan (m) / végane (f)	vegan
chocolat (m)	chocolate	végétarien (m) / végétarienne (f)	vegetarian
commander	to order		
cuisine (f)	cuisine, cooking, kitchen	viande (f)	meat
		addition (f)	bill
		aigre	sour
déjeuner (m)	lunch	assiette (f)	plate
délicieux (m) / délicieuse (f)	delicious	boisson (f)	drink
		bouteille (f)	bottle
dessert (m)	dessert	consommation (f)	consumption
eau (f)	water	couteau (m)	knife
entrée (f)	entrance, starter	cuillère (f)	spoon
		fourchette (f)	fork
faim (f)	hunger	goûter	to taste, try
fastfood (m)	fast food	nourriture (f)	food
frites (fpl)	chips, fries	plat (m)	dish, course
fromage (m)	cheese	régime (m)	regime, diet
fruit (m)	fruit	savoureux (m) / savoureuse (f)	tasty
gâteau (m)	cake		
glace (f)	ice, ice cream	sucré	sweet, sugary
goût (m)	taste		
lait (m)	milk		
légumes (mpl)	vegetables		
manger	to eat		
œuf (m)	egg		
pain (m)	bread		
pâtes (fpl)	pasta		
petit-déjeuner (m)	breakfast		
poisson (m)	fish		
recette (f)	recipe		
repas (m)	meal		
réserver	to reserve, book		

Shopping

acheter	to buy		
baskets (fpl)	trainers		
cadeau (m)	present		
caisse (f)	checkout, till		
centre commercial (m)	shopping centre		
client (m)	customer, client		
courses (fpl)	shopping		
coût (m)	cost		
coûter	to cost		
cravate (f)	tie		
échanger	to exchange		
jupe (f)	skirt		
magasin (m)	shop, shopping		
marque (f)	brand, mark		
mode (f); à la mode	fashion; fashionable		
monnaie (f)	change, currency		
payer	to pay		
poche (f)	pocket		
prix (m)	price		
robe (f)	dress		
taille (f)	size		
vendre	to sell		
vente (f)	sale		
vêtements (mpl)	clothes		
achat (m)	purchase		
chapeau (m)	hat		
dépenser	to spend (money)		
économie (f)	economy		
moulant	tight		
moyen (m) / moyenne (f)	medium, average size		
produit (m)	product		
supplémentaire	extra, additional		

Now try this

To learn food vocabulary, make a mind map of different food and drink, organised into categories, e.g. drinks, vegetables, desserts, etc.

12 In the town and transport

In the town

adresse (f)	address	rue (f)	street
appartement (m)	apartment, flat	site (m)	site
banque (f)	bank	supermarché (m)	supermarket
bâtiment (m)	building	tour (f)	tower
boulangerie (f)	bakery	tourner	to turn
bruit (m)	noise	trafic (m)	traffic
calme	quiet	traverser	to cross
capitale (f)	capital city	trouver; se trouver	to find; to be situated
carte (f)	card, map, credit card, menu	village (m)	village
		ville (f)	town, city
central	central	zone (f)	zone
centre (m)	centre	accès (m)	access
cinéma (m)	cinema	ascenseur (m)	lift
cour (f)	playground, court	attirer	to attract
		banlieue (f)	suburb
crime (m)	crime	bibliothèque (f)	library
direction (f)	direction	circulation (f)	traffic
endroit (m)	place	cité (f)	(council) estate
festival (m)	festival		
Fête de la Musique (f)	World Music Day	commissariat (m)	police station
feu (m)	fire, traffic light	communauté (f)	community
habiter	to live	construire	to build
haut	high, tall	escalier (m)	stairs
historique	historical	foule (f)	crowd
immeuble (m)	block of flats	habitant (m)	inhabitant, resident
kilomètre (m)	kilometre		
local	local	lieu (m)	place
logement (m)	accommodation	multiculturel (m) / multiculturelle (f)	multicultural
marché (m)	market		
musée (m)	museum	renseignement (m)	piece of information
parc (m)	park		
pâtisserie (f)	patisserie, cake shop	situer, se situer	to situate, locate
pharmacie (f)	pharmacy, chemist	vol (m)	flight, robbery
plan (m)	map, plan, project	voler	to steal, fly
police (f)	police, police station		
pont (m)	bridge		
port (m)	port, harbour		
poste (f)	post office		
prison (f)	prison		
province (f)	province		
quartier (m)	neighbourhood		
recommander	to recommend		
région (f)	region		
régional	regional		
restaurant (m)	restaurant		

Transport

accident (m)	accident
aéroport (m)	airport
aller (m)	single ticket
aller-retour (m)	return ticket
assis	sitting, seated
attendre	to wait
avion (m)	plane
bateau (m)	boat
billet (m)	ticket
bus (m)	bus
car (m)	coach
conduire	to drive, to lead
debout	standing
départ (m)	departure
direct	direct
distance (f)	distance
gare (f)	station
manquer	to miss (bus etc)
métro (m)	underground, tube
rapide	fast, quick
retard (m)	delay
retour (m)	return
route (f)	road, way, route
station (f)	(bus) stop, (tube) station
train (m)	train
transport(s) (m)	(public) transport
voiture (f)	car
arrêt (m)	stop
arrivée (f)	arrival
quai (m)	platform
siège (m)	seat
signe (m)	sign
signer	to sign
véhicule (m)	vehicle

Now try this

Learn the transport words by covering up the English and writing the English translations yourself.

13 School and work

activité (f)	activity
ambition (f)	ambition
apprendre	to learn
argent (m)	money
art (m)	art
artiste (mf)	artist
attitude (f)	attitude
bureau (m)	office, desk
but (m)	goal, aim, purpose
cahier (m)	exercise book
carrière (f)	career
chaussette (f)	sock
chef (m) / cheffe (f)	boss
chemise (f)	shirt
classe (f)	classroom, class
club (m)	club
collège (m)	secondary school
cours (m)	lesson, course
cravate (f)	tie
devoirs (mpl)	homework
échange (m)	exchange
école (f)	school
éducation (f)	education
effort (m)	effort
élève (mf)	pupil, student
entreprise (f)	company, business
équipement (m)	equipment
études (fpl)	studies
étudiant (m)	student (university)
étudier	to study
examen (m)	exam, test
faible	weak
formation (f)	training, apprenticeship
fort	strong, loud, good at
futur (m)	future
gagner	to win, to earn
garçon (m)	boy

interdire de	to forbid, ban
jupe (f)	skirt
langue (f)	language, tongue
leçon (f)	lesson
lecture (f)	reading
lever; se lever	to lift, raise; to get up
livre (m)	book, textbook
lycée (m)	sixth form, college
maths (fpl)	maths
matière (f)	subject
mériter	to deserve
note (f)	mark, grade, note
office (m)	office
ordinateur portable (m)	laptop
page (f)	page
pantalon (m)	trousers
papier (m)	paper
pause (f)	break (time)
policier (m) / policière (f)	police officer
porter	to wear, to carry
poste (m)	job, position, post
professeur, prof (mf)	teacher
projet (m)	plan, project
pull (m)	jumper
règle (f)	rule, ruler
rentrée (f)	start of school year
réussir (à)	to succeed, pass (an exam)
rêve (m)	dream
rêver (à / de)	to dream (about, of)
sac (m)	bag, sack
salaire (m)	salary
science (f)	science
scolaire	school
strict	strict
stylo (m)	pen
succès (m)	success
travail (m)	work
travailler	to work
uniforme (m)	uniform
université (f)	university
visite (f)	visit, excursion

apprenti (m)	apprentice
atteindre	to reach
bourse (f)	scholarship, grant
compétence (f)	competence, skill, ability
comportement (m)	behaviour
directeur (m) / directrice (f)	boss, headteacher
disponible	available
échec (m)	failure
emploi (m)	employment
emploi du temps (m)	timetable
employé (m)	employee, worker
enseignement (m)	teaching
enseigner	to teach
entretien (m)	interview
harcèlement (m)	bullying, harassment
intention (f)	intention
inventer	to invent
métier (m)	job
objectif (m)	objective
œuvre (f)	work, task
patron (m) / patronne (f)	boss
permettre	to allow, permit
poursuivre	to pursue
pression (f)	pressure
professionnel (m) / professionnelle (f)	professional
profiter de	to take advantage, profit from, make the most of
réussite (f)	success
se comporter	to behave
sévère	severe, strict, harsh
stressé	stressed
surveiller	to watch, keep an eye on
union (f)	union
veste (f)	jacket

Now try this

Write five sentences in French to describe your school. Challenge yourself to include as many words on this page as you can!

14 Holidays, TV and film

Holidays

affaires (fpl)	belongings, things
camping (m)	camping
chambre (f)	bedroom
château (m)	castle
clé (f)	key
complet (m) / complète (f)	full, complete
coûter	to cost
double	double
étranger; à l'étranger	foreign; abroad
expérience (f)	experience, experiment
fenêtre (f)	window
hôtel (m)	hotel
inclus	included
lit (m)	bed
mer (f)	sea
passeport (m)	passport
plage (f)	beach
privé	private
recommander	to recommend
région (f)	region
réserver	to reserve, book
se reposer	to rest
sol (m)	floor, ground
souvenir (m)	souvenir, memory
tente (f)	tent
tourisme (m)	tourism
touriste (mf)	tourist
vacances (fpl)	holidays
voyage (m)	journey, travel
voyager	to travel
vue (f)	view

accompagner	to accompany
annuel (m) / annuelle (f)	yearly
couverture (f)	blanket
critique (f)	review, criticism
disponible	available
étage (m)	floor
étranger (m) / étrangère (f)	foreign
louer	to hire
mémoire (f)	memory
pièce (f)	play, coin, room
sable (m)	sand
se plaindre	to complain
se souvenir (de)	to remember
valise (f)	suitcase
vol (m)	flight, robbery
voler	to steal, fly

TV and film

acteur (m)	actor
célèbre	famous
chaîne (f)	channel, chain
comédie (f)	comedy
émission (f)	(TV) programme
fan (mf)	fan, supporter
film (m)	film, movie
genre (m)	genre, type, sort
horreur (f)	horror
informations (fpl); information (f)	news; information
médias (mpl)	media
personnalité (f)	personality
programme (m)	programme
rôle (m)	role
science-fiction (f)	sci-fi
série (f)	series, soap opera
télé(vision) (f)	TV
titre (m)	title
tragédie (f)	drama
abonnement (m)	subscription
acte (m)	act, gesture
critique (f)	review, criticism
documentaire (m)	documentary
parole (f); paroles (fpl)	speech, word, speaking; lyrics
séance (f)	film screening, session
son (m)	sound

Now try this

Learn the words for different types of film and TV programmes. Think of an example you have watched for each one.

15 The issues in the world, the natural world and the countryside

aide (f)	aid, help	poisson (m)	fish	inondation (f)	flood
air (m)	air	pollution (f)	pollution	intégrer,	to integrate,
améliorer	to improve	protéger	to protect	s'intégrer	to fit in
animal (m)	animal, pet	recyclage (m)	recycling	justice (f)	justice
arrêter	to stop,	recycler	to recycle	libérer	to free
	arrest	réduire	to reduce	liberté (f)	freedom
association (f)	organisation,	responsable	responsible	loi (f)	law
	charity	ressource (f)	resource	lumière (f)	light
bois (m)	wood,	risque (m)	risk	lutte (f)	fight
	woods	sauver	to save, rescue	manifestation (f)	protest,
campagne (f)	countryside	soleil (m)	sun		to protest
catastrophe (f)	catastrophe	terre (f)	earth, ground	manifester	show
cheval (m)	horse	vent (m)	wind	menace (f)	threat
ciel (m)	sky	vue (f)	view	mener	to lead
côte (f)	coast	accueillir	to welcome	minorité (f)	minority
couper, se	to cut / switch	agir	to act	mondial	global, world
couper	off	arbre (m)	tree	moral	moral
crise (f)	crisis	baisser	to lower	nuire	to harm
dangereux (m) /	dangerous	brûler, se brûler	to burn	paix (f)	peace
dangereuse (f)		champ (m)	field	paysage (m)	landscape
destruction (f)	destruction	chemin (m)	path, way	perte (f)	loss, waste
eau (f)	water	chômage (m)	unemployment	piste (f)	track, trail
effet (m)	effect	climatique	climate	pleuvoir	to rain
électrique	electric	combattre	to fight	prévenir	to warn
énergie (f)	energy	connaissance (f)	knowledge	réfléchir	to think about,
environnement (m)	environment	conscient	conscious		reflect
espoir (m)	hope	conserver	to keep	refléter	to reflect
extrême	extreme	contrôler	to check	renouvelable	renewable
ferme (f)	farm	déchets (mpl)	waste, rubbish	représentation (f)	representation
feu (m)	fire, traffic	détruire	to destroy	représenter	to represent
	light	discrimination (f)	discrimination	résoudre	to solve
forêt (f)	forest	disparaître	to disappear	réutiliser	to reuse
global	global	durable	sustainable	rivière (f)	river
grève (f)	strike	s'échapper (de)	to escape	se soucier	to show
île (f)	island		(from)		concern for
informer	to inform	empêcher de	to prevent	sec (m) /	dry
jeter	to throw	enquête (f)	survey	sèche (f)	
	away	espèce (f)	species, type	s'occuper de	to look after,
lac (m)	lake	état (m)	state, condition		take care of
lapin (m)	rabbit	fleur (f)	flower	sombre	dark
lutter	to fight	frais (m) /	fresh, cool	tolérer	to tolerate
mer (f)	sea	fraîche (f)		unité (f)	unity
monde (m)	world	gouvernement (m)	government	verre (m)	glass
montagne (f)	mountain	humide	wet, humid	voter	to vote
nature (f)	nature	imposer	to impose		
naturel	natural	individu (m)	individual		
neige (f)	snow	industrie (f)	industry		
organisation (f)	organisation				
plage (f)	beach				
planète (f)	planet				
plastique (m)	plastic				

Now try this

Choose ten words to describe issues in the world that you are concerned about.
Learn them and then practise them by saying sentences describing the problem.

Answers

The answers to the Speaking and Writing activities below are sample answers – there are many ways you could answer these questions.

1 Physical descriptions

1 Il y a deux garçons et deux filles.
2 Ils sont contents.
3 Une fille a les cheveux longs et roux.
4 Un garçon porte des lunettes.

2 Character descriptions

A, D, E

3 Friends

1 A   2 C   3 B

4 Family

SPEAKING TRACK 78 — Listen to the recording

1 Dans ma famille, il y a quatre personnes. J'ai un frère aîné qui s'appelle Alex et il a dix-sept ans. Je le trouve assez gentil. Ma sœur est plus jeune que moi et je m'occupe souvent d'elle car elle est assez calme et elle n'a pas beaucoup d'amis. Mes parents sont sévères mais on s'amuse bien ensemble.
2 Je suis assez sportive comme mon père, alors nous jouons souvent au foot. De temps en temps, je vais au cinéma avec ma mère parce que nous aimons regarder des films. La semaine dernière, je suis allée à un concert avec mon frère et la musique était excellente. Le week-end prochain, je ferai du vélo avec ma sœur et nous nous amuserons bien.

5 Relationships

SPEAKING TRACK 79 — Listen to the recording

1 Quand j'ai du temps libre, j'aime bien faire du sport avec mes amis ou ma sœur parce que je suis vraiment sportif. Hier nous sommes allés au centre de sport où nous avons joué au basket ensemble, mais c'était fatigant.
2 Selon moi, un bon ami devrait être fidèle et indépendant. Mon meilleur ami, qui s'appelle Charlie, m'écoute toujours et me comprend, alors on s'entend bien. Demain, je lui parlerai de mes soucis.
The answer would qualify for a Grade 6 as it displays a range of appropriate vocabulary, three time frames with five tenses (present, perfect, future, imperfect and conditional), complex sentences including the use of *quand*, constructions with the infinitive, direct and indirect object pronouns, connectives, different subjects of the verb and intensifiers.

6 Helping friends with problems

SPEAKING TRACK 80 — Listen to the recording

J'aime aider mes amis car ils sont fidèles et agréables. Les amis sont très importants dans la vie alors il faut faire des efforts pour les aider. La semaine dernière, j'ai aidé mon amie Nadia avec une crise.

Elle souffrait de la pression au collège et elle mangeait des choses malsaines. Son régime était nul et je lui ai dit de manger de la nourriture saine. Demain, je devrai aider un autre ami, Mehdi, qui a des problèmes médicaux.

7 When I was younger

SPEAKING TRACK 81 — Listen to the recording

Quand j'étais plus jeune, j'étais très sportif car je jouais au foot tous les jours avec mes amis et je faisais du vélo le week-end avec ma famille. Nous allions souvent au cinéma où nous regardions des films amusants. J'étais vraiment heureux car ma famille était toujours là pour moi.

8 Identity

C, D, E

9 Everyday life

1 coach   2 break   3 lunch
4 bike   5 see a pet

10 Meals at home

B, D, E

11 Celebrations

SPEAKING TRACK 82 — Listen to the recording

1 Pour fêter l'anniversaire de mon meilleur ami, on va normalement au cinéma où on regarde une comédie. On s'amuse bien! L'année dernière, nous sommes allés à un concert de notre groupe préféré et nous avons beaucoup aimé la musique. Mon ami venait de télécharger plusieurs chansons de ce groupe et nous avons chanté avec lui.
(Grade 8/9 for full response, Grade 7 without last sentence)
2 Récemment, on a fêté la Saint-Sylvestre chez mon oncle et ma tante. Tout le monde a dansé et on a mangé un grand repas qui était délicieux. L'année prochaine, je voudrais passer le nouvel an à l'étranger parce que j'aimerais découvrir la culture d'un autre pays.
(Grade 7)

12 Food and drink

1 the last day of the holiday   2 not dry OR really delicious
3 ice creams   4 quite boring

13 Healthy diets

SPEAKING TRACK 83 — Listen to the recording

1 J'aime manger des légumes (car ils sont bons pour la santé) et j'adore boire du café (mais on dit que c'est mauvais pour la santé).
2 Je dois manger beaucoup de fruits et de légumes (mais je ne dois pas manger de frites. Je ne suis pas végétarien parce que j'adore manger de la viande.).
(Grade 2/3 without the brackets, Grade 5 with)

133

14 Sport and exercise

1 La semaine dernière, j'ai fait de la natation à la piscine avant d'aller au gymnase où j'ai passé deux heures avec mes copains. C'était très amusant et je vais y retourner demain. Malheureusement, mon copain Nathan s'est blessé quand il est tombé. Quel dommage!

2 La semaine prochaine, je jouerai au tennis avec mon frère et je pense que je gagnerai car il n'est pas bon au tennis. Après avoir fini, je vais faire de l'athlétisme car je voudrais être en forme. À mon avis, c'est très important car c'est bon pour la santé. (Grades 7/8)

15 Physical wellbeing

1 J'aime être en forme.
2 Mon sport préféré c'est la natation.
3 C'est bon pour ma santé.
4 Hier je suis allé(e) à la piscine.
5 J'aime marcher chaque jour (tous les jours) et le weekend, je marche pendant deux heures avec mes chiens.

16 Mental wellbeing

B, D
Hint: Look at those negatives!

17 Feeling unwell

1 Mon **père** a véritablement mal aux **yeux**.
2 Il **souffrait**, donc il est **allé** acheter des médicaments **homéopathiques** en ville.
3 Je ne suis pas malade.
4 Ma mère s'est blessée.
5 Elle doit aller à la pharmacie.
6 Mon copain a mal au ventre et au doigt.

Hint: Try not to leave a gap as each word counts!

18 Equality and sporting role models

Mon modèle est Harry Kane. Il joue au football pour l'équipe anglaise et il est toujours agréable. Je voudrais être comme lui car il est calme et fort. (Grade 5)

19 Sporting events

Selon moi, les concours sportifs sont très importants puisqu'on peut y participer afin de montrer sa passion pour le sport. Moi, je suis très sportif et je m'intéresse à beaucoup de sports différents. Pourtant, il y a plein de problèmes comme la violence des fans, surtout pendant les matchs de football, ou le prix des billets. Ils sont souvent trop chers. Quel dommage!
Il y a deux semaines, je suis allé voir un match de foot passionnant au stade en ville. Malheureusement, mon équipe a perdu et je n'étais pas content. Après avoir quitté le stade, j'ai parlé avec les fans de l'autre équipe et ils étaient vraiment sympa. Je ne suis jamais allé à une course de chevaux, mais le mois prochain, je vais aller voir une course avec mon oncle qui vient d'acheter un cheval. Je crois que ce sera génial. (Grade 9)

20 Me and my mobile

1 half brother   2 from time to time   3 watches films

21 Social media

22 The internet

1 J'ai acheté un nouveau pantalon en ligne la semaine dernière car c'était moins cher que dans les magasins en ville. J'ai trouvé ça très pratique.

2 Normalement je télécharge de la musique ou je parle avec mes copains sur Instagram. De temps en temps je partage des photos ou je regarde des films. Demain je vais regarder une émission amusante et je rirai beaucoup. (Grades 5/6)

23 Computer games

J'aime bien participer aux jeux en ligne et je joue avec mes amis presque tous les jours parce que c'est amusant. J'ai créé mon propre personnage dans un jeu de football et mon équipe a gagné beaucoup de concours. (Grade 5/6)

24 Pros and cons of technology

J'aime utiliser Internet chez moi. Mon réseau social préféré est Instagram. J'essaie de communiquer avec mes amis chaque jour. Le mois dernier, j'ai envoyé un e-mail à ma tante qui habite à Paris. Utiliser les nouvelles technologies ne l'inquiète pas et l'année dernière, elle a acheté un nouvel ordinateur portable qu'elle aime bien.

25 Hobbies

1 horse-riding   2 drama   3 in the evening(s)

26 Music and dance

Grade 2/3 answer: Je préfère la musique. J'aime écouter la musique pop. Je déteste la musique classique. Je voudrais jouer d'un instrument.
Grade 5 answer (includes reasons, joining words and interesting vocabulary): Je préfère la musique parce que je trouve la danse difficile. J'aime écouter de la musique populaire mais je déteste la musique classique car ce n'est pas intéressant. À l'avenir je voudrais jouer d'un instrument.

27 Arranging to go out

B, C, F

28 Reading

1 A   2 C   3 B

29 Television

Listen to the recording | TRACK 90

30 Going to the cinema

1 B   **2** A   **3** C

31 Celebrity culture

A, C, E

32 Role models

A, B

33 Places in town

Listen to the recording | TRACK 91

J'habite dans une grande ville où il y a beaucoup d'industries. Je n'aime pas habiter dans ma région car il n'y a rien à faire pour les jeunes. Il y a des magasins et une piscine, mais si on veut regarder un film, il faut aller dans la ville voisine où il y a un grand cinéma. A l'avenir, je voudrais habiter ailleurs parce que ma ville est nulle.
(This response is from a student who is working at medium to high grade because of the use of the conditional and Higher vocabulary like *ailleurs* and *ne … rien*.)

34 Things to do

Listen to the recording | TRACK 92

Samedi dernier, je suis allé en ville à pied car j'ai manqué le bus. Après avoir rencontré mes copains, je suis allé manger dans un petit restaurant près de la gare. C'était vraiment génial et on s'est bien amusés.

35 Shopping

1 A   **2** C   **3** A

36 Transport

Listen to the recording | TRACK 93

Mon moyen de transport préféré en ville est le bus car ce n'est pas cher, mais quand je voyage dans un autre pays, j'adore prendre l'avion car c'est rapide.

37 Travel and buying tickets

Listen to the recording | TRACK 94

38 My region – good and bad

1 lake   **2** festival of nature
3 castle   **4** only Sundays

39 My area in the past

A, C

40 Town or country

Listen to the recording | TRACK 95

41 During the holidays

1 B   **2** C   **3** B

42 Abroad

1 swim and play on the beach (with their two dogs)
2 visit museums (with his grandfather)

43 Types of holiday

1 C   **2** A   **3** B

44 Where to stay

I think / believe that holidays are very important, so I always choose an expensive hotel. Last summer we spent ten interesting days in America. We found the accommodation was quite clean. It was also great that breakfast was included! My parents will visit Canada in August but they are going to go camping, even if it will be less comfortable.

45 Booking accommodation

Listen to the recording | TRACK 96

J'ai réservé trois nuits dans un hôtel au centre-ville. J'ai trouvé la chambre confortable mais chère.

46 Holiday activities

A, E, F

47 Trips and excursions

1 advantages: historic castle; disadvantages: bad weather
2 advantages: excellent landscape; disadvantages: expensive

48 Asking for help or directions

1 B   **2** A   **3** A

49 Shopping for gifts

1 39 years old   **2** jacket
3 fashion   **4** dress

50 Tourist information

1 old theatre   **2** summer
3 closed at the weekend

51 Tourist attractions

Listen to the recording | TRACK 97

Dans ma région, il y a des sites intéressants pour les touristes comme le port où on peut regarder passer les bateaux. Il y a aussi plusieurs musées et un grand centre commercial qui est très populaire. Moi, j'aime me reposer sur le sable, surtout s'il fait beau.

52 Holiday problems
1 in May   **2** road accident   **3** three hours

53 Accommodation problems
1 C   **2** A

54 Eating out
1 C   **2** B   **3** B

55 Opinions about food

Moi, je préfère manger des glaces car elles sont délicieuses, mais je déteste le fromage, alors je n'en mange jamais. Ce soir, je vais goûter un repas végan pour la première fois et j'espère qu'il sera savoureux.

56 The weather
1 I like hot weather / when it's hot on holiday.
2 My dad loves the snow.
3 When it's cold, we go to the mountains.
4 If it's windy, my parents are not happy.
5 Yesterday it rained the whole day / all day.

57 Customs and festivals
1 C   **2** B   **3** B

58 Visiting a city
La grande ville se trouve dans le nord-ouest de la France au bord de la mer. J'adore cette ville car il y a beaucoup de choses à faire dans le centre et c'est très amusant. Je vais visiter la ville le week-end prochain avec mes parents car je voudrais acheter des cadeaux.

59 School subjects

Au college, j'étudie beaucoup de matières. J'apprends l'histoire que j'aime bien et aussi le français. J'étudie les sciences et les maths et l'année dernière, j'étudiais le sport mais je ne l'étudie plus.

60 School likes, dislikes and reasons

J'aime bien les maths et les sciences mais ma matière préférée est l'anglais car j'adore la lecture et j'aime écrire.

61 Timetable and school day

Ma journée scolaire préférée est le mardi car j'ai sport et j'adore être actif. Mardi dernier, on a joué au foot pendant ce cours et mon équipe a gagné. J'étais si content.

62 Equipment and facilities in school
1 Il y a une classe.   **2** Je vois des ordinateurs.
3 Il y a des élèves.   **4** Ils portent une chemise.

63 School uniform
1 Il y a deux élèves.
2 Je vois des livres.
3 Les enfants portent une chemise blanche.
4 Ils portent une cravate.

64 Class activities
C, D, F

65 School rules
A, B

66 Opinions about school

Mon collège est trop grand et il y a toujours beaucoup d'élèves dans les bâtiments qui sont anciens. Par contre, les professeurs sont très gentils et ils m'aident, surtout quand je ne comprends pas ou quand j'ai un problème. Par exemple, hier mon prof d'histoire m'a expliqué une idée difficile.

67 Clubs and activities

Dans mon collège, on peut participer à beaucoup de clubs et je vais au club de musique chaque semaine. Nous écoutons de la musique populaire et classique et la semaine dernière, j'ai commencé à jouer d'un instrument de musique. La semaine prochaine, je vais aller au club d'athlétisme pour la première fois afin d'améliorer ma santé.

68 Success at school
1 J'aime l'école.
2 Je trouve tous mes cours intéressants.
3 Mes professeurs m'aident chaque jour / tous les jours.
4 L'année dernière, j'ai décidé de bien travailler pour réussir.
5 J'espère trouver un bon emploi.

69 Options at 16
1 B   **2** C   **3** B

70 Schools – France and the UK
1 J'**aime** les **collèges** en France.
2 J'étudie les **sciences** et l'**informatique**.
3 Mon **ami(e)** adore la **géographie**.
4 L'école commence tôt.
5 Je finis très tard.
6 En Angleterre on porte un uniforme.

71 Future study plans
1 pass exams and study maths at university
2 an apprenticeship / became an apprentice
3 he earns money

72 Future plans
1 Jade   **2** Nathan   **3** Nathan
4 Diane   **5** Jade   **6** Diane

73 Part-time jobs and money

B, E, F

74 Opinions about jobs

SPEAKING TRACK 104
Listen to the recording

À mon avis, je voudrais bien trouver un emploi comme professeur car tous les jours seront différents et je pense que ce sera amusant d'aider les jeunes. Mon père, qui est prof de maths, m'a dit que c'était un excellent emploi.

75 Job adverts and skills needed

B, C, F

76 Applying for jobs

SPEAKING TRACK 105
Listen to the recording

77 Volunteering

SPEAKING TRACK 106
Listen to the recording

Oui, je voudrais travailler pour une association parce que je crois que c'est sympa d'aider les autres, surtout ceux qui n'ont pas beaucoup de choses. Mon frère travaille pour une association qui aide les personnes pauvres depuis deux ans. Ils s'occupent des gens qui n'ont pas de travail.

78 Equality and helping others

SPEAKING TRACK 107
Listen to the recording

Je ne crois pas, non. Notre société n'est pas égale car les hommes gagnent plus d'argent que les femmes et ce n'est pas juste. Je dirais aussi qu'il y a beaucoup de problèmes sociaux causés par le manque d'égalité dans le monde.

79 The natural world

1 A   2 B   3 B   4 B

80 Spending time in the countryside

SPEAKING TRACK 108
Listen to the recording

J'adore la campagne parce que j'aime regarder les animaux comme les lapins et les chevaux. Ils sont très gentils.

81 The environment and me

Dans ma région, il y a beaucoup de pollution de l'air car les voitures ne sont pas interdites dans le centre-ville. À mon avis, l'environnement est très important car je voudrais être en bonne santé et la pollution est dangereuse. Récemment, j'ai recyclé le papier et le plastique au collège et chez moi, mais je vais faire plus de choses pour l'environnement. La semaine prochaine je vais aller au collège à vélo et je vais arrêter d'utiliser la voiture quand je vais en ville.

82 Local environmental issues

SPEAKING TRACK 109
Listen to the recording

Dans ma région il y a trop de voitures qui contribuent à la pollution de l'air. Les rues ne sont pas propres et il est possible de voir beaucoup de sacs en plastique qu'on a jetés dans la mer.

83 Global environmental issues

SPEAKING TRACK 110
Listen to the recording

À mon avis, il y a beaucoup de problèmes dans le monde. Par exemple, il n'y a pas assez de nourriture pour tout le monde et il y a des pays où il ne pleut pas souvent, et il n'y a pas assez d'eau. Cependant, le problème le plus grave pour moi, c'est le changement climatique car on risque de détruire le monde si on n'agit pas.

84 Caring for the planet

A, C, F

85 A greener future

SPEAKING TRACK 111
Listen to the recording

J'ai l'intention de ne pas acheter de voiture et je vais essayer de manger les fruits et les légumes de mon jardin. Quand je pars en vacances, j'utiliserai le train ou le car parce que je préfère les moyens de transport plus verts.

94 Articles 1

le garçon, **la** mère, **les** étudiants, **le** printemps, **l'**Afrique, **la** France, **la** condition, **le** bleu, **la** decision, **le** père, **le** visage, **la** plage

95 Articles 2

1 **a** Allez au   **b** Allez aux   **c** Allez à la
   d Allez à l'   **e** Allez aux   **f** Allez au
   g Allez au   **h** Allez à la

2 **a** Je veux du pain.   **b** Avez-vous / As-tu du lait?
   c Il n'a pas d'eau.   **d** Je vais à l'école.
   e (Est-ce que) tu vas à la gare?   **f** Il va aux toilettes.

96 Adjectives

1 un petit chien noir
2 la semaine dernière
3 Mon petit frère est très actif.
4 Ma meilleure amie est petite et heureuse / contente.
5 Son frère est grand, sportif mais un peu sérieux.

97 Possessives

1 mon frère   2 son ami   3 ses amis
4 son sac   5 ma sœur   6 son amie
7 ses amis   8 son portable   9 mes parents
10 leur ami   11 leurs amis   12 leur voiture

98 Comparisons

1 L'Everest est la montagne **la plus haute** du monde.
2 La jupe est **plus chère** que la robe.
3 Demain, il fera **plus beau** qu'aujourd'hui.
4 **La meilleure** solution est de prendre le train.
5 Julie est **moins amusante** qu'Amit.
6 Le TGV est le train **le plus rapide**.

99 Other adjectives and pronouns

1 ce	**2** cet	**3** cette	**4** ce
5 ces	**6** cette	**7** ces	**8** cette

100 Adverbs

Maintenant, Normalement, De temps en temps, demain, ensemble, vite

101 Object pronouns

1 Il l'a envoyé.
2 Je ne l'ai pas regardée.
3 Il ne les a pas achetées.
4 Tu l'as vu?
5 Sarah l'a lu.
6 Mes parents l'ont achetée.

102 More pronouns: *y* and *en*

1 J'y suis déjà allé.
2 J'en ai déjà trop mangé.
3 J'y suis allé hier.
4 J'y vais de temps en temps.
5 On y va souvent.
6 Je n'en mange jamais.

103 Other pronouns

1 Mon ami **qui** s'appelle Bruno aime le football.
2 L'émission **que** j'ai vue hier n'était pas passionnante.
3 Le quartier **où** ils habitent est vraiment calme.
4 C'est le prof **dont** je vous ai déjà parlé.
5 Elle a une sœur **qui** est prof.

104 Present tense: *-er* verbs

Je **m'appelle** Yasmina. J'ai une sœur qui **s'appelle** Diane et qui **joue** au tennis. Je **préfère** faire du vélo. Je **chante** et je **joue** d'un instrument. Le soir, nous **rentrons** à cinq heures et nous **mangeons**. Ensuite je **parle** avec mes amis et j'**écoute** de la musique. Quelquefois, mon frère et moi **jouons** à des jeux vidéo ou **téléchargeons** un film à regarder plus tard.

105 Present tense: *-ir* and *-re* verbs

1 Le matin, je **sors** à sept heures et demie.
2 Le mardi, les cours **finissent** à cinq heures.
3 Mon ami ne **boit** pas de café.
4 Le train **part** à 8h20.
5 Nous **apprenons** le français.
6 Pendant les vacances, nous **dormons** sous la tente.
7 Mes copains **choisissent** des frites.

106 *Avoir* and *être*

1 a ai	**b** avons	**c** a	**d** ont	**e** avez
2 a sommes	**b** est	**c** suis	**d** sont	**e** êtes

107 Reflexive verbs

1 Elle se lève.
2 Ils s'amusent.
3 Nous nous demandons.
4 Elles se reposent.
5 Je m'appelle

108 Other important verbs

1 vais / I go to school by coach.
2 faisons / We go cycling in summer.
3 peut / You can go to the cinema in town.
4 veulent / They want to go to France.
5 dois / You must do your homework.
6 sait / She knows how to swim.

109 The perfect tense 1

Mercredi dernier, j'**ai pris** le bus pour aller en ville. J'y **ai rencontré** un ami. Nous **avons fait** les magasins. J'**ai voulu** acheter des baskets rouges mais elles étaient trop chères. Nous **avons mangé** des pâtes et j'**ai choisi** un café. Mon copain **a bu** un thé. J'**ai laissé** mon sac au café. J'**ai dû** y retourner et, par conséquent, j'**ai raté** le bus et j'**ai dû** rentrer à pied.

110 The perfect tense 2

1 Samedi dernier, je **suis parti(e)** tôt.
2 Le matin, je **suis allé(e)** jouer au football.
3 Je **suis sorti(e)** à dix heures.
4 L'autre équipe **n'est pas venue**.
5 Nous y **sommes resté(e)s** une heure, puis nous **sommes rentré(e)s**.
6 Je **suis arrivé(e)** à la maison juste avant midi.

111 The imperfect tense

It's written in the imperfect because it's about what someone used to do.

Quand j'**étais** jeune, j'**habitais** à la campagne. Nous **avions** un grand jardin où je **jouais** au foot avec mes frères. Le samedi, on **allait** au marché en ville. Il y **avait** beaucoup de magasins où j'**achetais** des cadeaux. Nous **mangions** des pâtes et nous **buvions** du café. On **rentrait** en bus avec tous nos voisins et nos achats!

112 The future tense

1 mangerai	**2** ira	**3** fera
4 partageront	**5** auras	**6** sera

113 The conditional tense

1 Je **voudrais** aller en France.
2 Si j'avais assez d'argent, j'**irais** au Canada.
3 Il **ferait** un long voyage.
4 Tu **aimerais** voir ce film?
5 Je **préférerais** manger au restaurant.
6 Si j'avais faim, je **mangerais** du fromage.
7 Il **voudrait** aller en ville samedi.
8 On **irait** à la plage s'il faisait beau?
9 Tu **irais** au match si tu restais encore deux jours.
10 Elle **voudrait** quelque chose à boire?

114 Negatives

1 1H, 2F, 3B, 4A, 5C, 6E, 7D, 8G
2 a Tu ne fais rien.
b Tu ne m'as jamais aidé à la maison.
c Tu ne fais plus tes devoirs.
d Tu ne respectes personne.
e Tu ne fais que le nécessaire.
f Tu ne peux aller ni au football ni au restaurant ce soir.

115 The perfect infinitive and present participle

1 a Après avoir regardé la télé, j'ai joué au foot.
b Après avoir fini ses devoirs, il est allé en ville.
c Après avoir écouté de la musique, ils / elles sont allé(e)s à l'école.
2 a en mangeant **b** en ayant **c** en travaillant
d en finissant **e** en faisant

116 The passive, the imperative and impersonal verbs

1 C	**2** A	**3** E	**4** B	**5** D

117 Questions, prefixes, suffixes, prepositions

Possible answers:

1 Où travaille ton père? Where does your father work?
2 Qui va à la fête? Who is going to the party?
3 Comment allez-vous? How are you?
4 Combien d'amis as-tu sur Facebook? How many friends do you have on Facebook?
5 À quelle heure rentrent tes parents? What time are your parents coming home?
6 Pourquoi as-tu pris le bus? Why did you take the bus?
7 Que voulez-vous faire? What do you want to do?
8 Depuis quand apprends-tu le français? How long have you been learning French?